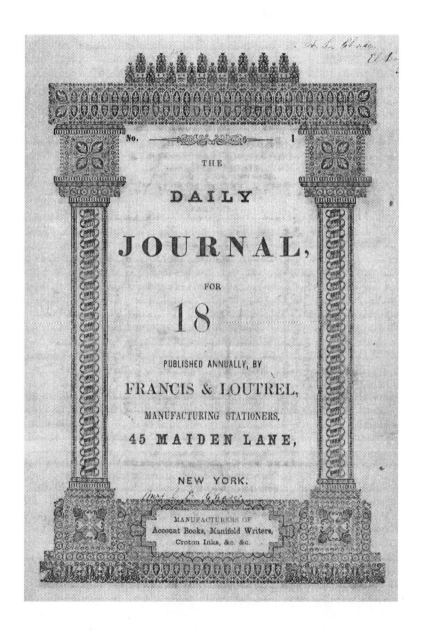

No. ———— 1

THE

DAILY

JOURNAL,

FOR

18

PUBLISHED ANNUALLY, BY

FRANCIS & LOUTREL,

MANUFACTURING STATIONERS,

45 MAIDEN LANE,

NEW YORK.

MANUFACTURERS OF
Account Books, Manifold Writers,
Croton Inks, &c. &c.

Augusta began transcribing her previously hidden notes into
bound journals made by Frances & Loutrel well after they had
established themselves in Eldorado, where it was much safer.

Augusta's Journal

VOL. II

The First Year in th Life of Eldorado, K.T.
1858

A BIOGRAPHY

BY

Marjorie Lund Crump
&
Ralph Eugene crump

authorHOUSE®

AuthorHouse™
1663 Liberty Drive, Suite 200
Bloomington, IN 47403
www.authorhouse.com
Phone: 1-800-839-8640

First published by AuthorHouse 5/14/2009

ISBN: 978-1-4389-3571-3 (sc)
ISBN: 978-1-4389-3572-0 (hc)

Library of Congress Control Number: 2008911619

Printed in the United States of America
Bloomington, Indiana

This book is printed on acid-free paper.

Contents

Volume II

Illustrations

ACKNOWLEDGEMENTS

Donnali Fifield of San Francisco who has edited for Forbes Publications and recently translated "March of the Penguins" and other books from French to English, painstakingly edited all fifty-two chapters (and more) …(a task of one and a half years)

My brother, James L. Lund, Esq., inherited the three original volumes from our mother, Hazel. Sometime in the 1980s he passed them on to me.

Dr. Ramon Powers, Executive Director of the Kansas State Historical Society in Topeka in the early 1990s invited us to use their library and gave us access to twelve volumes of the transactions of the Kansas State Historical Society, where several references of the territorial period verified some of entries, though it appears to us that Augusta has provided some of the best accounts of the first few years of Eldorado and its founding by her father and a few like-minded abolitionists in the summer of 1857.

Mrs. Kim Stagliano, a professional editor and author, edited this volume for punctuations, typos, etc.

The Kansas State Historical Society, headquartered in Topeka, KS, graciously gave us permission to use the two pictures of John Brown and one of Sara Robinson.

Historical PROLOGUE to Vol. II Beginning in 1858 - Pre Civil War

For thirty years, prior to the Civil War, the question of whether a state would come into the union slave or free was settled by the Missouri Compromise. In that way, a balance of power was maintained in the Senate. However, for ten years prior to the 1854 Kansas-Nebraska Act, the Missouri compromise failed to satisfy either North or South in deciding a territory's status once it becomes a state. As a result of this indecision, the North/South debate widened and became bitter. Senator Douglas proposed that Congress avoid a designation (free or slave) as regards a territory. When conditions of statehood had been met, the territorial population would vote whether the state should be admitted as slave or free and submit an appropriate state constitution. Dubbed "Popular Sovereignty," it was an untried doctrine and unintentionally set the stage for seven years of bloodshed out on the Kansas prairie, which soon became a prototype for our Civil War.

Before the ink was dry on the 1854 Act, southern politicians in Congress began encouraging proslavery immigration, and began making proslavery territorial appointments from top to bottom, made easy by a proslavery dominated U. S. Senate and a series of proslavery U. S. presidents.

The North, if they were paying any attention, seemed powerless to do anything about it and was slow to react. Oh, they were indignant but slow to move.

The Gold Rush of '48 and '49, peopled mostly by Southerners, had established for new immigrants the trails west.

For the first fifty years of the 19th century, while the North was wringing its hands, using its growing manufacturing base to create a true middle class, listening to sermons and lectures, reading editorials and Harriet Beecher Stowe, the South was doubling its size and accumulating three and a half million slaves mostly through natural reproduction, since importation had become illegal. Slavery was the ancient "old country" plantation system pushed by ambitious southern aristocrats, who owned most of the property, land and slaves: all indistinguishable as property and amazingly confirmed as such in the Dred Scott Decision. That ambition was exercised through their Senators, who themselves were major slave holders, elected to the Senate to represent the interests of the growing southern aristocratic elite; between 1800 and 1860 they did an outstanding job of it.

The stakes for the struggle took an economic leap as a result of two separate events: the Cotton Gin and the need to push the railroads west. A little before 1800, Yankee Eli Whitney invented mechanical means to separate cottonseeds from fiber.

His invention increased cotton production by a factor of ten. Cotton was not a dominant crop. Rice, indigo and tobacco produced their revenue. Before the Cotton Gin, for every slave working the fields, ten to fifteen were in the shed tediously and manually separating seed from fiber. This labor consumed the balance of the year after harvest. With Whitney's invention and its rapid distribution the cultivation of cotton exploded, increasing the demand for slaves, reaching 3.5 million, one third of the southern population, though fewer than 5% of the whites were slaveholders of any significance.

With Whitney's gin, the South saw that it had within its grasp the ability to dominate the world's growing cotton market, but they craved more land. Within a decade of Whitney, cotton became the most profitable U.S. product. Some Southerners envisioned a corridor Coast to Coast paved with cotton fields, worked by slaves, connected by railroads. By mid century, they had made excellent progress toward achieving that ambition.

Within the decade of Whitney's invention, Missouri and Louisiana were admitted as Slave States, having been cut from the vast landmass purchased from Napoleon, followed by Arkansas, Alabama, Mississippi and Florida from the same source. Georgia, of course, was an original colony. By 1846, when Texas came in "Slave," with its vast land area of a quarter million square miles, planters projected the need for another two million slaves and railroads. By the end of the Mexican War a corridor existed paved with eight new states, all "Slave." But to make it ocean to ocean they needed to connect to and acquire the California territory, which also seemed to be within their grasp.

Some Congressmen feared that if the U.S. did not exercise its "rights, the California territory would be seized and occupied by England" There was plenty of West Coast support for slavery, since so many original California Gold Seekers were Southerners. It was "nip and tuck" whether she would come in "Slave" or "Free." More California newspapers favored slavery than opposed it.

Led by the Railroads, the growth industry of the mid-19th century was transportation. There was pressure and urgency to expand the railroad network. The real plum of the expansion was the vast territory beyond the Missouri river, framed by the uncertain boundaries of the Old Louisiana Purchase, which, when acquired fifty years earlier had doubled our land mass.

Both Senator Douglas (Illinois) and his ambitious Senatorial adversary, Abraham Lincoln, had grown prosperous as lawyers representing railroads and their various interests. Each politician intended to persevere on behalf of his clients, particularly Douglas.

Both Lincoln and Douglas knew that before their westward expansion could be financed the railroads needed guarantees that their rails, equipment, freight, passengers, and general operation would be protected by agents of state and federal government, which included guarantees of safe passage through territories then owned or claimed by Indian Nations. They wanted to operate west of the Missouri river with all the advantages they enjoyed east of it. Senator Douglas intended to deliver those assurances by granting territorial status to an area called Kansas/Nebraska, a landmass stretching from the Missouri River to the Continental Divide. The ten-year congressional (political) debate hinged on whether this new territory would be admitted as a state, slave or free. The railroads didn't care one way or the other.

Some senators were willing to allow Kansas to come in as free, if they could get California or Texas as slave states. A good many citizens thought President Polk met the Texas criteria by provoking a War with Mexico, which brought in Texas with slavery.

Where congress abdicated its responsibility was in neither dividing the territory into Kansas as a slave state contiguous to a slave states Missouri and Nebraska as a free state, contiguous to free state Iowa. Rather the Act of 1854 would admit the combined "territory" without a designation, Free or Slave. A new untried Doctrine of Popular Sovereignty was intended to allow the territorial citizens to vote their own social or economic preference rather than prearrange it through Congressional debate, using the guidelines of the old Missouri Compromise. So long as proslavery elements could oppress abolitionists with violence and could dominate the territory politically, the U.S. Army stood by and declined to provide safety evenly for all settlers. Jim Lane, ex congressman from Indiana and a veteran general of the Mexican War, organized volunteer abolitionists into a local militia to successfully oppose and to always be larger and better armed than the existing proslavery militia in the Kansas Territory with financial and other forms of aid from dozens of like-minded northern leaders.

In only two years the population of the Kansas Territory became predominantly antislavery with a competing constitution banning slavery: the first territory to do so.

By 1858, popular sovereignty; i.e. the vote was unintentionally being used to deny the extension of slavery. All those abolitionists migrating to the territory turned the original purpose of the southern voting plan on its head. Occasionally the consequence of legislation works to the opposite of its intent, simply because the initial purpose of it is often designed to satisfy special interests. That was absolutely the case of Senator Douglas' legislation calling for "local" popular sovereignty.

By 1857/1858, Free Soilers had accumulated the popular vote. It was too late for slavery to prevail in Kansas. Their constitution was pending in Washington. Its signing would be one of the first acts of the new president, Abraham Lincoln.

From 1856 to 1861, this difference in Applied Religion in Kansas formed the Ante-bellum prototype for the tragic war between the States.

Pre-war, northern citizens agreed on moral and religious grounds that slavery must be abolished. They disagreed however on the means and the method. Would it be achieved through reasoning or bloodshed? For fifty years reasoning prevailed but so did slavery. The problem was profoundly complex as it was profoundly wrong to enslave. Though the debate lasted through several generations, by mid century it became obvious that the South would never be persuaded to give up slavery, short of war! By the time the Kansas Territory possessed a majority vote for a free state, most southern states had made two pivotal decision: one to continue slavery; two to declare a separate independent Confederacy. That forced them to a third decision: to fight for independence. In 1861, to defend their necessity, they struck the first blow at Fort Sumter.

In volume I of this Journal, Sam Stewart, Augusta's father, had attended a rally * in Detroit, where tub-thumping abolitionists spoke persuasively in favor of northern immigrants going to the New Kansas Territory to both outvote the pro-slavery element in the contest of popular sovereignty and the abundance of economic opportunity. Sam quickly sold his sawmill and general store on Lake Erie, bought a Studebaker (the body of a prairie schooner) and left with his two daughters, Augusta and Adda, for the new territory, where their first stop was Plymouth, which the girls quietly discovered was also a way station on John Brown's northbound "underground" railroad.

Traveling mostly solo for forty days on the way to Kansas, Augusta begins volume I as the family's optimistic notary. In Plymouth, close to the Nebraska line, their personal episodes of 1856 will later appear in the tapestry of territorial history; at the time some of their experiences are deemed so sensitive that the girls are advised to hide their journals and notes, particularly Augusta's entries about a letter and her episode with a young disillusioned officer planning to desert the army who invites Augusta's company, her first proposal.

He explains to Augusta that he's come to disrespect his assignment of harassing and oppressing the new arrivals, but only the abolitionists. In time Augusta comes to suspect that he and other Southerners she met lacked commitment. Captain Henry explains to Augusta that slavery really only favors an elite

*summer, 1856

minority, which stifles opportunity for the rest, thereby spawning whole social layers of resentment. He anticipates war and doesn't want to fight to defend an aristocracy. She declines his proposal, but never forgets it.

Within weeks of arriving in the territory, Sam volunteered to fight in one of "General" Jim Lane's free soil militia companies. After several small but successful skirmishes, Sam's company was captured by the U. S. Army and interred in a P.O.W. camp, run by pro-slavery elements.

The girls temporarily move a few miles north to peaceful Archer, Nebraska.

By January 1st of 1857, Sam and eighty more who were interred were released on parole.

14.

A TALK WITH MR. CHASE
February 1858

Frank Robinson, who, I've discovered, thinks he's now engaged to Adda, approached me as I was outside the tent hanging up some laundry and said after some small talk, "Augusta, I should like to have Chase as a brother-in-law. He's first rate."

"Well," I replied, "why don't you then?"

"Oh, I'm going to one of these days. If he doesn't cooperate, I reckon it will be his fault."

I said under my breath to myself, "Well, Mr. Robinson, you are rather presumptuous." In fact, I could barely contain my humor. Adda has confided to me on more than one occasion about certain reservations she has about Mr. Robinson. My conclusion is that Frank's romantic intentions toward my sister are not exactly reciprocated and the likelihood that Mr. Robinson will be my brother-in-law is at best rather remote.

On February, 8th Father, Frank Swift, Jerry Jordan, Mr. Otterson and Mr. Whitney left to survey a town site that they had previously located and staked out. They've agreed to call it "Arizonia" (rather than Orizonia.) It's located where the White Water and the Walnut Rivers come together a few miles from here.

The balance of the parts for our sawmill finally arrived. The load was so heavy that the freighters used a four-mule rig to pull their wagon, a standard practice. The steam boiler was not in this shipment. It is "on the way." Two gentlemen from eastern Iowa, Mr. Young and a Mr. Eastridge, a Scotchman, accompanied the freight. They are millwrights assigned by the Pennsylvania factory that makes the boiler to assemble the entire steam mill.

Our claim includes frontage on the Walnut River. Father wants to erect the mill close enough that logs can be floated (or pulled on the ice) from upstream woodlands. Mules will be used to pull the logs up the bank, where they will be stored before being cut. Father has accumulated a supply of cement from Eastern sources, and a huge pile of river-run gravel intended for the sawmill's foundation, which Mr. Eastridge and Mr. Young will manage. By providing "board and room" to travelers who are looking for a few day's employment on their way west, when the weather permits we give them a shovel and a large wood-framed screen, which they prop up at an angle down by the river.

They shovel river edge gravel onto the screen. With a washing, mud and sand go through the screen and in time a pile of gravel accumulates at the bottom of the screen, which is washed again with river water. At the end of the day, these men, using our small wagon and a horse, bring the gravel to the location Father has picked for the foundations, halfway between the house and the river. We never get more than two or three days' labor from these itinerants before they announce that they are moving on, or they just up and leave. On two or three occasions they've taken our shovel with them and I must buy another one from Mr. Howland. He says that the Stewarts are his best shovel customers.

Mrs. Weibley (the doctor's wife) came by this morning, February 9th. It's become a delightful part of our recreation—and distraction from our crude living conditions—to visit with new arrivals and old friends. Adda, Mrs. Weibley and myself have been planning for some time a visit with Mrs. Cordis. Her husband Tom, one of the town "founders," arrived last July. A little before noon today the three of us "marched" up the creek to the Cordises'. On the way we stopped to chat with the millwrights, Mr. Eastridge and Mr. Young. Mr. Eastridge, the older one, seems to be Father's age, maybe older and is obviously in charge. Though he is recently from Iowa, he was originally from Scotland, and lived for a while in Canada. He has a brogue so strong I can hardly understand a word he's saying and his mouth is so obscured by his bushy red mustache that I get no help by watching his lips. He just assumes that we "get it all" and he keeps on talking. He has a great sense of humor and punctuates many of his sentences with hearty laughter and words that make no sense at all, like "swith," "foosh," "aloss," "whurra," "braugh," and begins some of his sentences with "Ah, weel noo." He claims to have had several jobs, both in the Old Country and in the States, dealing with boilers, steam engines and steam-driven machinery.

Mr. Young and Mr. Eastridge seem to be making slow progress. Lord knows we need that mill up and running. We need planks for flooring and framing in place of logs for the many houses waiting to "go up." Mr. Howland is working up a big detailed order for lumber to build his new store, which will replace his tent store. Mr. Chase hopes to get the carpentry on that job and is already working on the framing of Jerry Conner's store down on the old Hildebrand claim. Chase knows that his carpentry prospects will pickup considerably when the mill starts.

Father is President of the Town Company and is in charge of selling town lots. Because he will survey them, if asked. Our house has become "Hotel Eldorado" for the newcomers who spend two or three days discussing land business with him. There's hardly a night goes by that some newcomer (or two) isn't lodging and eating with us. We need more space for the overnight lodgers, but won't get it 'til the sawmill starts up. Adda and I do the best we can to make our guests comfortable and that includes serving up two or three meals a day. Sometimes they pay, but mostly they don't. But it's all quite congenial. Often they have some supplies, which they contribute, or they will go up or down the river and shoot game, which is abundant, so it isn't as though we provide charity.

Well, we arrived at the Cordises' about noon, just in time for dinner and who should be there besides Tom Cordis? None other than Mr. Chase. Of course, I am so glad to see him in a social setting. When he is around our claim, with all the hustle and bustle, he assumes such a businesslike air, the carpenter-soon-to-be-contractor, the surveyor associate of my father's, not at all the romantic prospect for the eldest of the (eligible) Stewart girls. With occasional humor I wonder if he dared to pay the town founder's daughter a little warm, friendly attention, if it would somehow tarnish his professional status? Heavens forbid! Frank, on the other hand can't keep his eyes and his thoughts (and perhaps by now, I suspect his hands) off my sister. Since Chase and Frank Robinson are so close, why doesn't a bit, just a smidgen, of Frank's ardor rub off on Mr. Chase? It's a mystery and I'm left some days pondering: Is Mr. Chase part of my future? I would like to think so, but I can't seem to find a way to let him know. In fact, when I do get an opportunity, some demon inside me puts contrary words in my mouth, followed by actions that, when I review them later, I can see were sure to have discouraged a little friendly spark from Mr. Chase. Did Mrs. Cordis arrange to have Mr. Chase here? It would be appropriate since it's less than a week before Valentine's Day, and it is a delightful female trait to be a matchmaker. Well, we'll see.

We had a wonderful afternoon visit, talking about all

the new people coming in and the political goings-on. Eldorado is really getting to be quite the city. Midafternoon Mr. Cordis and Mr. Chase excused themselves for an hour or so. They said they were going down to check on the progress of the mill. Tom Cordis will make most of the ironwork on it, various straps and connectors, pulley supports, etc., and Mr. Chase, I'm sure, will do the carpentry. And I think Mr. Chase wants some advice about the well. He knows, and we all know, that the progress on the well is not acceptable to Father. Even with blasting there are some weeks they hardly gain a half-foot.

Part of the afternoon with the ladies was consumed in speculating on the rumor that Frank has announced his engagement to Adda. Now Adda was present during this conversation, but with a quickly contrived fluttery of charm and humor, she implied that it's all news to her. Here's what I really think: Frank Robinson thinks he is engaged to my little sister and maybe in a moment of weakness or generosity she has given him some encouragement and he has blabbed it about, telling all of his men friends that he is now engaged to the daughter of Eldorado's President. As serious as this step would be, I've never heard a "peep" about it from Adda.

Mr. Cordis and Mr. Chase returned from the mill. Their interruption made us suddenly realize that the afternoon had gone, vanished like the sizable pile of firewood the Cordises' friendly little pot-bellied stove had consumed this afternoon. There wasn't much of the day remaining. We'd had such a good time together, but it was time to go.

As we made our good-byes, put on coats, looked for gloves and scarves, who should volunteer to fight off the Indians and wolves on our way home, but my dancing instructor? There was enough daylight left for us to get home a little before dark. But we were in no hurry. Father was away and we'd have plenty of time to make supper.

As we stepped outside the Cordis cabin, there was a light, wispy, rather pleasant scent of wood smoke, some of it hanging thinly out over the river valley, a lingering reminder of our sociable afternoon. Mr. Chase said it reminded him of the wintertime aroma in the Massachusetts woods during maple sugaring time. Then he made a little speech about our ancient love of wood smoke, which, he said, is very old in our culture. It is all mixed up with our need for warmth and fire and food preparation, he added, and it is both a friendly signal to our nostrils and a sign of comfort. He said these pleasures are instinctive, ancient—all these observations and reminiscing seemed to come out of him in an instant. It was the longest speech I've heard him deliver. In fact, it was more words than I've heard from him since his arrival last November. I'm seeing a poetic side to my Yankee carpenter.

The western sky was a little overcast. The late-afternoon sun was clear in outline, as a red disk, through the clouds. The low clouds close to the horizon were layered in unbelievably soft yellows, bright yellows and yellowish-whites. Slightly above those were horizontal cloud-clumps of pink and purple edged in white, and as the cloud layers slowly moved south, they carried these colors and shades with them. There must have been a dozen shades moving between the bright pink and purple layers. This blaze of sunset dominated the entire low horizon.

As the veiled sun sank toward the western edge of the earth, it carried down and compressed these layers of colors.

Mr. Chase said, "You know, if a painter tried to paint that sunset, duplicating exactly those colors, no one would believe him. The art academies would dismiss him as a lunatic. No painter could replicate and blend those colors with enough honesty and skill to represent that sunset." We both agreed.

As the path turned a little west to follow the river, the sun's outline, now straight ahead, was almost gone. All that remained was just a segment of the circle, an upside-down pink-purple saucer slowly disappearing out on the western edge of the prairie, where there is no demarcation between land and sky.

Mr. Chase touched my arm lightly to signal he wanted a little privacy. That touch brought a quick warm spasm of joy and expectation, the gladness of life and, I should add, a little giddiness. Yet it was a bit frightening. I have always been suspicious of these emotions. I've been afraid I might not be able to control them. The question is, can we enjoy them and at the same time be in control? In one of those fleeting fantasies that only happens in our mind, I thought I saw Mrs. Gates back in Lawrence preparing herself not for the noon meal but for the arrival of her "soldiers," her long auburn hair mingling and filtering the afternoon colors of the sunlight coming through the glass bevels in those little triangular panes in her front door. Her eyelids almost closed, she was smiling at me while one of her favorite "soldiers" approached her for his greeting. She continued to smile at me as they came together in their embrace. Her face became radiant in the lingering sunlight as they commenced a long kiss. I watched with a mixture of disapproval and vicarious curiosity, mingled with a little envy. Though her romance was none of my business, she was so open about it that those scenes have never left me.

We held back and Adda went ahead. With his hand on my arm, it occurred to me that maybe our time had come for some talk about us, just us, perhaps a little affection, a little courting, perhaps a promise of just a little allowable intimacy. "Tonight," I thought, "he will finally find his voice for the two of us, but it needs to be more than a voice, it needs to be a key—A key, I felt, that could begin to unlock some mutual affinity, some latent affection, that exists or could exist between us and that, until now, has been missing. I thought his little speech about the joys of smelling a bit of winter's wood smoke, would prove to be a happy prelude. Perhaps tonight will be our time. We seemed to have made so much of our opportunity in Archer, starting with my dancing lessons at the various autumn balls and continuing for several weeks of Mrs. Strong's frequent and generous dinnertime hospitality to the boys, a hospitality made more congenial if they brought the wild turkeys for roasting. Yes, I think we made the most of those good times. Then things changed. And I thought, "If the quality of mercy is not strained, is the quality of opportunity equally pure?" If we fail to take advantage of the occasion, do we get a second chance? How much opportunity does God give us? Though we clearly should make the most of it, we seldom do. And God, I'm sure, has some little punishment to mete out for those who don't make the most of the moment. Perhaps when we are blessed with an opportunity, there is an obligation to make the most of it. Perhaps opportunity clearly carries an obligation.

These thoughts, however, did not preoccupy me so much that I failed to observe Mr. Chase's discomfort. Obviously he had something to say. But it was difficult for him. He mumbled a bit and spoke with half-sentences and haltingly even with those. But the long and the short of it is he harbors some dissatisfaction with our relationship. What's more, he's given it a lot of thought, though I suppose that is a good measure of his continued interest. In "his humble opinion," he says, I am not receptive to his friendly gestures and his many little kindnesses. That it is well known that action speaks louder than words and I have not credited him enough for his actions. Well, this certainly sparked my curiosity. Actions? What actions? I am disappointed by this turn of the conversation. Perhaps a better word is "disillusioned." I am put off by his remarks and by his attitude. Instead of finding some pleasantries, he chooses to complain. I don't improve this situation by asking him to recite examples where his actions have not been properly appreciated by me. And in all fairness, he did remind me of things, for which I had failed to show gratitude.

He posed a question. "Why," he asked, "do you suppose I came to Lawrence when I learned your whereabouts?" He added that he had found adequate carpentry work up in Rulo and, that it certainly wasn't his concern for the abolitionist movement that had brought him back into the Territory. In fact, he said, one of the terms of his being released from Lecompton was that he leave the Territory immediately and he mumbled something to the effect that if old Judge Cato got wind that he was back in Kansas, the judge might put out a warrant for him. While I was groping for an answer, he said, "I'll answer my own question. When you and Adda went away, the Strongs' house suddenly became quiet. Not quiet as in the absence of noise, but quiet in the absence of joy and companionship. When you and Adda were working for Mrs. Strong, I looked forward to coming over and to going to all those dances. After you left, I went to a few dances but it was less fun. "And Augusta", (there, he said it again for the second time in two months), "you know, we sort of learned to dance together. Neither of us was much at dancing 'til those balls at Archer."

"Well, I can't deny that. Indeed, I've called up the memory of those dances time and time again."

He added that after Adda and I left, there remained no attraction at the Strongs' for Frank and him, although they made an effort to remain sociable. "On one occasion, for old times sake, to see, I suppose, if we could resurrect the 'good old days' when the Stewart sisters were there, we shot a turkey, cleaned it and brought it to Mrs. Strong. She dutifully invited us to supper. Well, the meal was fine—but quiet—you were gone. Adda wasn't around to tease Frank and to keep the conversation lively. Mrs. Strong was most hospitable but her hospitality couldn't make up for your not being there. Even your friend, Mr. Potter, the southerner with his missing front teeth, seemed to be melancholy and attributed it to the absence of the Stewart girls.

"This gloomy meal at the Strongs'," said Mr. Chase, "took place on a cold mid-January day, an already 'awful day,'" he added, "because of the gray skies and freezing weather.

"So that day about a year ago," he said, "I decided wherever you were, I'd follow you, even if it meant risking Lecompton (prison) again, though, with most of the abolitionists out on pardon, I think I'm fairly safe and don't have to worry about that any longer. But I'd been willing to take the risk. I asked Mr. Strong if he could help me locate your father. That's how I found your address for the letter I sent you in Lawrence. Your tardiness in answering it made me quite apprehensive about my decision to come down to Lawrence.

"You see," he added, "these are all actions of mine that you seem to take for granted." I didn't help matters by reminding him that though Frank visited Adda, Chase failed to visit me. I didn't tell him that I might have been sick out at the Gates farm when the two boys were in Lawrence last summer.

He went on to ask, "Why do you suppose, I persuaded Frank Robinson, and also Buchanan and Benton, to come all this distance?" I started to say, and should have said, that Adda and I were so flattered that he and Frank Robinson did come, that we had talked about it for weeks, that we had looked forward to their arrival and said that we would be so happy with their company, but that's not what came out. What I said was, "I don't have the slightest idea" and I uttered it totally without grace.

He said, as an act of loyalty, he had stemmed some unsavory gossip about Adda and me up at Mr. Howland's store, but he wouldn't reveal what that gossip was or its source. Why he brought this up, I don't know.

He seemed to have a list of these complaints, interjecting

more than once in his not very romantic speech that he has "no hard feelings." This seems to me to be a male comment. I've heard Father use it when, indeed he does have some "hard feelings." I thought, with a bit of dark humor, that the next thing we will be doing out here on the prairie is slapping each other on the back, shaking hands like two old businessmen who have finally arrived at a settlement to a dispute, and mutually agreeing that, after all, there's "no hard feelings."

What troubled him the most, he said, was my remoteness, the thick stone wall he claims I've erected between us and that he finds impenetrable; and he continued with other grievances: that when he is present and we are alone and he is prepared for conversation, I seem indifferent to him, that this is a one-way romance, that his attention should be reciprocated, that I seem to be unable to return his attention, signs of loyalty, affection, etc., and that I hardly acknowledged his presence in Lawrence last fall—and "things have not improved much since I've come down here," he added.

Then he said something that really hurt . . . probably because it contained a kernel of truth, namely; that to him I come over as someone who prefers, to extreme, her own company. Now that simply isn't true but I can see how Mr. Chase could come to that conclusion.

Why is it that everybody thinks I prefer my own company? I don't enjoy being alone. When I experience too much solitude, clouds of depression and troubling loneliness set in. I guess I'm too good an actress. I don't show how much I want and enjoy company.

He said that I am so self-sufficient that I don't need anyone else. In what I took to be a compliment, but was perhaps one more item on his grocery list, he said, with a note of finality, that I had far too much self-confidence and independence to be truly

19

companionable.

He's part right on that score. I don't lack self-confidence. I have an abundance of that. When your mother dies (I was eight) and nobody fills that void, and you have a little sister to take care of, and a willingness to become housekeeper for your father, all the things that your mother normally does for you, you suddenly must do for yourself and others; these new responsibilities develop self-confidence. But for heaven's sake, self-confidence doesn't rule out normal desires for companionship. But I didn't say any of that to him. I'm simply writing all this later. Walking with Mr. Chase, waiting for him to finish his sentences, tolerating these long pauses only to have another complaint follow the pause. The wood smoke from the Cordises' stove had drifted down the valley, but it seemed more acrid now, less pleasant.

Well, maybe Mr. Chase is right. I could be friendlier, I could encourage him, I ought to be able to articulate some little signs of affection, some compliments and when I do, I should employ more grace. If I could show Mr. Chase some sympathy for what he is trying to say, it would certainly help but the type of sympathy he is looking for is so hard for me to express. Talking makes me feel vulnerable. I prefer to show my sympathy and my caring for others through my actions. When Mrs. Gates' little girl had small pox, I knew it was not enough for me to be sympathetic. I had to help Fanny get well and I did. It was I who pulled her through, not that tongue-clucking, quack from Philadelphia.

Well, if Mr. Chase knew, if he only knew how lonely it can be here evenings, while Father is away politicking or out running a line * for someone . . . But when it was my turn to talk, I simply took offense. I first responded by saying bland and noncommittal things like, "My, my." Finally I found some courage to speak

*A term surveyors use when they measure and establish a line that will demarcate a border or property

but what came out contained very little warmth. I accused him of coming to the wrong conclusion, that he lacked adequate sensitivity, and in my heart I'm a very warm, affectionate and friendly soul. This speech of mine was followed by a very long silence.

We had lost sight of Adda. The sun was totally gone now, but it wasn't yet dark, and for some mysterious reason all the clouds that had celebrated the day's end with such color, were gone now, and had taken south with them my romantic anticipations. It was so quiet that we could hear the snow and ice, clumped together in little frozen clods, break under our footsteps.

There are all kinds of quiet but this was an anxious quiet filled with gray unfriendly shadows of our own making. We continued towards home in disagreeable silence.

There was a little snow on the prairie, the wind having drifted it here and there.

The mild day was continuing into a mild twilight, but not a very pleasant twilight for Mr. Chase and me, and I wondered, in metaphor, if this walk was twilight for our relationship. As we walked in silence along the river's edge, I could catch faint glistening reflections from patches of running water on the surface of the ice. The water had bubbled up, broken free through little cracks in the ice that confines the river from bank to bank.

The evening moon, just a stingy silvery sliver, was low and distant in the south. I imagined I saw Mr. Chase up there in the distance, walking on its surface. He was talking, still exhausting, with little puffs of vapor, his never-ending list of complaints. I continued to watch Mr. Chase make his way along the moon's surface. I guess I got a little hypnotized, a little disoriented from being so disappointed that to break this spell, I spoke up or mumbled something. I don't recall what it was but Mr. Chase, who was not on the moon after all, asked me what it was that I had just said. I pretended to clear my throat. I couldn't find the generosity to give him the satisfaction of admitting that I had spoken. In fact, all this time he was walking next to me—between me and the river—with his hand still remaining on my left coat sleeve, where it had been all along since leaving the Cordises' cabin.

The promise implied by his touch, the same touching that a half hour ago (or was it years ago?) filled me with such hope and expectation, had simply become an illusion—all gossamer stuff but, believe me, I'm grateful for hope and illusion. Sometimes hope is all we have between the reality of dirt floors and the hope that in time we'll have the same wooden floors enjoyed in most civilized American homes, the hope that the Indians will be friendly against the reality that sometimes they aren't.

We still had some distance to cover and I thought, in metaphorical parallel, that I too have some distance to cover. If I expect to get to know this carpenter better, I'll have to find a better way than I've found so far in inducing him to get better acquainted with me. Do I want to walk alone? What's left of life's river with Mr. Chase? Or should I free myself from this Yankee who seems as cold as the ice out there? Or should I separate myself like the little patch of water that has bubbled up and separated itself from its frozen cap and is moving on? But a glimmer of hope popped into my head—a hope that he has not given up on me. For in spite of his grievances, for the most part he has made more effort than I. After all, he's here, not in Rulo or Archer, or Lawrence for that matter. And so my thoughts drifted to other suitors, not as serious alternatives…but as possibilities that flattered my vanity and puffed up my self-esteem. Erastus Howland came to mind, and Frank Swift and perhaps the most adventuresome prospect, certainly the most far-fetched one: the elopement proposed by Captain Henry, the Southerner, the latent abolitionist back in

Plymouth. I wondered for a moment where the two of us would be by now if we had pursued his plan. "Did he ever desert?" I wondered.

I enjoy Mr. Howland's company, but I feel no romance or affinity for him. He affords me ample opportunity to get to know him better. It has not been lost on me that Mr. Howland seems to find an excuse once or twice a week to come by our claim. He is a first rate flatterer. He flatters my handiwork (I made a towel and gave it to him as a present). He likes my baked bread—and when I can get good flour, I think it's pretty good myself. Even when Mr. Howland brings the supper, he flatters me by comparing his efforts to mine.

But I think Mr. Howland is simply looking for a business partner who happens to be female. Occasionally, he asks me to write up orders for him, and I do. But I'm never sure what his motive is. Does he just want a little help? Or is it a test to see if I would make a good wife for a grocer? And Mr. Howland seems to create a mystery about his past. I'm not sure where he is from; except I know it is the "North" and that he is a Christian, and an abolitionist (but not in the extreme.) He certainly has courage to come all this distance with his inventory of groceries, dry goods, etc. But where did he get the money to pay for all these supplies? Today is Valentine's Day. Now on Valentine's Day in every other civilized place, down through the centuries, the valentine has been carried by a messenger. In Eldorado it will be a bleak day because the town has no post office and all the young people are well aware of that, so I presume we won't exchange many valentines.

Well, I received a valentine after all. It was late in the day but before I commenced to prepare supper; a messenger appeared at our door with a roasted turkey from our friend, Mr. Howland, and tied to the roasting pan was a red valentine. I asked the messenger if he was delivering a "sundown" valentine, but I'm afraid the romance or humor of the question was lost on him. I added, "Business must be pretty good to afford Mr. Howland so much time for turkey shooting." I sent word via the messenger that Mr. Howland should join us for supper. He did, and he brought with him one of his customers, none other than Mr. Jacob Chase. We all spent the evening together. Something seems to have come over Chase. * Maybe that long walk and never ending talk along the river a few days ago allowed him to "get it off his chest." Perhaps that night, by reciting all of his frustrations he has purged himself of them? Oh, I do hope so. Maybe it's the spirit of Valentine's Day? He called me Augusta tonight. He usually calls me Miss Stewart. That is, when I can get him to acknowledge that I'm on this Earth. The courage it took Chase to call me Augusta is like the courage it took Columbus to seek the New World or drove Saint George to slay the dragon—but I guess I shouldn't be so snippy. After all these months, I probably should be a bit more grateful; as I get older I will learn to see grace as a virtue that I should acquire. That has been Father's advice from time to time. I'm beginning to understand that unlike Erastus Howland or Frank Swift, who are both quite sociable and enjoy conversation, Chase is shy. And with him I'm shy. If I want to get to know him better I'll simply have to be more outgoing and friendly. Well, that might be easier said than done

A few evenings later the young men of Eldorado had a meeting to organize a debating club. According to Mr. Howland, they made great progress. When I pressed him to reveal the greatness of that progress, he told me, "Well, we've agreed on a name, 'The Eldorado Lyceum.'" The meeting was held at Dr. and Mrs. Weibley's cabin. I was not in attendance. Adda was there, accompanying Frank Robinson, who had been invited. For the life of me I think Frank's only qualifications for this lyceum are

*From that 1858 Valentine's Day on, Augusta always called him "Chase".

that he is young and that he is a gentleman. I have known Mr. Robinson for some time and although he does possess some of the expected social graces, he is by no stretch of the imagination a debater. And he certainly is no scholar. I don't think he reads a book a year, whereas Adda and I use much of our spare time reading. In that couple, it is my sister who is the scholar. But, despite that fact, Frank Robinson was invited to this meeting and my sister, his fiancée, (you may be sure), was only there as his guest. She and Mrs. Weibley "did the honors" with the refreshments, which means Adda was privy to all their talk. Mr. Howland reported that during the meeting Adda spoke up and said that since there are simply not enough men (young or old) to makeup a proper and vigorous debating society, they had better not exclude a big fraction of the population, not to mention the available talent namely, the ladies. At this juncture, Adda may have gone too far. Mr. Buchanan made the serious mistake of laughing at my sister's suggestion. In the blink of an eye she challenged him to a debate. Now Adda, I will point out, dear journal, was suffering a felon on her finger. * I'm afraid the poison, in circulating through her body, had affected her reasoning. When asked by Mr. Buchanan, with a bit of arrogance, what debating subject she preferred, Adda answered, "Any subject that you care to choose, Mr. Buchanan,"— which she pronounced, according to Mr. Howland, as "Bee You Cannon" — "and, if we can find three honest judges in this town, you will learn to your dismay that I have beaten you, hands down!"

In the presence of the recently formed Eldorado Lyceum, Mr. Buchanan had no choice but to accept my sister's challenge.

God seems to have given my sister extra measures of confidence and courage along with her robust health and energy.

*A felon, also known as a whitlow, is an abscess under or near a fingernail or toenail

That confidence was honed by training in Detroit. We both had taken a course called, Rhetoric and Public Speaking and Adda had subsequently won second prize in a public speaking contest. She also won a Bible at Sunday school for her recitation and descriptive explanation of the Beatitudes. Now these were not the dry Beatitudes found in the King James Version but a more lilting poetic rendition. Adda had studied from a different translation, a translation published by the Mormons she found, and it contained two more homilies, which had been overlooked by King James scholars. Our Presbyterian preacher, from the famous Presbyterian college in New York, said he had never heard such a beautiful reading or interpretation of the Beatitudes. Well, that's my sister.

After Adda's challenge to Mr. Buchanan, the group spent several minutes arguing over what would be an appropriate subject for the inaugural debate. They referred to a journal on rhetoric, that Mr. Howland just happened to be carrying with him that evening. The journal, published by Dartmouth College in New Hampshire, suggested over a dozen debating topics but the group soon boiled their choices down to three:

1. Was the Mexican War simply a political contrivance by President Polk to get more land for cotton and slavery?

2. On the American frontier is there any evidence of the "Noble Savage," as depicted by James Fenimore Cooper or the French philosopher, Jean-Jacques Rousseau?

3. Do you see a connection between the suffering of the North American immigrant and Job of the Old Testament? And since my sister said she would outdebate Mr. Buchanan on *any* subject, neither she nor Mr. Buchanan was allowed to vote on the proposition.

According to Adda, there was a lively discussion about the debate topics. It boiled down to whether "us prairie chickens" could handle such weighty themes. It was my sister's opinion that we were up to the task.

On the second ballot the subject chosen and reframed for the debate was:

Resolved that the Noble Savage, as described by James Fennimore Cooper and Jean Jacque Rousseau, exists on the American frontier as in the jungles of the Belgian Congo.

For the Affirmative: Mr. Buchanan
For the Negative: Adelaide Henrietta Stewart
Date: 7 P.M. March 16, 1858
Place: Howland's Store
Judges: Dr. Marcus Weibley,
Mr. Erasmus Howland,
Mrs. Tom Cordis

15.

TWO VISITS FROM PAUL, THE OSAGE
February 1858

D r. Weibley was here today for a visit and I'm afraid we took advantage of his presence by asking him to look at the felon on Adda's swollen finger.

Reacting with concern, he decided to lance it immediately. He said he was concerned about the red lines on her hand and forearm: a sure sign, he told us, of beginning blood-poison. I won't put into this journal what spurted out of that finger.

The Doctor asked if I had any goldenseal. *   I said I thought so. He suggested that I make a poultice from it and wrap it around Adda's finger to draw out any remaining poison. He went on to say he wanted Adda to eat two raw vegetables a day and cut down any meat that was greasy.

The next day, in midafternoon, Paul came back for another visit. This time Adda invited Paul and the chief's son, Mas-Mas, and the "other one" into our cabin.

After some bantering and small talk, Adda asked, "Were your people, Paul, moved here from back East by the Federal Government?"

"No, we are the true Kansa. We've always been here."

*It's the ground-up root of the goldenseal that is used.

"Oh? How did you get here?"

Paul, "The south wind blew us here. We are of the south wind. We call our tribe the Wa Sash. We are the Deer People. No, we were not moved. Some of your people call us Osage. But we are just one tribe of Osage.

"Kansa in our language means 'wind' or 'wind god.' There are four great wind gods called, Wa Kandas: the north wind, the south wind and so on. We have a name for each of these four wind gods. And there are also three lesser wind gods like the Wa Kanda that blows near the earth and carries our scents, and the grass and moves the trees. The birds all fly with this Wa Kanda. There is a friendliness enjoyed between the birds and this Wa Kanda that we envy but don't understand. The middle Wa Kanda moves the clouds. He too can go in all four directions. Sometimes he is joined by a sister god that can make rain, snow and hail. And finally there is upper Wa Kanda or "Great Spirit", the most powerful god. He directs the sun and moon and stars."

Looking at us, Paul said, "You were brought here by the East Wa Kanda, the Wa Kanda, that blows the grass and the trees and the bushes. It's one more example of the gods' indifference to us. We have always lived here. Why did the Wa Kanda blow all you White into our land and across our land?"

"You mean each wind is a god?"

"Not exactly. A god makes the wind blow because he is a god, a god that moves. The wind is a god and the god is wind. Those twelve gods are always on the move. They are constantly reminding us of their power to move all things, like the grass or the clouds or the sun."

"Oh, that's interesting. You think a wind god moves the sun?"

"Oh, yes. The sun moves, doesn't it? What do you think makes it move?"

"The sun Wa Kanda has a contest with the East Wa Kanda and he is so powerful that he works day and night. At night he moves the moon. The moon changes its shape to fool the Wa Kanda, but it doesn't work. The wind god always finds the moon and pushes it in the sky."

"That is a beautiful explanation, Paul, and I think I understand it."

"No, you only understand the story because I am explaining it to you, but that doesn't mean that you really understand the gods."

"Can you pray to your gods?"

Paul, "Well, yes, we can," said Paul, "but we don't. We don't pray for favors. Only our elders are allowed to, we pray to express our fears. We are fearful of our gods but proud towards men. We don't ask for personal favors from our Wa Kandas. It is useless. Our gods are too busy and too indifferent. They don't care about us, so we must learn to get along with them. We are like fleas on a dog, and a flea's prayer to a dog would be useless."

Paul said that they had good reason to fear them. We have many worries, all caused by our Wa Kandas. In the upper winds, the winds that move the clouds, there are gods lurking there—some that speak and tell us that rain is coming—but we are simple people, so we need more warning, so his sister god has light that she saves from the sun Wa Kanda and she flashes this light, which tells us it might rain. The rain simply comes when the rain Wa Kanda has too much for himself. He isn't sharing it with us. He simply gets rid of it when he has too much. We need it for our crops, but we can't influence his generosity. Your people think we can make it rain. But we can't. And neither can you."

"Paul told us that when the gods get together, they are even more dangerous." In the wintertime the Wa Kanda that blows the grass joins the snow Wa Kanda. They get into a contest of strength and this can last several days. We fear those Wa Kandas alone. So you can imagine how we fear them when they get together."

Paul said that when he attended the Quaker mission school, he had come to see some similarities between his beliefs and ours.

"We don't understand our gods and you don't understand your god. When I was in the Quaker school, there were many stories about your god that the Quakers didn't understand, like the story of Job. Why did your god punish Job? Why does your god employ all of you Christians to punish the Mormons? They are also Christians, so why are they punished?

"The Quakers don't press their god on us Kansa. The Quakers are great people. They understand that their Wa Kanda probably won't help us. And the Quakers all have to die before they get any real help from their god, so they know they have to do the best they can on their own. So they have developed many skills. And they try to pass them on to us, so that we can do better on our own, too. The Quakers teach us to read and to be better farmers. They teach our squaws to sew with Quaker needles. They wanted me to be a carpenter but we move too much to bother with building cabins."

Paul paused, "We have talked too much," he said. "We are hungry. Can we eat?"

"I have some beans with some deer meat. Would you like that?"

Paul said yes to Adda's offer, but added, you Whites eat too many beans. You should eat more corn. We have ten, maybe twenty, ways to cook corn. Next time I visit I will bring you some soft hominy. We taught the Quakers to make hominy with ashes from their wood stoves. You should save your ashes. I know where you throw them. Ashes have power over corn. Do you know hominy?"

"Of course," replied Adda. "We just don't make it. But we would like to learn."

"Well, you need a special corn for hominy. I will bring you some seed and show you how to plant it. And I will show you how to cut the fish and put the fish with the corn to get it started."

Adda, "Paul, what does fish have to do with corn?"

"The fish is a small Wa Kanda. He knows how to make the corn grow."

"Well," said Adda a little haughtily, "we've raised a lot of corn without the help of fish."

"Yes, that's what the Catholics said when I was in their school. So I showed one of the priests that my corn was stronger, taller and with more cobs than his corn. He uses fish now."

"How long were you in the Catholic school?"

"A long time. The missionaries taught me. They wanted me to become a Catholic. Their teachers were very good but very strict."

"Can you read?"

Paul, "A little, but reading isn't important. All of the Catholics could read. They were always reading but when the sickness came, the Wa Sash left. When we came back many of them had died." Reading didn't keep the Catholics from dying," said Paul. "The nuns rubbed beads. Some of them died, too. Rubbing beads didn't help. There is no medicine in beads. I gave one nun, Sister Charlotte, some of our beads and told her, 'Sister, you are in Kansa now. You must rub our beads." It was my humor. We don't rub beads. Our squaws wear them!"

"What happened?"

"She chased me out of the school with a broom. Later she died. You see, all these gods are the same. You can read, you can pray, you can rub beads but if a Wa Kanda blows a sickness and you are in the way, you will die. They don't care about us. We just have to get along with them and show fear."

After Paul and his two companions left, Adda and I talked about it. Stimulated by Paul's story about the various wind gods, I rummaged through a box of old schoolbooks and found Virgil's Aeneid. There it was: Juno, worried about a Trojan invasion, conspired with Aeolus, king of the wind gods, to disperse the Trojan fleet. Another classical reference identified Boreas as an ancient wind god, the god in charge of cold north wind. Zephyrus blew wherever and whenever it pleased him, Auster was a warm wind with rain; Eurus blew from east to west. Boreas was the worst of them, spreading mayhem. Maybe he's behind these Kansas blizzards. Some sailors thought that the north wind only blew on odd days.

So imputing godlike power to the wind isn't new. Each culture invents its own version.

The next afternoon a prairie wolf prowled around outside, howling intermittently for two hours. The noise became a nuisance. Some of our other neighbors must have heard all this howling and reported it to the store, because in late afternoon Mr. Howland came down and proved to be as adept at shooting wolves as turkeys. After he had shot the wolf, I asked him to skin it. I thought the fur would make an attractive edging on my famous shawl. Who knows? Maybe another wolf will come calling and in time I might have the makings of a fur coat.

We had some high humor at suppertime. I served a baked meat loaf of ground venison with baked potatoes and stewed turnips. The meal was heartily consumed. Our guests included the wolf slayer, Frank Robinson and Chase. * After supper, I told the others about Howland's shooting our dinner. I asked them what they thought of my recipe for wolf meatloaf. Their response was to ask for sandwiches of it to take home!

For such a small community, we don't lack for a social

*After Valentines Day of 1858 Augusta always refers to Jacob Chase as simply, Chase.

life. Another religious meeting is scheduled at the Careys' for tomorrow night. But I don't know anything about this preacher other than he will be coming from Chelsea and is an itinerant. That fellow who was here at the Careys' three weeks ago was one of the best-educated, most articulate speakers I've ever listened to. How I wish he would settle here.

Father returned from Lawrence while we were at the Careys' meeting. The evening included some new arrivals, the Fairchilds, and Mrs. Martin, a pretty little woman from England with a delightful accent. She and her husband Henry Martin, who is also English, were among the July arrivals. They are a bit younger than Father, very formal but friendly. Another July arrival, Miss Glennis Bemis, who lives nearby in Walnut, obviously came over here tonight for a social evening—The boys all call her the "Belle of Walnut." She is Catholic, not Protestant. During the meeting she remarked to me that our prairie religion is quite different from the Irish Catholic service, adding that she didn't think it was necessary for the preacher to make certain remarks about the Pope.

A few days after the meeting at Carey's Father said there would be an election held at our house and in Chelsea on March 9th and wanted to have a caucus tomorrow to discuss voting details and make appointments. They appointed Tom Cordes, Mr. Carey and Mr. Keyes to be judges and Frank Robinson and Mr. Howland to be recording clerks.

The caucus was at our house and Mr. Keyes had a slightly concealed bottle of whiskey. Father has said on more than one occasion that he hoped that the elections out here would be less dependent on alcohol than they have been in Lawrence. As much as he respects Governor Robinson, one of the criticisms Father's had of him is that the Governor seems to condone the generous use of whiskey at elections time.

In February, a few weeks after we moved into the cabin Adda and I heard rocks or clods being pelted at the sides and roof of our cabin. Adda went outside to determine what was going on.

"Paul, if that's you, stop throwing those rocks and come on over," Adda yelled.

I went over to stand in the doorway behind Adda. Paul and his two usual companions walked over to the cabin. Paul was wearing old Army laced-up leather leggings and an old heavy mackinaw with most of the collar worn or rotted away. A remnant of the collar was flapping in the wind.

As Paul approached, Adda said, "Well, I see you have not shriveled up or gotten smaller by talking with us Whites."

"Yes, I have," he responded, "my people say it is just a matter of time until I will be a ghost."

Adda walked up to Paul and grabbed what was left of the worn collar of his old mackinaw. "Look, Paul, we are going to be here for a long time, so you and I are going to conduct an experiment. I'm going to weigh you and I'm going to write your weight on a piece of paper with today's date, and each time you visit us I will weigh you. I am going to prove to you that you are not losing weight or shriveling up." Adda began pulling Paul along toward Howland's Store, while explaining to him what the word "weight" meant. I was still standing in the doorway, wondering what in the world my sister was up to now. So I decided (after quickly putting on a jacket) to follow them. Presently we were all inside the store. In recent weeks Howland had acquired a platform scale. Adda grabbed a small hammer from a bin of tools and conspicuously dropped it.

"Why did the hammer fall, Paul?"

"Because you dropped it."

"Yes, yes, but why did it go down rather than up or right or left? Why does an acorn or a walnut fall straight down?"

"Because the tree doesn't need the nut any longer. The tree let's go of the nut; you let go of the hammer."

"Yes, but why does it travel toward the earth? Let me try to explain it in terms of your gods. There is a large god in the middle of the earth that pulls all things towards him He pulls harder on big things than little things. We understand this and can measure his power. We call this power, weight. You will weigh more than that hammer. This piece of medicine," pointing to the scale, "can measure that difference." To demonstrate the scale's use, Adda stepped up on the platform, added a little black cast iron disk to a hook on the right side, slid the little balancing weights on the arm until the pointer became floating. "One hundred and twenty-four pounds", she exclaimed. She stepped off the scale. All three Indians were standing around, fascinated by these antics of my sister the White, big-talking squaw. She grabbed Paul by his mackinaw and guided him to step up on the scale.

She moved the little adjusting weights. "One hundred and thirty-two pounds, Paul!"

On a nearby counter stood a neat stack of hard candy Mr. Howland had put up in one-pound bags. Grabbing one of them, she put it in Paul's hand. "Paul, what's in this bag weighs one pound. Your body has one hundred and thirty-two of these. Did the missionaries teach you to count?"

"Oh, yes."

"Can you count to one hundred?"

"Oh, yes."

"Can you count to one hundred and fifty?"

"Oh, yes."

"Well, when you get past one hundred, stop at one hundred and thirty-two. That's how many pounds you weigh."

Paul, showing a mixture of puzzlement, amusement and some understanding of what she was saying, repeated, "One hundred and thirty-two pounds!"

My sister asked Mr. Howland if he had a little
price tag or inventory tag. He produced a cardboard inventory
tag, which had a little wire running through a reinforced hole.
Adda found a pencil and wrote:

February 27, 1858

Paul - 132 Pounds Paul remained standing on the scale. Adda
pulled up a brass rod that was concealed in the hollow vertical
post attached to the back of the scale. The top end of the rod had
a little horizontal finger fixed on it, which Adda rested on top of
Paul's head. Adda read from the brass rod, "Five feet, six inches!"

She added that figure to the inventory tag, "Paul, today,
February 27th, you are five feet and six inches tall. You will never
ever in my lifetime or yours be shorter than 5 feet 6 inches. Have
you got that through your head? Do you understand? I have just
measured how tall you are. Your medicine man said that you'd
shrivel like a wintertime grape and get smaller. Well, every time
you come to our claim in friendship, I will weigh you and measure
your height. I can personally guarantee that you won't shrink. In
this medicine, I'm as smart as your medicine man. I know all
about weights and measures. I am absolutely a walking, talking
expert on them, and that is a powerful, White's medicine!"

Paul allowed himself a small grin of relief, but I'm not sure
he was fully convinced of my sister's "medicine."

After they had left, in a soft voice I said, "Well, smarty,
now you'll have those Red Skins up here all the time."

Adda looked at me with a condescending smile of
forbearance, "Sister dear, this is our job, our noble obligation, to
bring a little civilization to these natives." She lowered her voice
and added, "What do you think all these missionaries have been
doing out here since we bought this land from old Napoleon?
How would you feel if some priest or one of these prairie parsons

told you that each time you spoke a foreign language, like that Latin you're so fond of, you would begin to shrivel up, smell like an old Roman, and in time just evaporate. But before you'd disappear, your people would have some sort of social right to shun you and give you a name like 'Stinky Stewart'? And treat you like some sort of pariah?" Well, I guess I had never thought a thing like that could happen to me, but maybe she's right. My sister does seem to have a different way of viewing things.

Over the following months, Paul did indeed visit us, always irregularly, and if it was convenient, and it usually was, my sister would march Paul up to Mr. Howland's, ask for an inventory tag and register Paul's weight and height. After several months, we accumulated twenty or thirty of those little wired tags. They all hung in a cluster on a nail just inside the door.

Each time Paul visited, Adda would take down the little bundle of tags and spread them out on the table or the floor. She and Paul would arrange them chronologically, starting with the first tag, dated February 27th. By putting them in a series, she was also teaching Paul our calendar months and their sequence. After they had the tags all arranged, Adda would patiently point to the weight and height numbers to prove to Paul that his medicine man was working some superstition on him: The tags showed that Paul was in little danger of getting smaller—in fact, just the opposite was happening.

Long after the Osage had left their hunting site and returned to their reservation sixty to seventy miles east, taking with them, I might add, their putrid buffalo hides, which on warm days with a south breeze we could smell for miles, Paul would reappear for a visit with his new teacher and they would spread out their tags. The record of his growth proved that Paul was in no danger of shrinking. Whether he truly believed it was quite another matter, but there developed a certain friendliness, a social arrangement between two cultures, between Adda and Paul. Adda would hector Paul to stand-up to his medicine man and say that he wasn't going to dry-up nor blow away, and Adda also tried to explain to him that being able to speak English was a skill he should be proud of, that it was no cause to be treated as a half-breed among his people. And I must say that Paul listened. He was much impressed by this young Michigan squaw who could shoot a rifle, cook delicious food, ride a horse bareback and had so much "medicine" about weights and measures. Sometime the following week a traveler through Eldorado stopped for supplies at Howland's Store and in an exchange of news left copies of several eastern newspapers. A few days later, Mr. Howland brought over those, intending to visit with Father about the sorghum mill. He wanted to order five gallons to be put up in quart containers. But he didn't leave the containers. I don't know where in the world he thinks we can get twenty, one-quart containers.

One of the newspapers Mr. Howland gave Father was from Chicago and had an editorial that quoted Governor Chase of Ohio to the effect that if the U.S. Army troops stationed in Kansas to protect us settlers there, soldiers who had been paid for with taxes (not just the south) couldn't prevent us from being harassed, he considered it Ohio's right and duty to interfere."

Another of the northern papers described a New York City meeting of the National Kansas Committee, where $81,000 was raised. The Committee also received donations of goods worth $110,000. In addition, according to the report, some residents of Chicago had contributed $120,000 in cash towards the Free State immigrants. The article noted that the Committee planned to "adopt" and finance 2,000 immigrants from New York State to the Territory.

The elections were held here and in Chelsea with Mr. Carey and Mr. Keyes as judges. Frank Robinson was clerk here and Chase clerk in Chelsea. Father was elected to represent this district, which included Hunter and Butler counties, in the territorial legislature.

The March elections held here also chose candidates for the Minneola Convention where Free State delegates will rewrite our Constitution. Father said only seventy-two delegates would be chosen (added later: I counted eighty-four names on a copy of the Final Draft that included Father's. James Lane was president of the convention.)

This "Likeness" taken in Lawrence in November 1859 in Dagarian's studio, I was twenty years of age.

16.

I'M ENGAGED
March 7, 1858

March 1858 Father went up to help the Martins with raising their house. The work went all right, he said, but he was worried because some of the workers were drinking. He said, "I'd like to see one 'raising' in my lifetime without liquor. I might tolerate a drink after the work is done to celebrate, but drinking and construction can only result in either an accident or shoddy workmanship, or both."

It's the first week of March and the mercury this morning was thirty-five degrees. Though chilly, it is sunny and really quite pleasant. Frank Robinson calls our place "home" now. Well, I suppose Jerry Jordan does as well. I seem to be running a boarding house—or is it a prairie orphanage?

Howland came by with a Mr. Loren Jones and took dinner with us. We already had a full table. Some newcomers, who we hope will buy a claim and help us settle Eldorado, arrived today. They are James Young and his brother, Valerins, and a companion, Mr. Couch.

The voting took place at our house today, March 9th, to elect the local free state delegates to The Leavenworth Constitutional Convention. After Jerry and Chase voted, Father, the District Representative, asked them to go to Chelsea, which is north of here about nine miles up the river to see how the vote goes there.

In the election: Eldorado polled twenty votes. Mr. Cordis, Mr. Carey, Mr. Keyes were the judges. Tom Cordis and Frank Robinson were the clerks. The convention will convene in Minneola because the Free Stators are determined not to acknowledge Lecompton as the capital. There are only eighty to eighty-five delegates—Father being one of them. He has been elected to represent Butler and Hunter Counties at this convention.

After the vote was over, Father left for Lawrence and Leavenworth, carrying the election results from both Eldorado and Chelsea, and said we could expect him to return about "April Fool's Day."

The next day Chase came by on an errand, the first time I've seen him since the caucus February 27th. I'd really like to see more of him but obviously he doesn't share that opinion.

The following Sunday, March 14th, a party of about a dozen men came through Eldorado asking for directions to Arizona. I tried a little salesmanship on them over coffee and some cinnamon cake (from my "bakery"), trying to convince them that in Eldorado we have good fodder, plenty of land, and a growing community, and will soon have a sawmill and a syrup mill, which will provide employment for those who aren't farmers and also be a source of business for others.

It seems that these men who are looking for a town site have some sort of community—they called it a colony in mind—but when I inquired as to their religious or political affiliation, etc., they politely declined to inform me.

I didn't tell them that Father was also a founder of Arizona and that they'd be buying their town lots from him. I just said he would be available to do the surveying and land office filing. They seem to know of Father's political involvement, though none of them spoke up when I inquired if any of them had previously lived in Lexington or Plymouth or Holton. I thought it would not be discreet to ask if any of them had been in the prisoners' camp at Lecompton with Father. I recorded most of their names and since I have a list of the prisoners, I can look up their names later myself.

After they had left, I made an irritating discovery. I have been unsuccessful in hiding my journal from prying eyes. Frank Robinson informed me with a few snippy comments, about his impression of my literary style, which he calls "journalistic." He doesn't have the slightest idea what the word means. When I asked him to be a bit more specific in his observations, he used an analogy. He said I am too high-minded and that I'm trying to write like Shakespeare. "Well, I'm delighted to be compared to Shakespeare," I said. "Which of his plays or sonnets do you think my prose resembles?" There was a long hesitation. Then, "Frank," I said, "what of Shakespeare have you read lately?"

After another long pause, he finally said that I was trying to get my chair higher than other people's. I thought to myself I could be sitting on a toadstool so short a cricket could look down on me and still be "higher" than Frank Robinson. One of the prices we pay for companionship out here on the prairie is personal privacy. It is simply assumed that those of us who have something to be private about must automatically share it with others.

But I bit my tongue, and didn't say anything more to Frank about it.

We have some long skinny logs that Father wants split into "rails" and Frank is fair with the ax. Three weeks ago he wasn't paying attention and the ax opened up the toe of his boot. Luckily the sharp edge went mostly between his big toe and the next one. As a consequence, he is taking some good-humored teasing about the new ventilation in his old boot. He only has one pair!

The next day Howland came by to drop off some things I'd ordered from the store. Jerry is busy cutting logs, anticipating the construction of the mill. I noticed that Chase came down, spoke to Jerry and inspected our woodpile, but made no attempt to come in. I left the door open for a few minutes as a hint. I rather hoped he would favor us with a little visit. No such luck! He did go down and spend some time with Mr. Eastridge and Mr. Young, who are assembling the sawmill.

Just before supper two gentlemen came in and inquired about available lots. I invited them to stay for supper, again hoping that Chase would join us. They are from Arkansas, both Southerners, both favor pro-slavery. They are quite current about the progress the south has made toward having what they call a corridor of slave states from Georgia to California. I was embarrassed by not knowing that Arkansas was a state and had been since 1836.

Just as I was putting the supper on the table, Howland and Chase both came in, and I invited them to join us. So we all had a nice suppertime discussion with the men from Arkansas, even if they do have peculiar politics.

Later in the week, Howland and Chase "dropped in" for an afternoon visit. The two of them played a game of backgammon and generally ignored me, but nevertheless I noticed that they both seemed to want me to be around. Jerry Jordan also dropped in to see how the game was progressing.

Jerry made some small talk with Frank, who had been here for supper. During a lull in the game Jerry trying to be inconspicuous slipped me a note. I knew from his secretive manner that I needed to keep its content from the others, so I waited until they left before I read it.

I made sure I had a good candle and then with some suspense and anticipation, opened the note. Well, it was a love letter and though men outnumber girls, we don't get love letters every day, so I intended to give it considerable candlelight.

Here follows the contents, word for word:

Miss Laura Augusta, I take this method of addressing you on a subject, delicate indeed, but of vital importance to mankind generally, but particularly your humble admirer. The subject is framed in one word, Love. `

> *And my heart, the fomenter of that*
> *feeling, tells me that you and you only*
> *do I love. Question: Is that love*
> *received with favor? Or will you*
> *choose, God Forbid, to spurn me?*
> *Yours 'til death*

Jerry

Until bedtime I thought of nothing but the letter. I read and reread it until the candle became a sputtering nubbin. As I crawled into bed, I wondered, "Where in English literature is there poetry any better than this." Before dropping off to sleep, I decided that tomorrow I would reread the sonnets for comparison. Jerry's note rather reminded me of J. A. Henry's letter up in Plymouth, in which he proposed to desert the army if I would "fly" with him to the Kansas gold fields. Captain Henry's letter, too, was full of flattery. He said I should be the "Queen of the Castle." Quite a prospect. I might have been willing to be queen, if he could have provided the castle. Although it is a lesser virtue, flattery certainly has almost unrivaled charm and persuasiveness.

Jerry's flattery is different. It is short and to the point, but a good night's sleep automatically provided me with a response though I knew it would be difficult to compose an answer as sweet and sincere as his proposal, I must decline his offer but will try to equal his flattery with enough grace that we remain friends. Sometimes the saddest duty is to say, "No." I had hoped beyond my right to hope that his letter might have contained a valentine from Chase delivered by Jerry.

The days are warming a bit. It's March 18th and the mercury this morning was fifty-one degrees.

Jerry and Chase went to the doctor's to set a saw, and returned by noon with Howland. Before they left, Miss Bemis came by. She agreed to spend the evening and will stay the night. After supper, which Howland and I prepared, we had some fine singing, though we all agreed it would have been better if Chase had remained, either to sing or to fiddle. My friend, Howland, seems taken by "the Belle," Miss Bemis, and for good reason. She is so attractive and a very engaging conversationalist. She knows all the church songs and also some old English, Irish and Scotch songs, songs I have never heard before. She says she'd be happy to teach us her songs, and has already taught us several.

Howland "dropped" by again this morning (ahem, before Miss Bemis departed! She looked as lovely before breakfast as last night after supper.) He brought some hot cornmeal muffins.

Chase came in to warm up, he says, but I think it was to checkup on all the social goings-on of last night. We all told him he'd missed some fine singing.

He is working, on and off, on the mill, but progress is slow.

Late in the day, David Upham and Joseph Boyer, two boys from Lawrence, came into town. Adda and I knew these Stubbs boys quite well when we were working in Lawrence.

They said that Mrs. Gates is still supplying nourishment, both culinary and romantic, for the Mount Oread (Stubbs) Rifles, that she is well and as beautiful as ever. Neither Joe Boyer nor David Upham was on her "most favored" list but, like Adda and me, they were observers. We explained this as delicately as we could to Howland, Chase, Frank and Miss Bemis. Howland suggested that we were voyeurs. Well, this occasioned a discussion, but first I looked up "voyeur" in the dictionary. Yes, I suppose we "fill that bill."

The Stubbs boys had brought some mail, including a letter for me from Frank Swift. Frank says that things are relatively quiet in Lawrence. He sends gratitude for the rousing good time he had with us in early February, and writes that he remains intent on settling in Eldorado. I wonder if Frank has romantic interests here or does he simply think his fortunes would be better out here?

David Upham and Joe Boyer learned of our whereabouts through Frank and now it seems that they are also thinking about locating their own claims out here in the valley. They will be welcome additions to our growing prairie "metropolis."

They seem to know the Bentons, who have proposed that we all take a "potluck" and spend Friday evening celebrating their new house. "A capital idea," as the novels say. I think I'll take a big pot of baked beans with chunks of ham; I'll start soaking the beans right now.

David Upham and Joseph Boyer were invited and, of course, so was Chase—he had been the head carpenter on the Bentons' house, and Frank had been his "first assistant." Frank and Chase had conveyed the Bentons' invitation. When Howland heard about the supper and found out that Miss Bemis would be there, he offered to bring a stuffed roast turkey in exchange for an invitation.

So it was quite a party with all the necessary social ingredients: first, a potluck supper, which always seems to provide food in excess, romantic interests and potential romance.

We were having such a pleasant time. After supper the

group wanted Chase to sing. He came over and sat next to me while everybody coaxed him. Finally he relented. He said he would sing if Howland and Frank would join him. The "trio" asked for suggestions.

The first two we asked for were "The Lone Starry Hours" and "Farewell My Lily Dear." David Upham, who also has a fine voice, joined them in some reasonably good three-part harmony. This was followed by a lovely song, "Sweet and Low," by Miss Bemis, whose music and self-confidence fill the room. She said the words came from a poem by Tennyson. For an encore, she sang "Drink Me Only with Thine Eyes." "Its title" she said, "came from words from a very old poem by Ben Johnson", which made me recall Jerry Jordan's proposal of a few days ago. When we shouted for more, she sang "Abide with Me." I hadn't heard it since our first church service in the Territory, up in Plymouth two years ago. Of course, it's an old, familiar hymn, and I knew it well, but her perfect soprano rendition brought tears to my eyes.

David Upham asked Miss Bemis if she knew "Flow Gently, Sweet Afton."

She smiled, but before she could respond, Howland stood up next to Miss Bemis and said, "Before 'Sweet Afton' was a song, it was a poem, a Bobby Burns poem," and began reciting it in a Scotch accent. When he finished, Miss Bemis said, "Mr. Howland you stand here next to me. David you come on this side. I'm going to teach you both the harmony chords to this song. We might practice once or twice before doing it together."

She instructed Howland to carry the tune while she sang David Upham's harmony part. Even that duet, a rehearsal with just two voices instead of three, was beautiful. Then David carried the tune and she taught the harmony of the lower notes to Howland. Soon she clapped her hands and said, "All right, we are ready."

And the three of them standing close together sang "Flow

Gently Sweet Afton" in very melodious three-part harmony, so captivating that before they'd finished, Chase was standing next to Howland, their two heads together in low-note harmony. Adda squeezed in beside Miss Bemis and began to carry the soprano melody. My voice is a little lower so I joined David's part but an octave above his. Frank and Joe Boyer sang melody one octave below Miss Bemis.

Singing for the first time as a group was so special and so satisfying that we sang several of the stanzas over and over. We didn't want this rare harmony of our own making to end.

> Flow gently, sweet Afton, among thy
> > green braes
> Flow gently, I'll sing thee a song in thy
> > praise
> My Mary's asleep by thy murmuring
> > stream
> Flow gently, Sweet Afton, disturb not
> > her dream.

When we finished we were standing in a tight semicircle, and the Bentons had joined us. We had to disengage our arms, which we had placed about each others' waists to applaud our own performance.

Afterwards no one spoke.

Each of us knew that we'd just spontaneously created, in that song, some fine musical fellowship, but that it was evanescent, not likely to occur again.

To break the silence, Miss Bemis, conscious that she'd led us in this rare social achievement, said, "I think we need a few Irish tunes. If you know the words or the melody, join in," and she began a medley of four or five songs. When someone was strong with the melody, she sang a lilting soprano harmony. Our group knew all but two. In this fashion we sang the hours away.

During the entire evening Howland couldn't resist looking at Miss Bemis. The need to harmonize gave him an excuse to put his arm around her waist. She did not resist. In fact, she lowered one of her hands to cover his and as they sang, their heads were close together. I think he is smitten. They do make a lovely couple. It will be very interesting to see how this romance blossoms. If Miss Bemis chooses to stay in Eldorado, she will be most welcome. She and her parents are with the group camped across the creek. But she doesn't like camping, so we see a good deal of her.

She is here so much, in fact, that when Miss Bemis boards with us, she pays Adda ahead of time, and I might add, when she is with us, Howland always finds an excuse to join us. She does seem to encourage his attention, and I've noticed that she often visits him at the store. Adda has tried to mimic her pleasant Irish brogue.

Half of Miss Bemis' camp are Irish miners. We have heard that their outfit will definitely go west. So the next few weeks will test the "blood is thicker than water" theory. If she leaves with them, Howland will be devastated.

While Miss Bemis was teaching her music pupils old Irish songs, Chase dropped out of the group and joined me, sitting on the arm of my chair. He was blushing. He said in a soft voice he wanted me to know that I had recently made him very happy. I thought to myself, "What's happened in less than three weeks, since that long discouraging walk home from the Cordises' to make him so happy?" Though that walk had brought such gloomy clouds to an otherwise magnificent sunset it had allowed Chase to unburden himself.

Though I didn't know what he was talking about, I replied that I had decided to turn over a new leaf and devote my spare time to making him happy.

I was glad he was happy but the reason for it was a mystery. Trying to be a bit lighthearted I said, "You haven't been drinking with Dr. Weibley and the boys over at Conner's, have you?"

"No!"

"Then pray tell, what is it that I've done that makes you so happy?"

And now the plot thickens. It seems that Frank in nosing through my Journal read Jerry Jordan's letter, which I had pasted there. Well, this marriage proposal of Jerry's didn't fit into Frank's plans. Frank has said before that he expects me to marry his bosom friend Chase, perhaps even in a double ceremony. So it appears that Frank went to Jerry, though it was none of his business, asked him if I had accepted. Jerry told him I hadn't and added that he was thinking of leaving Eldorado and going to the gold fields. Then old Frank blabbed all this to Chase.

That's why Chase is happy, though he certainly took a long time to come out with it. I suppose it embarrassed him my knowing that he learned all this from Frank. Well now he knows about Jerry's proposal letter and seems to be taking heart from my response. I have written this up in half the time it took my bashful sweetheart to unravel it."

My "old" Latin teacher in Michigan had a phrase for this outcome: "Si finis bonus est; totum bonum erit"—"All's well that ends well." Shakespeare, I recall, wrote an entire play on the subject.

Adda and I agreed it was past our bedtime and reluctantly decided to excuse ourselves from such a lovely occasion. Chase and Frank said they would walk us home. It was a good time to go. While making our good-byes to the Bentons, I opened their door to see what the weather was like.

A gust of cold March wind caught the door and banged it backward out of my hand blowing in with such force it almost knocked me over. The singing had stopped and Howland had resumed reciting Bobby Burns. Raising his voice against the wind's noise, he said, "Listen to me, everybody, but leave the door open." Holding the door I peered out into a dark, moonless night, knowing that's the weather we would soon be walking home in he recited another Burns poem:

> The gloomy night is gathering fast,
> Loud roars the wind's inconstant blast,
> Yon murky cloud is foul with rain,
> I see it driving o'er the plain"
> The autumn mourns her ripening corn
> By early winter's ravage torn
> Across her placid, azure sky
> She sees the scowling tempest fly."

Continuing to speak loudly, Howland said, "Now close that door and come on back in. Let's have some more singing and afterward, we'll each recite a favorite poem before leaving."

I looked at Chase and Adda. We had all had a good time but we knew if we stayed, it was to humor Howland: to let him hold his audience a little longer, but mostly to let him have an excuse to spend more time with Miss Bemis. For his part Howland could have stayed all night. I suppose she'll come home with us. She hasn't yet given any hint that she wants to leave. Although her group isn't camped far away, she certainly isn't going to cross the creek in this weather, find their camp and crawl into a cold tent in the dark. She has said before that she prefers to sleep under a roof.

I knew the Bentons were glad to have us, just as they were glad to have a new roof over their heads, but it was getting late and it was time to go.

Chase bargained with Howland. "Give us one more poem,

then Frank and I will escort the Stewart ladies home."

Miss Bemis made a sign to me, indicating she'd like to go home with us. Just as I thought, Howland saw the signal and stopped his poem in midstanza.

I'm sure he reasoned that if Miss Bemis was coming home with us, he could be her escort. He said something to her, causing her to smile and nod her head. Soon the six of us, well, three couples, were trying to find our way home in the windy, black, moonless night. Adda and Frank were up ahead, only occasionally visible. Miss Bemis and Howland were behind, quite far behind. It was several minutes after the first four of us got in and closed the door before they came in. Though the house was warm, it was as dark in the house as outside. Someone had moved the candle box. It seemed to take Chase forever to locate the little, two-candle reflector mounted on the west wall.

Meanwhile Adda, with giggles, instructed Frank and Howland to behave themselves in the dark.

Chase finally got both candles lit. I located the coal oil lamp and lit it, turning the wick down as short as I could, to keep it barely lit. I like to write by its steady light, which doesn't flicker, but I hate the smell.

There was a note on the table:

We are guilty. We finished off your ham hocks and beans. Yes, we found the corn bread and it was as good as we've ever had. We must have gotten in shortly after you left. Thanks for leaving the beans warm on the stove. Before bedtime we threw some wood in the stove. I hope it's warm when you get in. We are in the loft. Try not to disturb us when you come in.

> Jeremy Eastridge
> Frank Gordy
> P.S.

We have some mail for you.

I wonder if Jeremy is Mr. Eastridge, the millwright's son.

I took the lamp over to the stove to tidy up that area, which our visitors had left in some disorder.

Adda busied herself locating the feather tick, which we keep rolled up, and handed it to Miss Bemis, who, from previous nights with us, knew where to spread it. Adda said in a soft voice (to avoid waking the loft occupants) that she'd find two quilts for her, adding, "If those two birds up there haven't beaten you to them."

Howland took his hat off and began to say something. I interrupted him, and as politely as I could, "No more poetry, please. We all need our beauty rest." That was also intended to be a signal to Frank and Chase, who caught the hint and made signs to leave. My message sailed over Howland's head. So love is not only blind, it's deaf.

Frank and Chase made their "good nights." I shot Howland a quizzical glance. He seemed oblivious to the fact that the door had recently opened and shut, that the occupants of this room had been reduced to four.

Miss Bemis removed her coat and hat and hung them on a wall peg. She smiled at Adda and looked at me with curiosity and consternation. Obviously she didn't know whether her grocer friend planned to stay with us—or if he was going home.

Adda and I were wondering the same thing. It was past midnight. We'd had a very full evening and all we wanted now was to go to bed.

Glennis had worn her dark brown hair in a long, full braid this evening. Reaching behind her head she removed a rather plain, curved turtle-shell clasp. Leaning forward and a little to her right, placed it on the table in front of Howland. He was seated in the middle of my long, straight-back bench, facing her. She began unpinning the white, tightly laced cotton shawl that she'd worn all evening and deftly removed it. Pinned closed in a V around her neck, it had covered her shoulders and upper arms. Leaning forward she handed the shawl to Howland. He folded it once or twice and draped it over his knee like a large napkin. Facing him and fixing him with a faint smile, she raised both of her milky white arms, now bare to her shoulders, and began undoing her braid. She was as charmingly conspicuous as she was beguiling while she was engaged in this ceremony that I considered was a rather intimate bedtime ritual. It took Glennis several minutes to complete the performance, which totally excluded Adda and me. I was standing some distance away and only occasionally glanced over at her. Adda was seated at the table. But as far as Glennis and Howland were concerned Adda and I could just as easily have been in the next county.

This certainly was not a casual routine between visiting girls at bedtime. I couldn't help but remember Mrs. Gates and her long, lovely auburn hair, which she too, often wore braided and would occasionally undo while her soldiers filed out after their evening meal.

Howland hadn't moved, oblivious to time but enraptured with the spontaneously enticing circumstance he was swept up in. Occasionally, he'd avert his eyes and focus on the turtle-shell clasp, as if watching her perform this private act was more than he could bear, was more than their relationship allowed, was more than he was entitled to. Yet he watched, transfixed.

Glennis' dark brown wavy hair cascaded down over her white shoulders, catching little reflections from the wall-mounted candles on her left, their flickering light dappling her hair in variegated shades of glistening brown. Howland sat stunned, hypnotized by her new and differently revealed beauty. He was obviously flattered to have been included, silently invited to be an observer, maybe even a vicarious participant in her nightly ritual.

If an epiphany of upon seeing beauty is possible, and I have read that it is, this sweetly seductive scene must have lifted him to levels of infatuation he had never experienced.

Glennis had worn a rather plain wool black dress, cut not too low, but square across the front exposing, which I'm sure Howland could amply see for himself, those delights that have beckoned and enticed the male since the beginning of time.

Glennis broke the spell by leaning forward, and with her left hand, sweeping up the turtle-shell clasp like a youngster picking up jacks while the ball is in the air. Pointing to her shawl, she extended her right arm until she almost touched Howland's knee. Seconds passed before Howland responded, as his eyes moved from hers to—elsewhere.

Finally, he understood. Unfolding the shawl he stepped behind her and as though they had done this before, she reached up and lifted her hair, inviting Howland to place the shawl about her neck and shoulders, which he did. She slowly rotated her body closely toward him putting both hands on his shoulders and standing on tiptoe, facing him, pressed herself against him. Howland bent down and returned Glennis' kiss. As they kissed, Howland slid his hands up her waist to pull her closer. In the flickering candlelight it was a lovely sight, but not as long or lingering as it might have been had Adda and I not been in the room; still it was much more than a thank-you-for-your-poetry kiss.

Adda, never at a loss for solutions to a social problem, went over to the bench, picked up Howland's cap and handed it to him.

"Come on down for an early breakfast. If you've got any fresh eggs, bring six of them, and before you come in, see if you can find six more eggs in our chicken coop." Pointing to the loft, she added, "I notice the boys brought us some Missouri bacon. We'll scramble-up some eggs with it."

She walked over and cracked the door open. She didn't want to open it wide—it was just as windy at our place as it was an hour ago at the Bentons.'

Howland finally got the message, stood up and walked over next to my sister. Adda, with a big grin, reached up and pulled the bill of his cap down over his forehead, "Think you can find your way to the store, big boy?" she asked him. As Howland stood by the door, he turned and faced us but looking at Glennis, in a rather husky voice began to recite:

> She walks in beauty, like the night
> Of cloudless climes and starry skies
> And all that's best of dark and bright
> meets in her aspect and her eyes.
> Turned and vanished into the night.

The next morning, I was the first one up. I made a fire, then read the two very (welcome) letters that our volunteer postmen brought by for me. I am informed that Mary Holbrook is now married in Detroit on New Year's Day. News travels slowly when you don't have a post office.

Adda and Glennis both stirred. They quickly got up and dressed. The boys in the loft heard our noise and, with an attempt at humor, asked if it was safe to come down.

In ten minutes Howland came in, saying he'd been up for hours, long enough to have baked some cornmeal muffins, but had waited to come down 'til he saw smoke in our chimney.

He handed Adda a warm, newspaper-wrapped muffin tin.

"Well," she said, "what about my midnight assignment? Where's the eggs?"

"Here's a baker's dozen."

He walked over, put an arm around Glennis and whispered something in her ear. She smiled and nodded in agreement. He must have invited her for a visit, because, after breakfast, they excused themselves and I saw them walk together up toward his store.

March 21 A glorious and memorable vernal equinox. After supper our other guests departed. Chase, Adda, Frank and I took a walk.

It had been an unusually warm day. The mercury almost hit seventy degrees, which produced a balmy early-spring evening. Though the sun had gone down, we were to be the beneficiaries of the now-lengthening struggle between daylight and darkness. And darkness was not to be the total victor. The last rays of the sun lit up our path. The full moon not only extended the lingering prairie twilight, it provided us with enough light for us to see our way back home.

Chase and I lingered on the path watching the moon make wavy reflections in the creek, slightly below us to the west. Frank and Adda went on ahead.

There was a fire on the prairie some distance south of us. It was far enough away to appear to be a slowly moving red glow on the horizon. We wondered if the Osage were up to some mischief. Standing on the bank of the creek, watching the prairie fire, Chase was slightly behind me.

He put his arms around me and drew me closer. I had thrown a light shawl over my shoulders before we left the cabin, but the dress I was wearing did not have a collar. I had put my hair up into two braided coils, which exposed the back of my neck. Chase buried his face on one side of my neck—and kissed me. This moment of tenderness and affection moved and surprised me. He has always been shy and formal around me, occasionally even distant, and in his presence, I too have reflected that shyness.

But tonight was pleasantly different. This is the first time Chase and I have been this near each other since our dancing days in Archer, which I have remembered so often and with such pleasure. For some time we just stood there, very close together, with his arms about my waist, gently pulling us together. I was too shy to turn and face him and I suppose he sensed this, since he could have come around and faced me, but didn't. Neither of us said much, using the excuse of observing the prairie fire as the reason for this rare intimacy, an intimacy I'd dreamed of but had feared and avoided, though without completely understanding why. And I'm sure Chase's bashfulness toward me is the result of my behavior and reflects my own strange social contrivances.

This kind of pleasure is a stranger to me and I fear it could either overwhelm me or prove unreliable or disappointing. But tonight, being close like this with Chase, our affection and as yet unspoken love aroused in me the loftiest of feelings. I was transported to emotional realms I'd not known before. Great plans began to materialize in my mind. We'd do great things out here on the prairie: raise a family of fine children, continue some of Father's enterprises, bring useful industry west to convert the frontier to civilization and put a stop to all this divisiveness and fighting.

I basked in this long, warm, magnificent reverie until I heard him speak again. My darling Chase suggested that we consider marriage and said if I was so disposed and agreeable, we could use this evening, the beginning of spring, as our engagement. I believe our vernal romance will grow and blossom as springtimes have eternally promised.

"As soon as your father returns," he said, "I'll make a formal request for your hand."

Chase's acknowledgment of custom made me happy and I agreed with his plan, as I have come to place great store in Father's judgment and wouldn't consider a marriage without his blessing.

My marriage might pose a practical problem for Father, as Adda and I have often dreamed of a double wedding, and perhaps Frank's persistence will finally win her over, though I hope not.

After we got back at the house, Chase wished me a fond good night. And as soon as he left, I told Adda the news and she said, "I don't believe it. Well, what I mean is, it's about time for you two. I've wondered what's he waited for? He followed you down to Lawrence, went back to Archer, and couldn't stand Archer without you. I'm sure he found out we moved but he had to find out where Eldorado was and make the trip, and we'd only been here two weeks or so when they showed up. But, Augusta, he's so quiet and reserved. ' think you can put up with that?... Well when's the big day?"

I told her that first he wanted Father's permission.

She interrupted, "Ya. What will we do, if you get married?"

I didn't want the answer but I asked it anyway, "What about Frank? You know he thinks he's engaged."

"Yes," Adda was quick to respond, "and that rooster used to think the sun didn't come up 'til he crowed."

"Does that mean you probably won't marry Frank?" I asked.

But Adda didn't answer.

The little walk tonight with Chase was as enjoyable as it will be memorable, probably the most enjoyable walk I've ever had or will ever have. And now, dear journal, good night.

17.

THE SORGHUM MILL
March to April 1858

There was great excitement here today. When freighters arrive in town to deliver goods, they usually come to Howland's Store. Then they begin their return drive or they roll on across the creek towards the Arkansas River, which they follow until they must make a decision for either Santa Fe Trail or the Kansas gold fields. But today, a freighter with four oxen pulled right up to our claim and unloaded some very large wooden crates, all of them from Pennsylvania. When Father, Chase and Frank Robinson got them pried open, all the parts for our syrup mill lay scattered around on the ground. We all became elated at the prospect that they would soon be assembled and our syrup mill would be up and ready.

Looking toward the sawmill site, Father, with a chuckle, said to me, "I wonder how long the millwrights will be able to resist their curiosity?" He no sooner finished his question and they were walking up the hill. Mr. Eastridge was particularly curious about it and later returned to their shed to get his own tools. Chase said he had special wrenches for pipe, special tools to cut and bend tubing, etc. When he returned, he not only busied himself examining each element, he soon began supervising assembly and was so good at explaining things that we hardly needed the manufacturer's manuals. Thanks to Mr. Eastridge and a quick perusal of the instruction book, I understand how the mill works.

As usual with Mr. Eastridge, there's always a note of humor. We invited the two millwrights to supper and towards the end of the meal Mr. Eastridge addressed Father, "Mr. Steewart, sorr, I believe the factory forgot to ship you an important element."

"Oh? Everything I checked matched the shipper's manifest. What do you think is missing?"

"It's so obvious I'm embarrassed to bring it up. You need a big copper fermenter for the mash; 'twood be an awful shame not to persuade some rum out of the left over mash after it's fermented."

"I've intended to feed the mash to the cows. It's better than fodder."

The old Scotchman got up, looked for his jacket and as he stood in the doorway, rubbing his mustache, said more to the prairie than us, "Foosh, all tha bra possibility wasted on cows." The next day we continued to examine the syrup mill. The parts included two very heavy rollers that crush the sugar or sorghum cane. They are driven by a large vertical axle that in turn, is driven by a belt that partially wraps around the flywheel of what seems to me to be a rather small steam engine.

The one cylinder engine stands vertical. Steam is admitted first on top of the cylinder, then on the bottom of it, so that the piston is alternately pushed down, then up by the 'live' steam, which the instruction manual tells us is very hot and under pressure. A vertically operating valve that's driven by the crankshaft alternately admits steam, top or bottom, to the cylinder. A crankshaft driven by the piston converts the piston's reciprocating motion to rotate a rather large flywheel, which is maybe four feet in diameter. Upon leaving the engine, the steam returns to water in a condenser and is then pumped back into the boiler.

Traveling in a horizontal circular path, the two rollers rotate in the bottom of a hollowed-out doughnut-shaped pan or trough about six feet in diameter and two feet deep, made from six sections of cast iron that will be bolted together. The metal rollers roll over and crush the chopped cane stalks thrown into this "pan." The pan's bottom is corrugated like a washboard, I suppose to help the crushing process. The sweet liquor squeezed from the cane comes out of three different spigots near the pan's bottom, goes through a strainer, then gets pumped up to the top of the boiler and into a separate chamber called the plenum: a large, flat, shallow pan that uses surface heat from the boiler to evaporate off excess water. This concentrates the raw juice and turns it into syrup or sorghum. One corner of the boiler pan contains a protruding spigot-valve from which the finished syrup may be drawn.

In Michigan, our relatives made maple syrup. They needed to boil off thirty to thirty-five gallons of water from the sap to get one gallon of maple syrup thick enough to use or sell. I don't know if the boys know how much water will be boiled off to make cane syrup. The manufacturer has included some manuals and I'm sure they will enlighten us. Making syrup and sugar is an ancient art and there are many books on the subject. The Pennsylvania supplier included two books in the packing. One is called "How to Assemble the Syrup Mill and Operate the Boiler" and the other on details of syrup manufacturing.

The first half the book describes how to produce the syrup, while the second half has details on how to reduce the syrup to sugar.

It's obvious from reading this book that reducing the

syrup to sugar involves a separate cooking process, during which it is necessary to know the temperature of the syrup as it cooks, almost minute by minute. Whereas water boils at 100 degrees centigrade, syrup boils at increasing degrees above 100 degrees centigrade as the water evaporates and the syrup becomes increasingly concentrated. The author recommends using a special thermometer, graduated between 100 degrees and 170 degrees, to continually test the syrup for its readiness to be converted to sugar. Apparently, to produce the best sugars, we'll need a French or Belgian thermometer used to measure the temperature of the syrup as it thickens. I don't know how in the world we'll ever get one of those thermometers, if we decide to also make sugar.

This writer claims that the best sugaring temperature is 168 degrees, and warns that just a few degrees above that when all or most of the water is driven out or is evaporated, which he calls denaturing, the sugar will caramelize, turn dark, burn, etc.

The author describes the sugaring process as a chemical reaction that, at first reading, seems complicated. He says that concentrated syrup made from sugar or sorghum cane will change its state from liquid to solid; i.e., syrup to sugar crystals when heat is removed. This process can be initiated (accelerated) by stirring into the cooling syrup a small quantity of sugar. He gives this example. When enough heat is removed from pure water at exactly thirty-two degrees Fahrenheit, liquid water goes to solid (ice.) The same thing happens when concentrated syrup is cooled: solid sugar crystals are formed.

It's unclear to me, because I haven't studied the text enough just how to set up the cooking and let the batch cool and, one hopes, yield a mixture of sugar crystals and syrup without burning it.

Of course what's most sparked our curiosity is using the sugar to make candy. The book provides recipes for over two dozen kinds of candy, including chocolate candies, like fudge, and flavored hard candies, with suggestions on how to make the flavoring, which can be from cinnamon, cloves, ginger, wintergreen, mint, etc.

In the next few weeks, Father and the boys assembled the syrup mill "element by element," but never without the supervision of Mr. Eastridge. They carried water to the boiler and fired it up using stove wood. That was a long process since the boiler holds so much water. A few days later they connected steam lines provided by the manufacturer to the little engine and got it running. It was surprisingly quiet until they hooked up the drive belt from the engine to the roller axle and got the rollers moving, then there was considerable clacking and banging, which I suppose will go away when we load the pan with chunks of cane stalks.

By pouring water in the large "juice" pan, father tested the little steam-powered pump to make sure it was working. When the raw cane juice gets squeezed, the pump is supposed to push the juice up into the plenum, which is located on top of and along side of the boiler's outer (hot) surface. Excess heat from the boiler's surface boils off enough water to thicken the syrup while it is in the plenum.

If the syrup isn't thick enough, we simply circulate it through the boiler top again through recirculating pipes and valves, back to the flat boiler pan in the plenum. Again, there are tests using a special thermometer to know when the syrup is thick enough for commercial purposes. If it's too thick, sugar crystals will form in the cooled syrup. The manual says this can be tested by dropping a spoonful of hot syrup into a cup of cold water. If a "ball of candy" forms, it's too concentrated: add more raw juice.

During this process, vapor from the condensing syrup escapes to the atmosphere.

By pouring water into the juice pan, father and the boys put the pump to the test. The pump forced the water in little pulsating squirts, up into the plenum, where it boiled off and evaporated successfully. In this case, using water alone, the plenum, pump and pipes all got a good cleaning before we commenced making syrup.

So, now we know the syrup mill works, we are spreading word eastward to locate sugarcane or sorghum for our first batch of syrup. Though it won't be until August or September when the crop starts coming in. Howland said that he thought the syrup made in Leavenworth was from cane, raised over in St. Dervin (Missouri.) He thinks the closest syrup mill is in Leavenworth.

On Friday, Howland came by well before supper. He was more polite than usual but soon got to the point. He wants to read my journal. I think he is curious about how I've recorded the Benton party and his blossoming romance with Glennis Bemis. Well, if I'm going to publish any of this someday, I see no harm in a friend's perusal.

It clouded-up this forenoon. Several Indians are camped down below on the creek. Maybe Adda and I will walk down and see what they are "up to." We are both curious about the Osage. Father's advice is to keep our distance from the Indians. I'm sure that's what he would tell us if he were here, but he hasn't returned yet from the Minneola Convention, where he went to work on the Free State Constitution.

I finished a response to Frank Swift's letter brought here March 18th via Upham and Boyer. I encouraged Frank to pursue his plans to come out here to Eldorado. I gave him a report about the syrup mill and I also told him that many of the parts for our sawmill are here but we are still waiting for more parts, including the boiler before we begin putting that altogether too. These are exciting and promising times.

And I told Frank as delicately as I could that Chase and I are engaged, although I would be flattered if Frank's interest in coming out to Eldorado was me but it would be presumptuous to think that. His experience as an officer in the Mount Oread Rifles seems to have made him much more mature than Chase or Frank Robinson, even though I think he's only two years older than they are.

C.C. Hyde, * a friend of father who has settled here, left this afternoon on his way to Lawrence and I trusted Frank's letter to C.C. Before Hyde left, he was here with Howland and I fixed a nice tea for the three of us. Howland says he's packed his wagon and is going up to the new town site of Toronto and will be gone until Saturday. I wonder what will keep him away so long. He enjoys being an investor with Chase and David Upham in developing "their town". ** I asked him if Miss Bemis was invited to see the new town site. He said he wouldn't be surprised.

Late in the day, Mr. Cordis came by for some milk, which with the extra cow, we now have a surplus. We get excellent butter and if the extra milk keeps up, I'll have to get out my book on cheese making. I remember all our relatives in Michigan making a soft white cheese that hardened and tasted better with time, but I didn't pay enough attention to repeat the process out here. We're using surplus milk to churn our own butter, occasionally selling it to westbound outfits: ten cents per pound in cold months and six to seven in summer, cheese sells here for about the same price.

On April 1st, all the available men in town raised Mr. and Mrs. Dame's house. It went up very fast because Mr. Dame had already been gathering all the parts, including the logs and the

*Mr. C. C. Hyde (from New York.) had also been in the Lecompton prisoner camp
**Toronto

doors. Chase and Mr. Dame had prefabricated the rafters, so all they had to do was to get them up and make them "plumb." Mr. Dame was one of the men who came out with father last Summer. He paid Chase a fair down payment which, I've observed, has given him a rather strange new independence.

When they finished raising the house, they all came down here for supper to celebrate. I served venison. I roasted an entire hindquarter of a deer; the piece Mr. Cordis gave me for a gallon of milk. I roasted that chunk for four or five hours. I must have used a cord of wood keeping the oven hot. But it came out just fine. I served Baked Beans the way the Boston Yankees like them, using a pint of Molasses and a cup of brown sugar in the process, and they were pretty good, if I say so myself. I also roasted the last of the carrots, but there was not of those enough to go around.

Day after tomorrow is the big debate and Adda has been practicing furiously. She has a pile of books that she uses for reference. When she feels constrained in the cabin, she goes outside and gives long speeches to the cows, to the clouds, to anything.

She is so confident. Last night she said she will beat Buchanan by a comfortable margin, but said she doesn't want to humiliate him. He still owes us for his lot and the surveying work father did on his claim.

Mr. Buchanan has spoken to father about getting into politics. He is an amiable person, though given to little deceptions. For months he paraded around here as a single man, was a boon companion with all the bachelors, etc. Then all of a sudden, a few weeks ago, just before the big debate, up pops a Mrs. Buchanan! She came in unannounced on the Lawrence stage, a very attractive young lady about my age, maybe a year older. Well, I suppose he knew she was coming. Mr. Buchanan became a bit subdued with his misses around. I haven't visited with her, but I will. I wonder if, one of these days, another stage will roll in with two or three Buchanan children. Wouldn't surprise me.

Though father said he'd be back by April first, he has not returned nor have we had word that he'd be delayed.

April 3 The "Famous" debate went off in grand style. The evening had a big turnout and, as predicted by my confident sister, Adda won by the unanimous vote of the three judges—and by a large margin. Since a week ago Tuesday she's been bragging that it will be a long time before "Bee-you-cannon" will debate again in Eldorado. However, I heard glowing reports about Adda's performance from Chase, Howland and others. They said Adda spoke without notes and was so convincing that Mr. Buchanan didn't even bother with his summary rebuttal, which the rules allow.

For the debate, I helped Adda fix her hair in a long braid and she wore a plain tight-fitting white blouse and her plaid skirt, with shoulder straps made of the skirt material. Chase said Adda wanted to accentuate how much younger she was than Mr. Buchanan. But what I think was, Adda really wanted the judges to know that female brains with public speaking skills could sometimes triumph over simpleminded male puffery. But I hope she hasn't offended their hospitality. After all, the Lyceum is an exclusive men's debating society. That's why none of us ladies of Eldorado were invited, so we didn't attend.

This evening, after the Lyceum meeting, all the boys went up to the Cordises' to plan another debate. They came by on the way and invited my sister. Before she left, I told Adda not to press her luck! As the local champion, she could hardly wait to get there.

After they left, the cabin got very still, except for the wind, which seems to increase about sundown. The mercury was at thirty-eight degrees Fahrenheit at noon. When they left for the Lyceum meeting, it had dropped to thirty-four degrees. I hope it doesn't frost, though it will be some time yet before we start to plant.

April 5th and a fine day. Some wind at intervals. At noon the thermometer said fifty-eight degrees Fahrenheit. Earlier this morning, Adda and I ran an errand that took us up to Zimmermans' house. We saw a deer (perhaps it was an antelope) quite close to their place. On the way home we passed by the Benton's; the mister had shot a deer and he gave me three large pieces: one for us and one each for Frank and Chase.

When we got home, Frank and Chase were making some measurements around the mill site. Adda asked how the well was coming. "We're over the easy part," replied Frank, "now we're down to chiseling and pounding in bed rock, and it's very slow going. Even using blasting powder, we only sunk it six inches last week."

The next day Chase came by to say that a man stopping over at Careys' brought the news that the Minneola Convention moved to Leavenworth a week ago Tuesday; I supposed that father would head for home when the Convention * adjourns.

The Boys seem to think they've graduated in their well-digging efforts. David Upham has become the powder and blasting expert. According to Frank, some weeks ago they asked Howland to order a stone drill or stone chisel that miners use to sink shafts. Like a wood chisel, it is really quite straightforward in

*Sam Stewart, Rep. Butler & Hunter County, signed this Draft (April 3, 1858): 1ˢᵗ six articles dealt with land use, definition of township, etc. Every township section numbered 16 and 36 to be granted by State for exclusive school use. Article 1, Section 5, "There shall be no Slavery in this State unless for punishment for a crime." Annals Kansas, p. 230 and Andres, *History of the Convention*.

its use. At first glance it seems to be simply be a round shaft about twelve inches long. Well, on close inspection, it's not round, it's a hexagonal shaft about one inch in diameter and its surfaces are not flat but fluted, concave or dished out, like a miniature Greek column. The chisel end of the drill is exceedingly hard, enabling it to cut through stone, making stone dust and small chips in the process.

Whereas a wood chisel has only one cutting edge, this stone drill has two blunt cutting edges at right angles to each other intersecting on dead center of the shaft or bit. The shank or shaft is held in the left hand and struck with sharp blows from a hammer or top maul by the right. This constant pounding drives the drill, little by little, into the stone. Our Eldorado stone is sandstone or limestone though not as hard as granite, operating the drill requires much more skill than meets the eye.

It is slow, tedious work to pound a hole six inches or so deep. After the boys pound a hole that deep, they fill it with powder, stuffing a fuse into it. The boys then scamper out of the hole and light the fuse. A little flame follows the fuse to the powder. The explosion is intended to crack and loosen the adjacent rock, which they further loosen with a heavy hand pick. Some of the blasts do loosen up the rock adjacent to the hole, but just as many simply go off like a large firecracker, having no effect. The boys then have to repeat the blasting. Chase says that there are "tricks in every trade" and admits that the three of them are real novices. At their current daily rate, Chase calculates that it will be Thanksgiving before the hole will be deep enough to hit water. Of course, we don't know if there is actually any water there.

Two or three of Eldorado's citizens have had mining experience and occasionally they drop by to measure our progress, offer suggestions, but according to Chase, none of them want to drop down into the well shaft and pound the drill. They've been at it on and off for a week but the well is only about two feet down into the stone, which is five or six feet below the topsoil. Chase said he's offered to trade some carpentry for help in digging the well and he thinks in time he'll be getting some help when they want help from him.

Occasionally the bit gets stuck. The dust and small chips of stone accumulate during the drilling. The dust is supposed to travel up out of the hole via the concavities along the chisel's hexagonal sides but if removing this debris isn't attended to, the drill soon gets wedged inside the hole. That happened today while Frank was pounding and progress came to an abrupt halt. Getting the drill out of the hole is a big topic of conversation. Chase is worried that it will still be stuck when father gets home. It isn't that the chisel was expensive; it is that it is a rare tool in these parts. Without it all progress on the well stops.

The news of the stuck stone chisel seems to have reached Tom Cordis, Eldorado's blacksmith. He came down this afternoon with a long-handled adjustable wrench and with two or three persuasive twists loosened up the stone chisel and work was recommenced. Tom told the boys that in commercial mining, the drill bit has loosely connected to it a wrench that manually keeps the drill in slow, constant rotation as the drill pounds. In commercial mining he added, drilling is a two-man job: one holds the chisel and rotates it slightly with the wrench, as the other pounds, and they trade off tasks.

Tom suggested to the boys that they consider using a wrench and take turns at the drill. He also advised blowing out the hole occasionally and brought the boys an old hand-operated bellows that with a couple puffs will clear the dust. Tom thinks the holes need to be drilled deeper to contain more blasting powder. He says these shallow holes allow the powder to explode vertically up out of the hole rather than loosen the stone horizontally at the bottom of the hole. The boys listened to his advice and have been using it to make better use of the powder.

A week has passed. It's April 14th and father has not returned from the Leavenworth Convention. It must be taking longer than expected to write (or finish) the Free State Constitution. We heard he "lost" one of the horses, Puss, the big Canadian.

The next day in the afternoon, Adda and I walked over to the trail near the timber as the clearing for the trail affords us a good eastern view of the prairie. This would allow us to catch the first sight of father. But he didn't appear, so we went back home and made the evening meal.

After supper, we returned to our post and continued our "vigil." Father must have been detained trying to recover the horse. That will be an interesting story.

It was well after sundown when we abandoned the role of welcoming committee and in the quiet prairie twilight returned home.

Who should be there in a heated game of Smut with Frank and Chase? Father!

He interrupted the game to greet us.

He brought letters for both of us, the reading of which distracted our curiosity as to how he got past us on the trail and what happened to the horse.

On April 17th, Adda posted with an eastbound train another article for the Flint (Michigan) newspaper. Later in the day, Frank Robinson came in from Junction in company with a sick man who has asked to stay with us until he gets well. It seems that Frank has been telling a story in these parts that I am a practical nurse with natural born talent. I guess he remembers the notoriety I enjoyed nursing Mrs.

Gates and little Fanny back to health.

I asked the man what seemed to be his problem and he said he thought he had the Ague. "Suppose you tell me," I said, "how you feel rather than putting a name to what you think ails you."

"Well," he said, "I have fevers, and my face and body gets hot. The fevers are followed by chills, and then I start to shake." My big fear, which every settler fears, is cholera. We don't know what causes it but we think it's contagious. We know there is no cure for it, at least out here on the prairie. If you get the disease, you suffer terribly and you die. I know I didn't want a cholera patient on my hands and I was a little vexed at Frank being so generous with my time and possibly my health and maybe the health of Eldorado, and I told him so. But I agreed to see what I could do for the sick traveler.

When Dr. Weibley was here last, he gave me a bottle of pills made by Dr. John Sappington, an old friend of his over in Missouri. The doctor said the pills are made from quinine and they work for Ague. So I gave my patient two of Dr. Sappington's pills and told him the medicine would not only treat his Ague but would make him sleepy.

By resting he will recover. Dr. Weibley said that the pills are flavored with sassafras. I read in (our) Gunn's Book, "The New Family Physician," that most flavorings, like vanilla, sassafras, oil of wintergreen, etc., all induce drowsiness. Well, sure enough, my patient dropped off to sleep. He slept the balance of Friday and all through Saturday. I put him in father's bed.

Sunday morning, he was feeling better, but I made him take two more of Dr. Sappington's pills and stay in bed. By afternoon, he was up and about and asking when supper would be ready. Can you imagine that! I hadn't invited him to supper but he wanted to know when it would be ready!

Late in the day, the sun came out and it got quite warm. I suggested that he take the bedding outside, hang it on the clothesline and air it out, which he did. Afterwards he came in and offered to pay for his medical treatment, saying he'd be leaving tomorrow. I was tempted to invent some sort of charge for my services, but I didn't. I certainly admit that I felt good about my role in his regaining his health.

Instead of money, I asked him to do a chore for us. Pointing to the cows in our pasture, "If you know how and where to wash them first, you can milk the two cows" and I handed him two pails, one with warm soapy water. We're very fussy about washing the cows' bags with warm water and I think the cows like it."

No sooner had he grabbed the two pails, than I had second thoughts about this assignment. If he had some sort of contagious disease, I certainly didn't want him handling our cows. In Gunn's Book several paragraphs deal with "domestic and sanitary economy," which speaks to the virtue of cleanliness, clean water, clean cooking utensils, and the avoidance of bodily contact with contagious diseases. So I called out, "On second thought, you've just recovered from the ague and one of our cows is very touchy. She might kick you or knock you over, so Adda or I will do the milking." Thinking it over, I knew he couldn't strip those cows the way Adda and I can. I don't know why in the world I asked him to do it in the first place.

I paused, thinking about what other task he could do for us. "You can chop some of that wood for the stove, but don't exert yourself to a sweat." I proceeded to tell him the wood size I need for the stove and the size kindling I like to start the fire. "The ax for splitting the wood is there," and I pointed to it embedded in the chopping block, "and the hatchet is near the kindling wood."

He laughed and said, "Looks like you got a shiny new axe handle."

"Yes." "How many handles has this old axe head used up?"

"One in Michigan and two out here."

"Reminds me of my Uncle Adolph. He used-up four wives and said wives were like ax handles." I've heard it before and don't think it's a very nice observation. I'll be glad when he is gone. But in all fairness that man must have cut two weeks supply of stove wood, including a large rick of softwood kindling. I've never had such a supply of kindling. I will feel quite prosperous not having to scrimp on kindling in starting the fire. And I can't wait 'til I can tell Dr. Weibley what a prairie nurse I have become. Of course, his quinine pills and the warm bed rest did the trick. I simply dispensed the pills and enforced the instructions.

Tuesday morning my patient took his leave and I have not seen him since. He did say that he had a little ringing or roaring in his ears and in the fashion of the Lawrence doctor I cocked my head to one side, pursed my lips, looked him sympathetically in the eye, clucked my tongue, probably the way he was taught to cluck it in that fancy Philadelphia School of Medicine. I later remembered that Gunn's Book said that too much Quinine or impure Quinine would have some tempering side effects, like dizziness or ringing ears. In my new found professionalism, I declined to tell him that. Oh, well, neither would Dr. Weibley. And I didn't even get the man's name! Didn't care. Anyone who compares axe handles to wives should soon be forgotten.

Using our old reliable friends, Tempus and Fugit, father and Frank have been plowing some. They plan to plant over a hundred acres, mostly corn. Of course, this will be father's second crop. Father planted several acres the summer he came out here. He still brags about that corn, saying it was the first corn ever planted in this area.

Jerry Jordan has started to build a house. He's laying a foundation of heavy slabs of stone pried loose from the riverbank. I presume it's his house. It's a good sign that he's staying here. I'm so glad he took no offense from my response to his very poetic proposal of marriage. If he had left, father would not have been pleased and I would have heard about it. Their time together in Jim Lane's Company and surviving the winter in Lecompton in the Prison formed a strong friendship. It's obvious and we all know it, but you never hear the two of them talking about it. Jerry's been bringing logs down river and has accumulated quite a pile. Father told him that they are making such progress with the sawmill that he should wait and make timbers from his logs, not build a log cabin but a framed house. That indeed seems to be Jerry's intention.

In the meantime he was using our ox team to haul the logs up from the river to the saw. One afternoon a few days ago, he said, he took a little rest and walked up the oxen yoked up and chained to some logs. When he went back to his work, Hildebrand was there. He's the squatter who sold his claim to the Eldorado Township and moved into an old trapper's lean-to a little south of here by a creek. Hildebrand was in the process of unyoking the oxen. In fact, Jerry said, he had the yoke off. Jerry said there was quite a confrontation. Hildebrand claimed that those two oxen were just roaming around on the prairie, that they had been abandoned by some settlers or freighters, which is not common but it does happen, and that he had claimed them several days ago. Jerry said it was hard to be polite with the old bird. He tried to explain to Hildebrand that the oxen, and for that matter the yoke and the harness all be longed to the Stewarts, telling him that we bought the team and the rig in Iowa City two years ago.

Hildebrand then became very angry, used terrible profanity, and when Jerry turned his back to ignore him, Hildebrand pursued him and proceeded to grab his neck and started choking him until he could manage to get free.

Jerry showed us the marks on his neck, and I must say, it's a bit swollen.

18.

ELDORADO'S FIRST SAWMILL
Spring 1858

I've kept this note separate from the journal, but am adding it now because of an episode today involving an interesting young woman who visits us occasionally. When Miss MacIntyre comes to Eldorado, she pays Adda in advance if she takes a meal, and she almost always does. Now and then she also spends the night and is quick to pay for that, as well. She's from Little Walnut, a small settlement between Eldorado and Chelsea.

When Pete Gillespie, who spends time in Walnut and Chelsea, was here last, I asked him if he knew her. His response was "Yes, yes, I know her." But then he paused and added, "And so do several of my friends." At that moment something came up and though I wanted to I couldn't pursue his enigmatic answer. She appears to be without a husband or family, is not traveling either west or east with an outfit, and so is someone I wish to "study" and keep track of. She was in Eldorado for the whole of last weekend (April 25th and 26th) and as usual she boarded with us but, as was the case during her previous stays, she didn't seem to have any specific business or social reasons to be here.

Today at the noon meal she came by and politely asked if we could find room for her at our table. David Upham, who is six or seven years older than me, and seems younger than Miss MacIntyre, was also taking his noon meal with us, so I said, "Yes, of course, we'd be delighted."

Miss MacIntyre, who has a slight Irish brogue, but denies being from Ireland, spent the entire afternoon with David. They took a long walk north along the river together and soon got beyond sight. About an hour before supper they returned arm in arm and asked Adda if they could join us for the evening meal and spend the night.

"Of course," Adda responded. "We have plenty of room."

While we were cleaning up after supper, Adda said, "You know, Augusta, I think Miss MacIntyre has a 'past' and I'm curious to see if I can learn what it is."

About two dozen Osage braves are roaming around our place and it makes me a little nervous. Father and several men are off looking at claims north of here. Chase came by for the noon meal and we "limbered up" the Sharps by conspicuously firing off four cartridges, just in case those Osage have covetous intent.

Finally, today, May 3rd, after long delays, while we waited for certain parts, some from factories in the east and some made here by Tom Cordis, and after endless tinkering and testing, Mr. Eastridge and Mr. Young started-up the saw mill today, but were not quite ready to saw logs, which I will explain.

We began the assembly February 8th when the parts arrived, minus the boiler, so we've been at it, on and off for almost three months.

The boiler arrived early March and was bigger than I expected. It is a big black cylinder about five feet in diameter and nine to ten feet long. A firebox with a door is riveted to the front of the cylinder. A rear section supports a smokestack. The boiler rests on a raised cast iron platform, which Chase says will be bolted to the cement foundation, which has been ready for at least a month. "This boiler," which Mr. Eastridge pronounces "byler", is called a Scotch boiler the world over, because the Scotch invented it.

Mr. Eastridge, who in these start-up hours has taken full command, said he was very pleased with everything's performance, "pair-ticku-larly" the boiler's, though with all that water to heat up, it takes hours to get up a "head" of steam.

The millwrights knew the steam engine would work, for they have had it running, on and off, for the past two weeks, but unconnected to the saw blade.

The saw's axle is housed in two large bearing boxes from Brooklyn, New York, each resting on a concrete pilaster and has been in place for at least a month. The bearings containing the axle are really impressive. Four large bolts anchor each bearing box, and each box has a little oil cup that leads down to lubricate the saw's axle. The manufacturer included a one-gallon container of oil for these bearings. They say it's whale oil, but it doesn't smell fishy.

The saw blade is huge, with an axle four inches in diameter. Chase says this saw blade is the largest in the Territory. That sounds like an exaggeration, but the blade is very large and turns fast, dangerously fast. Chase thinks it rotates a thousand times a minute; too fast to count.

Father wants to be able to cut logs lengthwise, even logs as wide as three feet, and do it "in just one pass". Well, this blade can certainly do that.

We've accumulated a large inventory of wood, which the boys have stacked into two piles: one of hardwood for making planks for doors and flooring; and the other is softwood, pine and cottonwood that will be used for making siding, wall studs and rafters.

They have been studying a book published by a factory in Chicago, that describes an entirely new style of house-building called framing. The author proposes to replace the log cabin with houses built by using lumber cut to standard sizes and shapes. The walls are made with vertical pieces of lumber that are connected both inside and out with horizontal or diagonal planking and all the parts are held in place with nails. Indeed, this Chicago outfit is building these frame houses in such a way as to be able to ship them in sections to other locations. The company then sends out carpenters to erect the buildings. Their system is called prefabrication.

Mr. Eastridge calls the axle bearings "journals." This morning when everything was running, he checked them by putting one big hand lightly on top, one at a time. He closes his eyes, tilts his head to one side and pauses, trying to see if they are running hot. Sometimes when he breaks-in a journal bearing, he says if the alignment isn't perfect, it will get too hot and the lead in the bearing begins to melt. Looking at father, his nod indicated that the bearings were operating to his satisfaction. It was too noisy to talk. When they were mounting the bearing boxes, he and father, spent hours making sure that the saw's axle was exactly parallel to the engine's crank shaft by using some of father's surveying equipment. Of course both men have done all this before.

Mr. Eastridge likes to give spontaneous speeches about the boiler and all of the sawmill's parts, but he speaks with such a thick accent, we all have trouble understanding him. I asked father in a soft voice, during one of his speeches, if he understood a word the old engineer was saying. "Well, enough for my purposes."

Mr. Eastridge's Scotch brogue, his bushy rusty brown mustache, the way he waves his hands, occasionally performs a little foot-shuffling jig as he changes position or points to some mechanical part, all in my opinion conspire to impose such humor in his delivery, that it's difficult for me to take him seriously, that is, when I can understand what he's saying in the first place; but the facts speak for themselves. After all these months of tinkering, testing, trying one element at a time, finally, everything in assembly works.

We'll all remember this day! Under the close supervision of Mr. Eastridge, who is everywhere —oiling anything that moves, inspecting the bearings, counting the engine's rotation, tapping the big clock-faced steam pressure gauge, noting the boiler's pressure, peering into the boiler's firebox, dabbing black grease deftly on the engine's piston rod as it moves up and down— finally by late afternoon the boys ran the first log lengthwise through the saw. I said finally, because it's been eighty-eight days since the first parts arrived. First it took the millwrights and the boys two weeks digging the pit, installing the forms, mixing the concrete and pouring it. Thank heavens we had all that clean gravel available. I was glad that father was here to participate and supervise when they began to mix and pour the concrete for the saws' foundation. The whole process was much more complicated than I had expected. As soon as it arrived, the special lumber that father had ordered from a Leavenworth mill was assembled according to drawings that father said had been in the family for years. Chase, Jerry Jordon and others began building the hollow forms extending into the huge seven foot deep pit that had been previously excavated right down to bedrock. To be sure that he got consistent batches father had posted a sign containing the exact formula, which he wanted used for mixing each batch.

Each canvas bag of Chicago cement weighs 100#. For each bag of cement father wants three volumes of clean gravel using the cement bag for measurements and two and one half similar volumes of sand, all thoroughly mixed with six gallons of clean water. Each batch, the formula says, yields about 5 1/2 cubic feet of wet concrete. Chase had supervised the building of a large shallow wooden box for the mixing. It seems to me it took one half hour to mix and pour each batch. After two days of work I counted twenty-five empty cement bags. Except for corners and two bearing supports on opposite walls, the foundation will be about ten inches thick. The four corners and two bearing supports are much heavier.

When I reported to father that night that over the last two days the boys had mixed and poured twenty-five batches, he checked his drawings. He said, "You're not quite half done."

"How do you know that?" I asked.'

"Well, each batch is close to five and one half cubic feet and the drawings say we need about 300 cu ft to fill the foundation forms: 300 divided by 5.5 is about 55 batches. Let's hope it doesn't rain in the next two days...and by the way...save those empty canvas bags."

Then thirty days were consumed waiting for the concrete including the two large pilasters, the walls and floor of the pit to "cure" or harden enough to carry the loads of the engine, saw mechanism, and any log they are cutting. While the concrete was curing, Mr. Eastridge went back to Iowa on another job leaving Mr. Young to work with Tom Cordis who was making several metal parts for the mill.

Mr. Eastridge is currently sketching a design for a horizontal roller mechanism to feed the logs into the saw, and a guide to hold them tight against the saw blade.

Chase says making this guide, which Mr. Eastridge calls a fence, will be easy. Tom Cordis, who has already made several metal parts and the frames for the mill, said that the fence would be adjustable allowing the mill to produce planks two inches, three inches and four inches thick. Those planks will later be cut into salable timbers of varying widths; i.e., two by six, four by four, etc.

Father told Chase he had forgotten to order a "pee vee," a specially forged large iron hook or tong that's mounted on one end of a long wooden handle made by the Peavey Company in St. Paul, Minnesota for the logging industry. Father said he had several of them in the sawmill that he sold back in Gibraltar, Michigan.

The "pee vee" he explained "is used in sawmills to manually rotate long heavy logs. The first saw cut produces a flat surface along one face of the log. The "pee vee" is used to rotate the log ninety degrees, which puts the log's new flat surface, face down so that it slides along the saw's steel table for the second cut. These first two cuts are called bark cuts that produce planks salable as siding or used for rough flooring, laid on the dirt, bark down.

Until father and Tom Cordis can build a mechanism driven off the steam engine to pull the log through the saw we are using a mule, which is a nuisance because he requires constant attention.

Well, without a "pee vee" father showed the boys how to use a wooden lever and leather belt looped around the log's end to rotate the log for the first two cuts.

From the second cut on, one of the boys must use a metal lever made by Tom Cordis to keep the log tight against the turning saw blade. This produces planks of constant thickness.

Tom Cordis' moveable fence will eliminate the need for this manual lever and Mr. Young says that will make each successive plank more even in thickness than the planks we're getting now.

This afternoon two major items remained to be improved. The first is the big wide drive belt that stretches from the engine's flywheel to a similar wheel on the saw's axle. This belt delivers power to the saw blade and must be tight between the engine and the saw's axle. The second and final item is a large one-piece assembly holding a pulley wheel and a lever mechanism. Although this assembly was bolted onto the metal frame between the engine and the saw's axle, it is adjustable. This pulley is in line with the belt and has deep flanges to act as a guide for the belt to keep it from moving to and fro. The drive belt, which went on loose is made tight by adjusting the vertical position of this pulley, which Mr. Eastridge calls a clutch and seems very concerned about it and the lever that engages it. For safety, the manufactory's manual instructs that this pulley and lever be adjusted after the belt has been installed.

This was all done according to the book's instructions, but with the engine running, when the pulley was swung down to tighten the belt, according to Mr. Eastridge, not enough power was delivered to the saw to cut wood.

This was disappointing to Chase and all the boys who have been involved in this long assembly process. They obviously expected to saw perfect wood once the belt was installed and the engine was running.

Only father, who grew up building and running sawmills, and Mr. Eastridge were unperplexed. After a hasty conference, Mr. Eastridge ordered the engine to be stopped. He crawled under the belt and with his own brand of Scotch profanity began adjusting the lever assembly that moves the pulley guide up and down until he was satisfied that his adjustments made the belt tight enough.

This tinkering, adjusting and a final test run, all came together late this afternoon when the crew sawed up the next log, not for planking but to make sure everything worked. It did. With that accomplishment father, who seemed pleased with their progress, announced, "It's time to quit," and invited everybody to supper.

During the meal all we talked about was the sawmill.

Father said, "Tomorrow we'll make our first commercial cuts and it will be essential we all know our jobs and work together." He assigned specific jobs to each boy and asked the two millwrights to supervise the operation.

Though Jerry Jordan added wood to the boiler's furnace twice during the night, it took over an hour to get the steam pressure up to where it satisfied Mr. Eastridge. I went down to the sawmill twice this morning to watch them, spending about half an hour there each time, marveling at the way they all worked together and the speed with which they cut wood. The saw makes a terrible racket and spews out prodigious amounts of sawdust and bark chips, which fall into the deep pit directly under the saw blade. This debris will be burned in the boiler's furnace. At noon I took a nice picnic down to them. When they stopped to eat, they seemed to want the steam engine to continue running. The clutch, which I've already tried to describe, disengaged the saw allowing it to cease rotating. Apparently it's best to keep the engine hot and the boiler steaming when the saw is idle for a short time. Once the big blade stopped rotating, its incessant scream stopped too. Without all that noise it's more comfortable to be around and we can talk to each other without yelling. I have a major concern. Unless a lot more care is exercised than I saw today, The workers could have an awful accident like the loss of an arm or a hand, and it could happen in the blink of an eye. I think I will inquire of Dr. Weibley if I can keep a supply of morphine.

After lunch they started-up the mill again and sawed logs until late afternoon.

Mr. Eastridge and Mr. Young had announced some time ago they intend to go home, as soon as the mill is running satisfactorily. Mr. Eastridge brought up again during the afternoon break that it was his superior talent that got everything working.

This was followed by another of his educational speeches about the boiler. But, again, he spoke with such a heavy accent and with so many of the other distractions I've noted before, that if I get half of what he said, I'd be surprised.

Your boiler, he says, has fifteen large steel tubes, each tube is about five feet long, each one big enough for a man to put his fist in. All of the tubes are in the lower half of the boiler, totally surrounded by water and have a slight upward tilt towards the back of the boiler. When the firebox is open, the front of these tubes are visible.

In the Old Country, says Mr. Eastridge, these are called "fire tubes"—and for "gude" reason. The flames, heat and smoke from the combustion that takes place in the firebox all travel turbulently up through the tubes, with some combustion taking place in the tubes, which is why we call this a fire tube boiler. The smoke in the tubes gets discharged through an exhaust plenum in the back of the boiler, and leaves, often with swirling sparks via a smoke stack several feet tall. Mr. Eastridge says we should build a brick smokestack to extend its height by twelve to fifteen feet. "'Twill draw better and give the wee sparks time to extinguish themselves," he says. The heat in the tubes is conducted into the water and accumulates until the water is so saturated with it that a phenomenon takes place inside the boiler that is understood by only a few Scotch scientists. The water changes its character, in two ways. One, it becomes a gas, a very hot, scalding gas. And two, a pint of water makes a thousand pints of steam, if unconfined. But the role of the boiler is to confine the steam in the space above the water, so all that heat creates explosive pressure. The Scotch have studied this and have learned to harness it, like we harness horses to put them to work. It's the steam pressure pushing the piston in the engine up and down that does the work. Mr. Eastridge said he suspected that this boiler is at least twice as large as it needs to be for our engine. Father explained that in time we would build a flourmill and run it with the surplus steam.

Mr. Eastridge says all the locomotives of the world are driven by Scotch boilers, as are all the large water pumps. Mining the world over would come to a halt without steam from Scotch boilers to run their lifts and ore crushers. All the factories that are commencing to switch to steam power to rotate their machinery, like textile mills or gristmills are getting that steam from Scotch boilers. He said before he left Scotland, over fifty steam ships were operating on Scotch and English waterways. "Aye," he says, "the work of the world is getting done by these bra Scottish inventions."

Mr. Eastridge is convinced the boiler is one of man's best inventions and is not at all surprised that the Scots invented it. The boiler converts the energy in anything that burns, like wood, coal, oil, corn cobs, into heat and transfers that heat through the fire tubes into water. He said while we waited for our cement foundation to cure, he was in Iowa installing a boiler that will operate exclusively on corncobs, and he added something surprising. "In India, the Hindus burn dried cow dung in Scotch boilers; could that really be true? Cow droppings! He must be teasing us. "Give me a pint of steam under pressure and I'll move the earth," he declared.

It was the Scotch, he says, who discovered how to measure steam pressure. "Yet nobody knows how to measure its energy, but since the Scotch are so curious and inventive, surely some Scotchman is working on that measurement.

"The world is becoming so dependent on the talents of wee Scotland that it is putting a strain on what we can do." Just as Scotland's Presbyterian ministers are being asked to save the world's heathens, he says—and he thinks that they are up to the task, now his countrymen are being imposed upon to provide its mechanical salvation. "Losh! We can bairley turn out ministers fast enough but now we are being called upon to produce mechanics to run steam-driven machinery having already provided the boilers." He paused. Looked pensive and added, "My own brother runs steam locomotives for the Rooshians."

He continued to muse a bit, rubbing his mustache. "Why us? Why the Scotch? Well, it all derives from our Presbyterian superiority, helped somewhat by a chemistry of our own devices, whiskey. It's in such limited supply west Missouri," he observed, "that it is absolutely alarming," and that shortage will obviously be a major restraint in developing this Territory."

It was getting late and I had to return to the house to start supper. Adda and I thought it would be nice to have something special tonight to celebrate the first wood cut by the sawmill. We had invited the millwrights, the Martins and the boys.

Shortly before supper father came into the cabin, smelling of sawdust. Though he wore a cap, he had sawdust in his hair. But before he cleaned up, he came over to the stove where I was putting the finishing touches on the meal, put his arms around me. "Sweetheart," he said, "that sawmill is going to make our family very comfortable."

"You know," he said, "just those ten logs we sawed up today will amount to over four thousand board feet. At twenty-five dollars per thousand board feet, we grossed one hundred dollars." Father thought that when we are better organized, able to use machinery to move the logs from the yard to the saw and so on, we could soon double or triple today's output.

"Let me give you a little arithmetic assignment. If we gross three hundred dollars a day and allow for maintenance and various work stoppages, so that we work 250 days a year, how much business will we do in a
year? Of course," he added, "that's gross. We have to pay wages for

a boiler operator, a firewood supplier, a sawyer or two, someone to control finished inventory, and a mechanic, and I need to pay off a balance owed on the sawmill." I know father can do all that in his head but it takes me longer. "Seventy-five thousand dollars!" he said. "You and Adda can start looking through the catalogs for some nice dresses." Father seemed so pleased and optimistic.

"Yes, I'm sure we'll do well" I said, "but only if our customers have the money to pay for our lumber. And before Adda and I start buying fancy dresses from Chicago, I think it would be better to put some flooring down in our own house before next winter."

"Don't worry, Augusta, we'll get your flooring and your dresses. As for getting paid, that's what banks are for. Our customers will borrow the money. In a year or two Eldorado will have a first rate bank, mark my word."

A short while later Mr. and Mrs. Martin arrived. Jerry Jordan, David Upham, Chase and Frank Robinson had been here working all afternoon with the millwrights.

Mrs. Martin and Adda began to set the table. Adda had spread wood chips and fresh, fragrant sawdust on the table—probably the first west of Lawrence—as a festive gesture to celebrate the initiation of the mill. Well, everybody noticed it; everybody had a comment to make. Father was in such a good mood that most anything would have pleased him. Mr. Young and the Martins thought the sawdust was novel and nice but the old Scotchman didn't seem either mystified or impressed by the symbolism.

"Fronkly, Muss," he said to Adda, "when yoo've eaten 'as much sawdoost as I 'av, it's 'ard to be amoosed by it, ef yool pairdon my obsairvation."

Addressing Father he said, "Muster Stewart, fust, let me congratulate you for possessing such a fayne Scottish name, and that you even spell it corractly." Pausing, he reached into his large back pocket and produced a pint bottle. With a flourish he plopped the flat half-full bottle on the table. Mrs. Martin had put small, decorative, sherry glasses by each plate. She'd brought them with her.

"Muster Steewart, sorrh, allow me to offer two toasts: one to your success in the lumber business and the second, to the generous hospitality of your two bra lassies who have taiken such gude care of us all these weery weeks." He walked around the table doling out enough from his bottle to fill each of Mrs. Martin's little sherry glasses, muttering things like a wee drappie fer ye." When he put the bottle down, I noticed the label said the whiskey was from Missouri.

Mr. Eastridge, remained standing, and raised his glass. He stretched so far across the table to clink glasses, first with Father, then Mrs. Martin, and all the others; I thought he would fall over it.

The Martins have been regular visitors to our house, all this spring. When Mrs. Martin visits the sawmill with Mr. Martin, she calls Mr. Eastridge "Ducky" and he loves it. Lately, Adda has succeeded in mimicking Mrs. Martin's English accent, and has been using it whenever she takes lunch to the millwrights or is asked by them to do some favor. Adda has become such a favorite of Mr. Eastridge's that he jokingly has offered to take her on as an apprentice if, he says, she got her hair cut, so she could pass for one of the boys. Then he would make Adda a boiler operator, first class.

Mr. Eastridge finished his toast, but chose not to be seated. In fact, he remained standing so long, I got up and put the food on the table, and father offered a blessing. For some reason Mr. Eastridge continued to stand.

The big Scotchman said he'd like to add a few Presbyterian words. But the only words I understood were the first few which were, "Deer heavenly Father ef I could osk yer attension ..." Mr. Eastridge interrupted his prayer to drain his glass, wiping his mustache with his sleeve, then went on with his prayer. We had all bowed our heads when Mr. Eastridge began praying. Raising her head slightly Mrs. Martin smiled at me and gave me a slow wink that suggested indulgence; it was all I could do to stifle my laughter. Absolutely, I dared not look at Adda.

During supper Mr. Eastridge announced that today's superior performance convinced him that his work was done, that he would file the appropriate report with the factory he represented and that he and Mr. Young would be leaving in the morning. He then gave Father and the boys another detailed lecture about "byler" maintenance, this time about the importance of maintaining the proper water level as viewed in the thick sight glass mounted on the front of the boiler.

After supper, the Martins went home and the rest of us retired for the evening.

Before I went to sleep, I was so happy that we were finally realizing one of father's dreams, which has been to bring some useful industry into whatever settlement he founded, I thanked God for his favors.

Well after midnight, we were all awakened by a strong high whistle, accompanied by a clattering sound coming up from the boiler shed. Adda got up and lit one of the coal oil lamps.

Chase, Dave, father and Adda all dressed and went down to the mill. Adda carried the lamp. After some time the whistle and the clatter subsided, then stopped altogether and the prairie resumed its customary nighttime quiet.

When they returned, they were in unusually good humor for people, who had been awakened from a sound night's sleep. Adda said that Mr. Eastridge and Mr. Young had gotten roaring drunk in a final celebration.

Chase said, "Though Mr. Eastridge was drunk, he was sober enough to explain that the one thing he'd failed to do was to test the boiler's safety valve, so he thought he might as well make a celebration of it. Chase added that Mr. Eastridge claims the safety valve was invented by one of his relatives after several lethal boiler explosions." And Chase told us, "that it was originally called the missionary valve because it saved so many souls.

"So" Chase said the millwrights decided to test it. They had heaped wood into the boiler's firebox, until the boiler got up a head of steam. Of course, that didn't take long, since all that water in the boiler had been hot all day. They didn't run the engine, because that would have consumed the steam. So in no time the safety valve began to blow. When steam escapes, it creates the high- pitched whistle to attract attention." That's what woke us up.

"According to Mr. Eastridge," Chase said, "a heavy, coiled spring in the safety valve tries to reseat itself
against excessive steam pressure. This ongoing contest between the valve's spring and the steam pressure creates the drum-like clatter until enough steam escapes to lower the pressure, and the spring is able to take over and keep the safety valve closed.

Chase said Adda went over to Mr. Eastridge, put an arm around him and mimicking Mrs. Martin's charming English accent, said, "Well, Ducky, why don't you bys go to bed now, eh?" and they laughed and crawled into the two bunks in the shed that they've been using all these weeks.

In the morning, the millwrights left for home. We'll miss Mr. Eastridge.

During the night, the boys had taken turns staying up "on watch." They kept the fire going in the boiler all night, so it wasn't long this morning before they had steam up and I could hear the saw resume its whine. They worked all day cutting Jerry Jordan's logs into timbers for his cabin. I've had a toothache on and off for a week. One of my molars has a large cavity, which Adda says gives me bad breath. "How do you know?" I asked her. She has one, too, she says, and Frank told her it gives her bad breath. She suggested I try what she does to reduce both the toothache and the bad breath. She chews a whole clove and then puts it in the cavity.

We hear there's a traveling dentist in Lawrence. I'm wondering if we can get him to come out this far. Otherwise we'll both have to go to Lawrence and get our teeth fixed, a prospect I'm not looking forward to. Chase came by for breakfast this morning. He suggested that we take a walk later today if the weather stays nice, and proposed that we go along the river up to the little draw just beyond the spring. He said he's been watching a large patch of raspberries ripen and thinks some of them should be ready for picking.

He came back in the midafternoon. We took a little bucket and walked over to the river until we came to the raspberry patch. Sure enough, some of the berries were ripe. We filled the bucket.

I noticed a stand of wild grapes growing nearby. The vine roots followed down along the cracks in laminated stone of the riverbank, then dropped into the water. "The grapes aren't ripe but we'll know where to come when they are."

Although it was a pleasant walk, the man I'm engaged to was being very quiet and taciturn. His claim is just north of the berry patch and he wanted my opinion as to where he should put the cabin. We came to the spot and talked about it, but the matter has remained unresolved.

Chase said little as we returned. It seemed to me he passed up an opportunity for a little romance. In fact, I had hoped that was his real reason for suggesting the afternoon walk. As usual, I was mistaken in trying to figure out his intentions.

When we got back, David Upham was visiting with Adda. As it was getting near evening time, he asked if he could join us for supper, so of course we invited him to stay. One of his fingers was bandaged. We asked him about it and he said he'd had a felon and the doctor had lanced it.

"We were going to have ripe raspberries in cream for dessert," I said, "I'm going to see to it that you get an extra portion."

Gunn's book of medicine tells us to eat more fruits and vegetables to avoid boils, felons, etc. I proceeded to give him and Adda a speech about raspberries. The only health problem Adda ever has, that I can detect, is an occasional boil or felon, always on a thumb or finger. It is the 17th day of May and most unpleasant. It has rained on and off all day. When it isn't raining, it's hailing. In midafternoon, three men came in for shelter and to warm up. Frank Robinson was here and he helped me fix supper for them. They are Cherokees. * The three are very polite southerners. I invited them to spend the night. We didn't talk politics during supper. Adda and I know intuitively that the southerner has his mind made up as to the slavery issue. They left after breakfast and paid me rather generously for our hospitality. I wonder if they'd been so generous if they had really known under what type roof—abolitionist—they spent the night?

Mr. Alfred Payne came in today, May 18th. He was a fellow prisoner with father at Lecompton, and Adda and I came to know him in Lawrence. I hadn't seen him since last March a year ago. Judge Lambden was with him together with Mr. and Mrs. Henry Martin and their child. As a shareholder, Mr. Martin has a great deal of interest in the progress of the sawmill. Although we have everything we need for the sawmill to be a success—plenty of wood, a nearby river to provide the water to transport the logs down to us from various timber sites, and labor to run the mill...we lack paying customers. Cash is our big shortage, and I'm sure Mr. Martin and Father are discussing this item. He and father talked all morning about technical and business matters.

These three were bound for the gold fields in the Rocky

*The name given to Southern white men who live in the Cherokee Nation.

Mountains. They went down to the sawmill for an "inspection" then came back for the noon meal.

At lunch, Mr. Martin rather formally said that he was glad that the mill is now working steadily. He was full of compliments for father and Chase. Referring to Mr. Eastridge, observing with his own English accent, that for a man who can't speak a word of the King's English, the Scotchman had greatly impressed him with his work getting the boiler, the saw and all the parts correctly assembled and working so well.

After the meal, Mrs. Martin helped Adda and me clean up.

Although Mr. Martin enjoyed visiting the mill, his main interest was to vote the Free State Constitution—up or down. Since Eldorado is the largest town in the area, the local voting will take place here, but also in Chelsea.

We heard later that the voters have approved the Leavenworth Constitution. Does this mean that we Free Stators now prevail in the game of popular sovereignty? It's too good to be true. The U. S. House of Representatives must first accept our constitution and that will call for a debate, and much acrimony from the Southern Congressmen. If Congress passes it, the U. S. Senate will then vote on it, and I don't know just how many of them have a proslavery constituency. If we can get over those two hurdles, we will need President Buchanan to sign it and, knowing all the speeches he's made favoring slavery, I'm not optimistic. We'll see what happens now. I guess we could wait 'til he leaves office, but we said that when John Fremont ran against him two years ago on an abolitionist ticket— Buchanan beat him. "Sufficient unto the day is the evil there in."

Besides the election, another big "event" happened today: My intended seems to have Rocky Mountain Fever. A train of gold seekers * (they call themselves Argonauts) have come to town, arriving here earlier today. The gold hunters have camped on the other side of the creek.

They are going to "Pike's Peak" and are getting up quite some excitement here. They have set up their camp here for a few days before traveling on to the Rocky Mountains. They are spending their time looking for "subscribers," plying them with whiskey and tall talk. Chase said tonight that the train would take five or six from Chelsea and Eldorado. Father asked him if he would be "on the train" and he said, with an air of mystery, "I shouldn't wonder." Father remarked. "I'm surprised that these men are going out so early in the year. The grass hasn't grown high enough yet to graze their animals during overnight stops."

Dave Upham invited himself to breakfast. While he was here, he let it slip that Chase is not going to the mountains.

I overheard his remark and was so relieved. I resented that he knew, but that I didn't.

Dave Upham asked me if I could fashion a poultice for his left hand. He's still nursing that carbuncle, even though the doctor has lanced it once already. The medicine in the poultice is supposed to draw the carbuncle to a head, though it may require lancing again. My Gunn's medical book says that boils and carbuncles are the result of an unbalanced diet. I tell these men that but they don't seem to pay me any heed, though Dave sure looked like he was putting my ideas into practice a few days ago—he certainly finished off that extra helping of berries I gave him.

Mr. Bray came in this morning, voted, and then offered to trade some buffalo meat for a gallon of milk. We had some good-humored bantering as we tried to determine how many pounds of buffalo meat I'm entitled to for a gallon of milk. In the end I got more meat than I bargained for, so I saved a big "chunk" for

*In 1858 gold was discovered at Cherry Creek near present-day Denver, setting off a gold rush, which lasted for several years.

Howland and another for Mr. and Mrs. Cordis. It's my opinion that too much meat and the absence of other foods, such as fruits and grains causes all of these felons, carbuncles and boils (or biles, as some people call them) that seem to plague us.

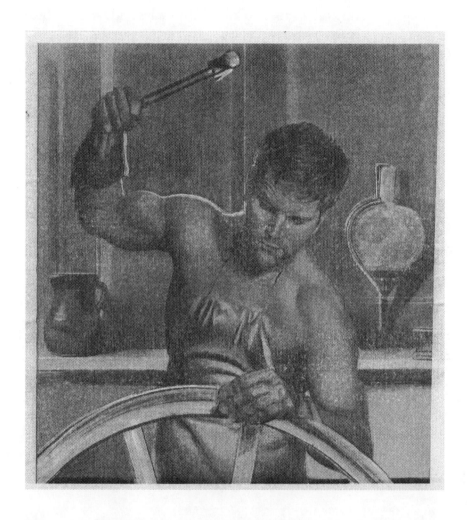

Tom Cordis, Eldorado's first Blacksmith. He also forged many parts for our Sawmill (Eldorado's first).
Illustration by Alan Reingold

19.

MR. DEMPSEY, THE IRISH MINER
May 1858

Our claim has been a beehive of activity for the past two weeks since we've had the sawmill running. When the boys aren't sawing logs, they are digging a well. Carrying make up water for the boiler from the river, has motivated them to get on with digging a well between the cabin and the sawmill. Progress through the top soil was fine, but when they hit rock and had to resort to chiseling, things slowed down to the point where father suggested that they be more innovative, i.e., use more blasting powder, drive the blasting holes deeper, and look for help among the itinerants.

Two days ago, Chase fashioned a sign and hung it outside our cabin advertising for "Journeyman Miners."

This morning an Irishman, from the camp on the other side of the creek, stopped by asking in a straightforward tone, "Who's the party looking for a miner?" He said his name was Dempsey. He was of medium height, with a full allowance of curly, shiny black hair, a large round open face, and a big smile, which he uses to punctuate his rather eloquent conversation. I noticed he had big hands, thick fingers and large muscular forearms. I was with Mr. Dempsey but a few minutes to realize he was a very ambitious, self-confident man. He said that even though he was from "the west," meaning the west of Ireland, he wasn't cut out to be a farmer. Anyway, Irish farms, he said were nothing but sources of poverty and despair and in any case, poverty is an Irish constant. "If the famines don't kill us, the English will."

I interrupted him and asked, "How are the English involved in Ireland's problem?"

Mr. Dempsey shot a silent, puzzled glance at me, that asked the question. "Where have you been, to ask such a question? Ireland is an English colony, has been on and off for 800 years, depending on what they want from us. Right now, they want the land. With wool prices where they are, sheep yield more to them than the Irish taxes."

Ireland's best export is her sons and daughters, so some of us were exported to the English-owned mines. The owners paid our way. Well, that is, they advanced us the boat fare and we 'worked it off,' when we got there. I worked the mines in Wales. Some of my relatives went to mines in England, out near Bristol."

"How long were you a miner?" I inquired. He said, "Oh, years."

"How many?"

"Well, I lost track. Anyway, it's well-known fact that a year underground is equal to three above."

It seems he's with a small outfit going west to the gold fields and will be delayed here while one or two of their wagons get repaired. He says about half his party is Irish. "The rest are American Prods but entirely different from the English Prods we all knew in the Old Country." I suppose that's Irish slang for Protestants.

He says he has a brother who, before he became a citizen

over here, fought in the Mexican War on the U.S. side. His company came out on this very trail but

afterwards he decided to return east and is now a coal miner in Pennsylvania. "My brother told me the Mexican War was the best thing that ever happened to the Irish immigrant. Two-thirds of the Army were immigrants and, half that, Irish." He added, that even one of the generals was an Irishman.

Almost as an afterthought he added that several of his relatives had already come over here a generation ago. "They were recruited to dig a canal, and got their way paid, though they had to work it off when they got here.

"Some of my mother's relatives worked on the Erie Canal and used to send money home. The nice part about that was when one canal was done; there would be word of another. Back home, to be able to say you had a relative working on the American canals made your family a little more important."

Mr. Dempsey said that his countrymen were now coming over to work on the railroads. "There are Irish-American clubs in New York that help our lads get citizenship, in exchange they promise to vote Democratic—a small price to pay, eh? And if the English immigrants in the U.S. vote Whig, that's enough for us to vote for the Devil, even if he's a Democrat."

He has a wife and two daughters camped on the other side of the creek. His wife, he said, has people in Baltimore.

All the while we talked he was alert, looking around. He looked east to the river, then out beyond to the prairie and north across the creek. Finally, he said, "I don't see any mine or any signs of mining."

"We have a steam sawmill between here and the river, and we are digging a well close to the boiler shed. After going through four or five feet of topsoil we hit stone." With some humor, he shrugged and pretended not to be interested. He said it would lower his status as a Welsh miner, a deep, underground miner, an expert on tunnels and blasting, if word got back to the Old Country that he had been working on a common water well out in North American Indian country.

"Our country doesn't have a post office, and the telegraph wires stop at St. Louis, so your secret will be well kept." I asked him when his two youngsters last had a gallon of milk, and paused. My question seemed to revive his interest in our need for an experienced miner.

He walked down to the site of the well shaft. The last I saw of him, he was climbing the ladder down into the well.

Tonight at Supper all I heard was "Dempsey." That in two hours he drove more holes than Chase and Frank and Jerry had driven in a week. "He knows where to place the holes to get the best results from the powder shots," said Chase enthusiastically. "We have been wasting powder by using it incorrectly."

Chase, who likes to sing, was also impressed by Dempsey's voice. It seems that while Mr. Dempsey works, he sings, and according to Chase he has an endless repertoire of Irish and Welsh songs. Some of the songs, Chase said, are romantic and traditional, others are humorous to the point of being "riskay." "I've never heard such singing, such music. I suppose that being down in the well did add a quality to the sound."

Chase said that he held and rotated the drill bit, following Mr. Dempsey's instructions, and in the process had learned several new songs.

"What were they?" asked Adda.

Before supper was over, we were all singing, "The Last Rose of Summer," "The Rose of Tralee" and a rather lilting but sad song about a Martha.

"Let's invite the Dempseys and Glennis Bemis to supper one of these nights and have some more harmonizing.", I suggested.

I said that Mr. Howland and I had recently had a big discussion about what we needed to do to keep this outfit in Eldorado.

He has convinced them that if they wait a week or two the grass going west will be much better for their animals. The Irish told him that on the way out here their oxen were so tired and hungry it was hard to get ten miles a day out of them. They tried feeding them oats and wheat, an expense they hadn't planned on. When we came across Iowa in July, the grass was at its greenest and all the food elements that our oxen needed were in that summer grass. We never once gave them grain. Didn't even think about it.

So their need to wait for the grass to grow means that Mr. Dempsey might be around for a while to help with the well. Perhaps before he leaves, we'll get it deep enough to "draw water."

This morning Dempsey came by for an early cup of coffee and mentioned that he is teaching Jerry (Jordan), Frank and Chase the proper way to operate the stone drill, which he calls "pounding the Swede."

"Why do you call it that?"

He paused, gave a delightful percussive laugh and adjusted himself in the chair to suggest that his answer would take a few minutes.

"In the Welsh mines," he said, "the biggest expense is chisels. The English owners try to get them made of English iron but their iron lacks the necessary mineral ingredients to make a good chisel. If they make them hard enough at the chiseling end the shaft breaks off in little pieces at the other end where the drill gets pounded, and English steel resists being annealed at the pounding end, which would solve that problem," he said, "so English owners have to resort, with great resentment to Swedish chisels."

The iron in Sweden has minerals in it that make a good chisel or the Swedes are clever enough to add them to make a good chisel. The tool must be hard enough to cut stone but not so hard that it shatters and also must be malleable enough from the pounding to absorb the blow and pass it down the chisel's shaft.

"The English bring these Swedish chisels down into the mines by the ton and since we've learned to recognize good Swedish steel, when we use them, we call it pounding the Swede. We make twice or three times the progress with Swedish chisels than Limey chisels. I think you have a Swedish chisel," he said with approval.

With a smile, he reported that Chase and Jerry were learning to operate the chisel, but he didn't hold out much hope for Frank. "He hits his thumb about as often as he hits the chisel, and he has trouble holding the chisel in one hand and pounding with the other." He laughed, "You know some of us can't tap time to music and comb our hair at the same time and your friend Mr. Robinson is in that camp. He wouldn't last a week where
I come from."

I poured Mr. Dempsey another cup of coffee and pushed the cream pitcher closer to him, as he added some sugar. "How much more pounding and blasting do you think it will take before we hit water?" I asked him.

"It's hard to tell. After several fait of solid rock we're saying some softer stone, and vertical cracks, which will give us more headway each time we blast. It could be several more days before we hit a pocket of sand or gravel or something porous enough to carry water."

I thought I would hazard a risky question. "Mr. Dempsey," I asked, "do you think we could prevail upon you and your family to stay long enough for us to hit water? You see, if Mr. Chase goes to the mountains for gold, we really will only have Frank, Jerry

Jordan and Dave Upham, and they also run the sawmill. So if we are sawing and the sawmill is running, the boiler needs more water than we like to carry up from the river. It would be so much more convenient if we could use well water.

He said he couldn't make any promises. "We'll just have to see. Some of our wagon wheels still need repair, but that shouldn't take long, and by now the grass between here and the mountains ought to be abundant enough for the oxen."

Mr. Dempsey commiserated with me, though, saying that if he and Chase left, we couldn't count on getting much work out of Frank. He's not good on the chisel and he's barely able to bucket up the chips and broken stone after we've finished a blast and he's no good with the pick either. When he swings it he's a menace to everyone around him."

Mr. Dempsey interrupted. "Yesterday Frank hit his thumb again. I was in the hole with him when that happened. He was pounding the Swede, and I was preparing a powder shot for a blast. This time it's so bad that the doctor thinks he might lose the part of his thumb that's under the nail. The doctor had to put a little hole in the nail to relieve the blood pressure. If it gets infected, he will lose part of his thumb, the Doctor told us."

Mr. Dempsey thanked me for the coffee and got up to go down to the well site. After he left, I had some time to myself and I wondered what Adda is getting into with this Frank. He's slow "upstairs," and now I'm finding out he also lacks manual dexterity, to the point where he even seems to be a danger to himself. Chase has told me quietly that Frank is not much of a carpenter, either. But I'd had no idea that Frank was so clumsy. Still, Frank is handsome. I think with Adda the mutual attraction has to be romance. A while ago I asked her what she talks about with Frank and she said, "Well, we don't talk much but he's quite affectionate and he likes me. Sometimes, Augusta, he likes me too much. There's just no end to what he wants from me—well, on second thought, I guess there is an 'end' to it but that would certainly get me in trouble."

I told Adda something mother had told me long ago about our Aunt Swiss, mother's sister. She died while mother and I were living in Albion, New York. "Adda," I said, "at that time, you were staying with one of mother's sisters in Genesee, so you didn't know her. But one of my early memories is of Aunt Swiss' lingering and agonizing death. Years later, I asked mother what had caused Aunt Swiss to die so horribly. I've never forgotten her answer. I didn't understand then, but there are lots of things we hear from adults that we don't comprehend at the time, but still remember. mother told me: that Aunt Swiss' downfall was that she'd followed a man to Hell".

Midmorning I took the promised gallon of milk and a little crock of butter over to the Irish camp and had the pleasure of meeting Mrs. Dempsey, a beautiful Irish lass from Galway, who, like her husband, pronounces it "Gaul Wee," accenting the first syllable. She appears to be only two or three years older than myself, but I must be wrong, since she already has two girls ages eight and ten, and as lovely as their mother.

The Dempseys had pitched a small, dirty, gray tent alongside their wagon. There are, by my count, ten wagons clustered together at this camp. Directly after I located her wagon I met Mrs. Dempsey and her two daughters, who came out of the tent, looking rather neat and clean for traveling youngsters.

I suspect earlier in the morning she must have used a little talcum powder. There was about her a pleasant fragrance, a personal body scent that the talcum powder hadn't quite masked, but modified. In the blink of an eye, that pleasant fragrance stimulated a memory of my mother when, years ago on a warm day, she had finished some household task. We were both together in the kitchen. I might have been six or seven, but my mother's personal fragrance is absolutely indelible in my memory; and in a sudden nostalgic instant, the image of my mother came and went.

"Are you Mrs. Dempsey?" I asked, and as she nodded, her quick eyes caught the tan-and-brown crockery jug of milk I was carrying. She said, "Glory be! I haven't seen a jug like that since we left Galwee. We carried and kept everything in those crocks: water, milk, vinegar, syrup and, in very rare prosperity, whiskey.

"Yas, oh yas, I'm Maureen Dempsey. Well then, you must be Mrs. Stewart. Francis told us about his big mining job on your claim across the creek," and she laughed at her own joke.

I didn't bother telling her I was Miss Stewart, but her remark made me hope that someday, before I'm thirty or forty, I'll be Mrs. Chase.

Mrs. Dempsey is about Adda's height and weight. Her smooth white face was framed with almost luminescent naturally wavy black hair. She must have just finished engaging in some strenuous activity. Her forehead was damp, and her hair, what I could see of it, looked moist. Most of her head was covered with an attractive orange-and-yellow bandanna, secured in the usual fashion with a little knot just above her forehead, but little humid ringlets of her hair, which was darker than mine, were adhering to the back of her neck.

I was taken by Mrs. Dempsey's quick irrepressible smile. "You and your husband have such social graces. You smile so easily," I said, trying to be complimentary without appearing to patronize.

There is quite a similarity between the Dempseys and the Bemis family, and also between Mrs. Dempsey and Glennis Bemis. Both the Dempseys and the Bemises seem different from the other Irish outfits that have gone through. The groups from

Belfast, who call themselves Ulster men, had much lighter skin and hair—almost Scandinavian.

Mrs. Dempsey told me about how they arrived in this country. When they sailed into New York harbor, she said, she realized intuitively, that they had reached a "land of plenty." In the New World there would be no English sheriff or landlord to drive them, like cattle, off their land. Everybody in Ireland, she said, had a relative, particularly in the West, who had been driven from their farms by the British in their attempt to turn all of Ireland into a vast pasture for English sheep. She said the English have unlimited contempt towards the Irish in Ireland.

"And if that wasn't bad enough, a year or so before we left the potato crop failed. The potato was our mainstay. We had all been farmers, making do on small parcels of land. Oh, it was such beautiful land but when we couldn't raise potatoes, starvation took us by the thousands. "In Ireland, we speak of a new baby as, 'another mouth to feed,' and we say it about old folks, too. I'll never forget the moment when we came into New York harbor. The four of us were all together at the ship's rail. I looked at our daughters, then I looked at my husband, and I said, 'Never, never again, will I refer to a loved one, my own flesh and blood, as another mouth to feed'."

I smiled when she said that, and I shouldn't have. Smiling was not the right response. She was deadly serious.

"Everyone in Ireland has a relative who starved to death, some whose mouth was green from eating 'dandelions,' like all those damned English sheep that the English were importing to replace us on the land."

I was shocked at such language. Then I realized that it wasn't profanity: It was a profound condemnation, but a bitterness that was now forever behind them.

"Compared to the Old Country this land is so abundant.

Coming west we've had all the meat we've ever wanted, just for the shooting, and when we have more than we can eat, we can trade it for other food. The antelope, the buffalo, the wild turkey, my land, for the last five hundred miles we've been living in God's free butcher shop." I had never thought of it that way, but she was right and it was so nice to see such gratitude expressed in such a novel manner and with such a pleasant accent.

"Francis says he still looks over his shoulder for a constable whenever he shoots game. What really put Francis in Wales was not the lure of the coalmines. Several years ago Francis went out in the hills above Galwee and shot a wee bunny for supper. He was immediately arrasted for poaching and charged with possessing a gun. It was, simply a little single-shot, shotgun. We Irish can't even own a gun in our country. The English are in the minority, yet somehow they've managed to make all of our laws and enforce them as well. Well, thank heavens the court bailiff was one of our relatives, though the English sheriff didn't know that. While Francis was waiting trial, he somehow managed to escape. He quickly went down to Cork and signed up to work in the English owned mines in Wales. That's how he got his mining experience. Half the miners in Wales are Irishmen who committed some minor offense, was convicted by an English judge and transported to a foreign land."

I asked Mrs. Dempsey if she had met any of the travelers camped a little north of them. She said she didn't think so. I told her that I thought that some of them were also Irish. I suggested we all have a cup of cool milk, and then take a walk up there.

We went up to the camp, where the two Bemis families are staying. Well, it turns out that Mrs. Dempsey does know the Bemis party, including Glennis, whom we all call, for good reason, the "Belle of Walnut Valley." The Bemis party of ten or twelve came last July. Some of them plan to go to the gold fields.

I would prefer to have some of them stay and stake claims. But Mrs. Dempsey thinks that is unlikely. The Bemises had bad luck as farmers in Ireland, she said, but several of their men folk had also learned the mining trade in Wales, knowledge that they think they can put to good use in the mining camps out west. And Mrs. Dempsey said that she and the other Irish immigrants were also concerned about their children's schooling. "We want to put them in real schools, schools run by proper Catholic priests. In Ireland the English try to abolish our religion and our native language. They have closed down all of our the Catholic schools, but the priests continue to hold classes, not in schoolrooms, but behind stone walls and hedgerows, and that is dangerous for the priests."

Most of the policemen there, she said, were "Prods."

Oh, I do wish they'd stay in Eldorado. They don't seem to care much about abolition, though they certainly care about politics. Even if they're Catholic, I think we'll be able to get along.

I am fascinated by their lilting accent and can understand them much better than Mr. Eastridge, the Scotchman—though he's been here a while. I must say, the wagons and traveling gear of the Dempsey camp looked rather dilapidated. I can see how they would need repair.

While I was there, I had noticed a large ox yoke, lying nearby. In the custom adopted by most of the pioneers out here, they had turned their animals out on the prairie to graze.

Problem is, unbeknownst to them, this area is over-grazed by outfits stopping here. Father anticipated this traffic when he located Eldorado at the intersection of the California, Arkansas and the Santa Fe trails. In fact, we didn't realize just how popular these trails were until this spring when the number of wagon trains passing through increased sharply. There are trains with freight on the Santa Fe, much of it is westbound military supplies. Of course most of those freight wagons, come back through here when they return eastward. Gold hunters also pass through here. Some of them use the Santa Fe to get to the Kansas gold fields around Pike's Peak. Some of the trains turn onto the Old California Trail, which is several miles west of here and leads in a northwesterly direction. I'm told those ruts are quite deep from all the westbound Southerners who went to California in '48, '49 and '50.

And we also have some north-south traffic on the Cherokee Trail. It connects with the Arkansas Trail about seventy-five miles south of here. The Cherokee Trail northbound from here becomes the Fort Smith/Arkansas/California Trail but around here we know it simply as the California Trail.

Since we are on the frontier with no significant settlement to the west for some five hundred miles, these outfits often camp here for a day or two, patronizing Howland's Store, making repairs and just resting. They take care of needed blacksmithing, including wheel repair, horseshoeing, etc. at Tom Cordis'. Before they leave, they use the springs along the Walnut River and our local creeks to fill up their water barrels. For those who plan to follow the Platte River to the Mountains, this will be the last good water they'll get 'til they get mountain water, which could be a month.

We appreciate all of this business, but one of the prices we pay is that the prairie grass for some distance around gets pretty well grazed off particularly if a large train of ten or twenty wagons comes through and decide to stay for a couple of days. Their animals are pretty hard on the grass. By now, the grass across the river ought to be so high you couldn't see under an ox's belly standing in it, but it isn't anywhere near that tall. But I didn't discuss that with Mrs. Dempsey this morning. I felt I had not known her long enough to tell her that.

Mr. Howland, Eldorado's first grocer, obliges me by shooting
the wolf that was making a nuisance of himself.
Illustration by Alan Reingold

20.

ELDORADO'S FIRST FUNERAL
May 1858

Two days ago, Frank Robinson brought an Irishman to supper named Mr. Curl. Mr. Dempsey had told him about Frank Robinson's thumb and suggested that he could make some money by helping us dig the well until Frank recovered use of his hand.

Mr. Curl took no food at supper, which was unusual. He did not look well and I told him so. After supper Frank agreed to walk him over to Dr. Weibley's. When he returned, he reported that the doctor thought Mr. Curl was a very sick man and had wanted to "keep an eye on him," so Mr. Curl stayed up at Dr. Weibley's place for the night.

Yesterday at breakfast time, a youngster arrived with a note from Dr. Weibley saying that Mr. Curl had died during the night. This poor soul leaves a wife and five children. Chase suggested we take up a collection to help Mr. Curl's widow and family pay for their return fare to the States.

Dr. Weibley's note asked if Adda and I could come and help with the corpse and he also asked could we make the funeral arrangements?

"We? Why us? For heaven's sake, does he think this is a

funeral parlor; that we are undertakers? That just gets my goat."
I'm afraid I became a bit indignant and felt we were being taken
advantage of. I thought maybe I should just send the doctor's note
to the Irishmen across the river. Frank brought him, uninvited, to
our house to look for work, but the man and was too sick to take
supper with us. Now he's dead. And now Dr. Weibley asks us to
take care of the funeral!

After I calmed down, I told Chase that Adda and I were
going up to the Cordises' to discuss where to bury the poor soul
since I knew Tom Cordis had Father's plat * plan. I asked Frank if
he would go and explain the situation to Howland, so Howland
could help, and I also asked Chase if he could find enough plank
lumber to build a suitable coffin. Thank heavens we've had the
sawmill running.

By the time Adda and I got there, Chase, Howland and
Frank were already there in Tom's blacksmith shop. Mr. Cordis
had recently hired two newcomers. I could tell from their
participation that they had all been informed. I suggested we all
go into their cabin so we could include Elizabeth Cordis. Adda
and I had intended to ask if she would help us with the corpse.

The first problem to solve was where to bury him. Father's
plat plan, doesn't reveal an area set aside for a cemetery. Of course,
there's plenty of land. We simply needed to pick a suitable spot
and we did.

Adda and I showed Mrs. Cordis Dr. Weibley's note and
she agreed to help prepare Mr. Curl's body for burial.

Frank said he would notify everyone in town and in the
Dempsey camp that Mr. Curl's funeral will be tomorrow at 2 PM.
Tom Cordis agreed to say the appropriate words. Although he
was reluctant, Adda persuaded Frank to find six men to bear the

---

*A map of the town site allocating areas for residence, commercial, parks,
town hall, etc.

pall. Chase and Howland volunteered to finish the casket a few hours before the funeral.

"There's two or three more things needed to get done," I said. "Someone needs to put the body in the casket and it needs to be gotten up to the grave site a little before the funeral."

Tom volunteered a horse and his utility wagon, the one without sides. His two helpers offered to pick up the casket at our place, take it over to the doctors, put Mr. Curl's body in it and get it to the gravesite.

During all this planning, we almost overlooked the grave digging itself. The older of Tom's two helpers said he would go over to the camp to see if he could locate some able-bodied Irishmen willing to dig a grave for their countryman. He thought they could dig half of it by sundown and have it finished well before the funeral.

Tom Cordis said that we would probably need to pay for that service. I spoke up, "Father has a small account he's set aside from the sale of the town lots, but I don't have access to the money." Tom's helper thought if he could use the town's president's name that would suffice until the cash was available.

Adda said she would fetch the widow Curl and her children to take supper with us. We'll find room for them at our place tonight, though the children might have to sleep outside in our big wagon.

A little after noon yesterday Elizabeth Cordis, Adda and I left for the doctor's place with some apprehension about what would be expected of us. With the experienced help of Mrs. Weibley we did our civic duty. It troubles me to note, though perhaps it's none of my business that the doctor had far too much to drink to be of any help. I can't imagine that the death of a patient, especially one who's from out of town, would be the cause for a drinking bout. His poor wife seems so reconciled to his behavior. It's my observation that the good doctor doesn't have to look very hard to find an excuse to drink.

Mr. Curl had been dead over twelve hours so by the time we began, his body had gotten very stiff: "rigor mortis," Mrs. Weibley called it. He was not a small man and it really became a gruesome contest trying to get some of Dr. Weibley's clothes, a clean shirt, a tie, and a coat, on Mr. Curl's uncooperating body. He refused to bend at the waist. It was almost impossible to move his arms when we tried to put on the shirt. Then we had another difficult time getting him into the coat. As Adda tried to get shoes on him she said, "Let's just bury him barefooted. Surely St. Peter won't demand shoes as a condition of entering heaven." All of this wrestling and dressing of the body took place on the kitchen floor of the Weibley's cabin.

While Adda was down there still working on his shoes, Mrs. Weibley thought we should shave his face. He did not have a customary full beard but he did have quite a stubble, which made his face appear even grayer than it had looked the night I saw him.

We found it difficult to shave him by bending over him, so Elizabeth Cordis simply sat down on his chest. Kneeling next to her I held Dr. Weibley's shaving mug that contained a round bar of soap. Using the doctor's brush and some hot water, I lathered up his face but was careful to keep the suds out of his eyes. Elizabeth scraped and shaved his poor cheeks and chin; it seemed unusual to me that a random "nick" or two didn't produce the usual bleeding. Try as we could to rotate his head to shave below his ears, Mr. Curl's neck was stiff; unyielding, resulting in a deeply cut ear that had he been alive we'd had some serious bleeding. While all this was going on, I would talk to him, cajole him to cooperate, to move when we requested it. He wouldn't budge. My talking to him distanced me from the reality that we were working on a corpse. I couldn't really accept that Mr. Curl was dead. The fact that both his eyes remained open didn't help matters for me. I continued to expect some response from him, a smile, a grimace when we cut his ear, yet getting none really didn't convince me that he was dead—really dead. Oh, in my head I knew he was dead but that other parts of me kneeling on the floor, helping Elizabeth Cordis shave his face didn't believe it.

When we had finished shaving Mr. Curl, we covered his body in an old gray Army blanket that smelled like it had been the doctor's horse blanket. It took three of us to pull Mr. Curl outside to the Weibley's "front porch," wondering aloud, as we placed him there, how they would get him into the coffin tomorrow. Then Mrs. Weibley made tea, and the atmosphere lightened considerably.

But before we sat down for tea, Mrs. Weibley was pleasant but insistent, since we didn't know what it was that killed Mr. Curl, we must carefully wash up. We scrubbed our hands and forearms all the way up to our elbows with very hot water and a rather pungent brown soap provided by the doctor's wife, which she called, carbolic. It left a slight brown-purplish stain on our hands and arms, reminding me of the color our hands used to get back home in Michigan when we shelled black walnuts in the fall. But that was ages ago. Mrs. Weibley laid out a beautiful tea set of pure white china, delicately decorated with a pattern of small light pink cyclamens. Mrs. Weibley's little ivory-colored linen napkins looked more like doilies than napkins. When I remarked about the beauty of her china, she said she and her husband had purchased the set on a trip to Chicago. "It was made in France, in a town called Limoges," she said. It is the loveliest china I have ever seen. I must remember that name—Limoges.

We made quite a sight, the four of us, with our white faces and brown arms and hands, handling Mrs. Weibley's fine white china, each of us stirring our tea with her polished, sterling silver spoons. She said the sterling had belonged to her mother, who had given it to her when she married the doctor, after he finished medical studies in Boston. The tea was delicious. I made mine a little sweeter than usual—a small reward for my part in a gruesome task. The ladylike companionship was quite a contrast to what we had been doing a quarter of an hour earlier. I remarked on Mrs. Weibley's sugar, which was small tan-and-brown crystal pebbles. which she said was imported from Jamaica in the West Indies, but that she used it so rarely that she was delighted to have a reason to serve it. As the two of us were quietly commenting on the luxury of this sugar and the beauty of the setting, Elizabeth Cordis with an impetuous laugh, interrupted us using an exaggerated English accent, said "Nawthing's too good for the Lydies Auxiliary Undertykers and Embalmers Guild of Eldorado." Her remark, delivered with such an outlandish accent, immediately provoked shrieks of rollicking laughter, that wouldn't stop. Uncontrollable tears gushed to Elizabeth Cordis' eyes, as she relished her own humor. She doubled over with spasms of laughter, and as she straightened up, she slapped her knees first with her right hand, then her left hand. I couldn't help thinking that those two knees would be black and blue by tomorrow.

Mrs. Weibley was seated in her old rocking chair. And for a few seconds, as her rocking to and fro became more animated with each gasp and burst of throaty laughter, I had serious concern for the safety of her elegant tea service, so serenely spread out on the little wicker table in front of her—and I also had some concern for the safety of Mrs. Weibley herself. I was worried that the next time she rocked forward she would be pitched out of her chair, hurtling in the air like those lady acrobats at the circus, or maybe while rocking backwards, she would tip over and fly out in a flurry of skirts, landing in her wood basket by the stove.

Meanwhile, I was having my own fit of laughter that just went on and on. Each time I opened my eyes and saw either Elizabeth or Mrs. Weibley another spasm shook me.

Normally Adda is a ringleader in affairs of this nature, not that she was subdued this time, far from it, but it was Mrs. Cordis and Mrs. Weibley who instigated and kept alive all this hilarity.

Anyone passing within a hundred feet of the doctor's house would surely get the wrong impression of what was going on, especially if they saw a well-dressed corpse horizontal on their front porch. As our laughter subsided, we were reduced to little gasps and giggles. We dabbed at our eyes with Mrs. Weibley's little linen napkins.

I suppose all of this low comedy was simply relief from our earlier somber and rather distasteful task, which had taken much longer than any of us had expected, probably because, except for Mrs. Weibley, we were such amateurs at the undertaking business.

Attempting to prolong the joviality, Mrs. Weibley tried to find humor in telling us about other "episodes" that had befallen her to "take care of," as the doctor's wife in previous communities where they had lived without an undertaker.

She repeated over and over how grateful she was for our help and our warm sisterly companionship. This shared experience was to make the four of us the best of friends.

Adda, Mrs. Cordis and I finally took our leave. As we were standing around, in the "good-bye process," Mrs. Weibley, who is such a dear woman and old enough to be my mother, exclaimed that we shouldn't wait for another Irishman to die in order to have an excuse for another tea party. Her comment precipitated another laughing spell, though quieter than the first one.

Adda and I walked Elizabeth Cordis home. As we left for our own place to make supper, we were feeling much better than we had on our way up to the doctor's. Our anxiety was gone, replaced with the certain knowledge that, even as amateurs, we had completed an important task, and now that it was over, it really hadn't been all that difficult. As we chatted on the way home, I brought up something that had stuck in my craw: Tom Cordis' remark that we should expect to pay the men for digging Mr. Curl's grave. I asked Adda why, after the four of us have voluntarily given up our afternoon to perform undertaker's work, why should they get paid for their grave-digging service? I complained to Adda about this, but after awhile we both agreed that we probably wouldn't have much choice about it, and we might as well "pay the piper."

It was a bright spring afternoon and we enjoyed the walk together, even though we knew, without saying so, that tomorrow's funeral would not be as pleasant. It would be our first funeral in Eldorado, and what a tragedy: a widow and five children. We had the Funeral this afternoon. After Adda and I cleaned up from the noon meal, we went up to the site, which was on a slightly raised knoll overlooking the Walnut River Valley. We were relieved to see that the grave had been dug and Tom's old flat wagon bearing the coffin, was already there, fifty feet or so uphill from us. Adda and I walked up to the wagon. The bark cut planks that Chase had used to make the coffin were so poor and irregular that I could see Mr. Curl's corpse through the cracks and crevices. I got a little sunlit glimpse of Mr. Curl's gray-white face in profile. His right eyelid had shrunk; retracting back into the eye socket, so that his eye appeared wide open, more open than it had been yesterday. I was still resisting the idea that Mr. Curl was dead. Now his open eye only reinforced this notion that he was still alive. As I watched him, I fully expected his eyeball to rotate in its socket and look at me. I steadied myself against the wagon, but his eyeball never moved, even when for a second a fat green blowfly nervously landed on it. And that wasn't all. Trapped inside the coffin were several of these buzzing green blowflies very busy examining Mr. Curl. I suppose they were looking for some safe place to lay their eggs—in Mr. Curl's ear perhaps or in one of his nostrils. That's when I decided that this shabby coffin needed a shroud. As luck would have it, the old gray Army blanket that we had used to cover Mr. Curl yesterday was under the coffin, placed there, I imagine, to keep it from sliding to and fro. We quickly retrieved the blanket and draped it as a pall, its four corners hanging diagonally down well below the bottom of the casket. When the funeral party assembled, Chase, Frank, Howland and three men from the camp, all Irishmen I presumed, very formally and with solemn slowness, slid the casket to the wagon's end and hoisted it up on their shoulders. In unison, as though they had rehearsed it, they somberly carried the casket down to the gravesite. I must say that the blanket concealed the shabbiness of the coffin and lent a certain ancient dignity to the ritual.

After a hushed conference, the men decided to lower the casket out of sight before the service. Using two ropes slung under the casket, they lowered it down into the grave. I draped the blanket over the loose earth, which was neatly piled on the west side of the grave.

Fifteen, maybe eighteen people had congregated, standing in a group near Adda and me and Mrs. Cordis. Mr. and Mrs. Dempsey, their girls, and old Mr. and Mrs. Bemis and Glennis were there. Of course, they were part of the Irish camp and had come to pay their last respects to their companion from the Old Country. I didn't recognize some of the others from the Irish group.

Not by plan but by circumstance, we were all facing west. The sun was quite high and quite comfortable on our faces. It was a pleasant spring day, but far from warm. The reliable Kansas breeze was, I might add, also in attendance.

Mr. Cordis stepped to the head of the grave and faced south. I hardly recognized him. He was wearing a long dark frock coat, and was bareheaded revealing his forehead, which was white from not being exposed to the sun and which was a sight I'd rarely seen before. He carried two small black books in his hand, which was so large that it almost concealed them. He conspicuously cleared his throat. "Friends." he said, then paused as he confidently surveyed his flock. The long pause produced an eerie silence. "Absent an ordained preacher or a circuit rider, I'm afraid all of you—and Mrs. Curl and the Almighty—must contend with having one of us to perform this ancient ritual. I will do my best to give this man as proper a Christian service as my Methodist leanings will allow.

"God in his benevolent wisdom does not burden us with many mysteries, and our daily lives are made comfortable and predictable by everyday affairs. But those few mysteries that we do have are profound. And we are gathered here today on this prairie frontier—on the western reaches of our ambition and so far from civilization that we lack most of its amenities—to confront one of the darkest of our mysteries: death. "Death is an unfathomable mystery but the death of this young father, dead before his time with children to care for is incomprehensible. Who among us can understand it? And so we join the family of Job, as we try to comprehend God's ways and try to find logic in untimely death.

"John the Disciple didn't understand it either," he said, opening his Bible. "In trying to explain death to a grieving widow, he turned to the words of his teacher, reminding her that it was Jesus, not himself, who said, 'I am the resurrection and the life: He that believeth in me, though he were dead, yet shall he live. And whosoever liveth and believeth in me shall never die.'"

There was a long pause. The soft prairie breeze irreverently flipped several pages of Mr. Cordis' Bible before he closed it. The silence was broken by the sobbing of the widow and of her friends, who were trying to comfort her. The two older children were crying. Mrs. Curl had also brought her two babies to the funeral. Mrs. Cordis was holding one baby and Mrs. Weibley the other; both too young to understand what was taking place.

Mr. Cordis, looking at all of us, opened the other book, the smaller one, and read: "In the midst of life we are in death." He glanced up at our small group, standing by the open grave, "Now, that is something we can comprehend. But I must tell you this passage from the Book of Prayer is a parable. It is taken from an old Latin antiphon and means that death is always close to us, never far away. For the adventuresome, it comes even closer. For the pioneer, dear friends, as we all know and are gathered here as witnesses, 'in the midst of life we are in death.' Death is our constant companion, our uninvited companion. And that is a reality we can comprehend, another risk we all considered when we responded to the great Christian cause that brought us here. And so we therefore commit his body to the ground:

> Earth to Earth,
> Ashes to Ashes,
> Dust to Dust.

Nothing mysterious about that."

He moved a little to his left, and put a comforting hand on Mrs. Curl's shoulder. At the same time he whispered something to Glennis Bemis. She nodded, and then stepped forward in front of the grave. Facing south she began to sing a hymn. I was so struck by the music, and by the clarity of her beautiful soprano voice, which sailed out on the open prairie like the sound of Gabriel's trumpet. The music was so compelling that at first I didn't recognize the words. She was singing the Lord's Prayer set to music I had not heard before. And towards the end when she sang, "For thine is the kingdom, and the power and the glory for ever," I thought, "now, Mr. Curl, if you have a soul, now is the time, under such rapturous music, to leave that body and go—go to Jesus."

There was a slight commotion among the Irish, both those I knew and the strangers. During the song they had bowed their heads. Now they were making the sign of the cross. They all knew the music.

Glennis stood there for a moment in silence, then began a second hymn, also new to me. I strained to catch the words. She must have sung a dozen words before I realized it was in Latin, perhaps a ritual hymn of the Catholic service. This was quite short and had lower notes, mostly in a minor key, but was hauntingly beautiful. When she finished, the Irish again crossed themselves.

Mr. Cordis handed both books he was holding to Chase, who was standing nearby. In a gesture that invited us all to do likewise, Tom bent over, cupped up a handful of our rich Kansas earth and dropped it down into the grave. As it hit the top slats of the coffin and thumped along the sides, the eerie but concrete sound brought us back to reality, breaking the spell of the service.

The spades and shovels, used to dig the grave, lay nearby. We picked them up and all took turns scooping some earth into the grave, fulfilling the ancient prediction:

Earth to Earth

Dust to Dust

As I stood there, still a little weepy, feeling my moist cheeks being cooled by the breeze, I knew I wasn't crying for Mr. Curl. I didn't know him. I was remembering my mother's death when she was taken from us, hardly beyond her youth, in a long lingering illness that left me—and Adda—motherless. You would think that time with its healing power would have long ago covered up the devastation of her loss to our family, but that's not so. I missed her warmth, her companionship. I missed her then. I miss her now. That's what brought tears to my eyes. The sadness of Mr. Curl's death called to mind my mother's untimely death. I wonder if it's normal, given the stimulation of an event like this funeral, to mourn all over again for a loved one, even one who has been gone a long time, like my mother, now dead over ten years. I tried to recall the biblical passage that begins, "And in the fullness of time," but wasn't able to remember more than the first few words.

After the service, I asked Glennis Bemis about her second hymn. "It was an Ave Maria, a hymn to praise Mary, the mother of Jesus," she said, "We Catholics have a dozen Ave Marias. The music for the one I sang was very old, written by the German Johann Bach."

As the gathering began to disperse, I turned to join Adda so we could leave together, a young man approached us. As we walked away, I tried to be inconspicuous in satisfying my curiosity but I couldn't wait: I unfolded the note.

> Dear Mrs. Stewart,
> I am Luke Toomey. My brother and I are with
> the Dempseys. You've met them both. Mr.
> Dempsey is digging your well.
> We dug the grave and will be much
> obliged if you could pay us each one dollar.
> It is too bad that Mr. Curl couldn't have
> had his proper last rites and a wake, yes, a
> proper Irish wake, which is not all weeping
> and wailing.
>
> Luke Toomey

My first thought was: These Irishmen are so ungrateful. Not a one of them offered to help with the body or the "undertakings" and now they're expecting us to pay to bury one of their own. That's the limit. Then I looked at the note again, and reread the sentence about having "proper" last rites and thought if Mr. Cordis, bless his soul, hears of this apostasy or blasphemy—I can never remember the difference—he won't hear it from me. And if they think just because we are the town founders, we are going to pay them two dollars for digging a grave for one of their own, then I'll charge them four dollars for the grave site, the coffin, and our undertaking services.

After a while my irritation with his letter was replaced with some truculence and righteous indignation, of which we Stewarts seem to have an abundance. The idea of charging them four dollars became rather intriguing and humorous. I could see myself calling the "Ladies Auxiliary Undertakers and Embalmers Guild" together and dividing the proceeds of our first funeral, four ways. The more I thought about it, the better I liked the idea. But I thought I'd better see what Adda has to say. She reminded me that we had laid the matter to rest yesterday. And she was right.

Midmorning the next day, well after breakfast, Adda (that is, "Mr. Adamont Stewart") was working on another article to send to a newspaper back in the States. Earlier this winter, Adda had submitted an article to a Michigan newspaper. The editor wrote, saying they didn't usually accept writing from females on such important subjects. She rewrote the article and signed it Adamont Stewart claiming she, well he, had relatives in Flint, which was true. The editor accepted the article.

Chase was here figuring lumber he would need for a job he's working on. He got up and, as casual as you please, grabbed a stick from behind the stove, walked over to the east wall and, using the stick's blunt end, pinned the head of a snake in between the two logs where the snake had concealed itself. He took out his knife and swiftly cut the snake's head off.

The head, which was dark red, tumbled to the floor. Chase stretched out the body of the snake. It was almost as long as Adda is tall. This old fellow had been lying between two logs in the wall, concealed by the shadows between them. How long had he been there and how often had he visited? I had no idea that we were sharing our lodging with such a creature.

We measured its length and speculated about its age. Chase said its age is equal to the number of rattles. This snake is called a Kansas copperhead rattler. It had eight rattles and a little tan bean on the end of its tail, so that means it was probably eight or nine years old.

I asked Chase what he thought this fellow ate. Chase, who's also curious about such things, opened the snake's belly with his knife. We found two partially digested mice. I wonder if the snake caught the mice in the house or out on the prairie. Lord knows there are plenty in both places.

As though that weren't excitement enough for one day, within an hour Chase spied another snake not quite as long as the first one. He dispatched it in the same fashion. From now on I don't think I'll ever be able to live in this house without examining the chinks and gaps in our log walls or plank flooring that could conceal a snake.

Chase threw the snakes out back. "It's a well- known fact that even a decapitated snake won't die 'til after sundown."

There is a notion hereabouts that wild pigs kill and feed on snakes, but I haven't seen any of these roaming pigs nor have I talked to anyone who has. Next day, both snakes were gone.

Snakes are a problem though I notice people seem reluctant to admit it, or even to discuss it. Yet when I bring up the subject, everyone has either had a frightening snake encounter or has had a family member who has been bitten. And everybody has a suggestion for how to treat a snakebite. The important thing seems to be to find the pin-sized bite site quickly, then open it with a sharp blade and suck out the venom. If the knife cut is deep enough, the bleeding also helps flush out the poison.

Thursday, May 20 mid-afternoon Chase abruptly left the cabin saying he had almost forgotten about a meeting. He didn't explain what the meeting was, but I knew there has been two or three advance men here in the valley drumming up recruits for a mining party that's due to depart this coming weekend. One of them has been around Howland's offering free whiskey and big promises to potential Argonauts, so I had my suspicions.

After the meeting, Chase came by and suggested we take a walk. When we got outside, he began in a vein unusually enthusiastic for him, explaining the details of this mining party that he has been thinking about. Then he blurted it out, "Augusta, I've changed my mind. I've decided I will go with this outfit. They've invited me and I'm convinced they have enough professionals including some surveyors for success. Of course, I'm not a charter member but they want carpenters—I hope you aren't too disappointed."

He said a group of citizens met last October in Lecompton to organize this party from the territory, not just for prospecting but to layout a major town site in the Rockies near the gold strike. Twenty-five chartered members each invested $500.00, which has been used to fit-out five wagons. Most of those men will be mounted and well armed. Actually there are two parties, he said. The other one is from Lawrence and has been organized by a William Parsons. It's larger than our party, with forty chartered members. Their aim is mainly mining. He said "Our party left Lecompton May 10, will spend at most two days here and will leave Saturday. The other party will be through here later." I questioned, "Saturday? Why that's in just two days."

"Yes, I know," he replied.

Chase and I had a nice long walk, a nice, long, sad walk. I asked him over and over why he had to go. From what he said I gathered that he wants to strike it rich out there and then come back and start a construction "outfit." Well, I must admire his ambition. But still I don't want him to go. I tried to reason with him. I appealed to his sense of duty. He knows we are busier than ever in trying to get a source of well water close to the saw's boiler and I'm not at all sure that Mr. Dempsey will stay long enough to finish the well. And when there's lumber to be sawed, we need three or four experienced hands to operate the sawmill properly.

It was a warm mellow spring evening, unusually warm. On the same path and on the same spot where in March we decided to get married, Chase kissed me for the first time. It was a long kiss, a sweetheart's kiss. For fear I might never see him again, I clasped him to my breast and kissed him as sweetly as I could and told him that I loved him. I was torn between the despair of losing him and the joy of our embrace. Both emotions brought tears.

He said that he might not be able to say a proper good-bye Saturday morning if the wagon train left early.

I told him over and over that I loved him; that I loved only him that I wished he wouldn't go, that it wasn't safe out there, etc.! And what I also meant, but couldn't verbally convey, was that I dreaded the loneliness I would feel after he left. I admit I'm given to fits of self-pity and melancholy, I knew when he's gone I'd be racked with despair.

"Will you come back to me?"

"Yes, of course," he said, but his answer seemed to lack commitment.

Oh, he was serious but the tone of his words sounded more like a business promise, like, "I'll be here tomorrow to hang your door," than like the vow of a man who is engaged. My question made of us two separate people. Chase's pledge to the train's advance man was stronger than his pledge to me, and he was obviously committed to keep that pledge. Duty is a terrible test.

On our way back to the cabin. I thought of the discussion Adda and I had with Father on the eve of his departure to fight with Jim Lane and the Plymouth Company. Father's reason for going had boiled down to duty, and, I might add, the pursuit of that duty landed him in the prison camp.

As Chase and I walked back to the cabin, I had this gnawing intuition and it disappointed me that none of my reasoning or pleading would change Chase's mind.

That evening after supper, I wanted to speak to Adda about Chase, but she seemed busier than ever, condensing an article from her journal. It seems she's received some more encouragement from the newspaper in Flint to submit another article. I wonder if she's writing up the funeral? The train left as planned midmorning (May 22, 1858) and my sweetheart with it. Chase explained that this party was organized last October in Lecompton. One of the organizers was the Reverend Eli Moore who preached our first service August 24, two weeks after we arrived in Plymouth. The group intended to found a town site in the Rockies near the gold fields.

He was able to come by the house twice this morning and we had a few more farewells. I'd like to say they were fond farewells, but for me there was nothing fond about it. I was both surprised and delighted that their outfit got off to such a slow start. Now I know how women have felt down through the centuries when their husbands, fathers or sons marched off to war, or to a distant land to "seek their fortune." In every heart is the nagging, question: Would they ever see each other again? And the reality is, sometimes they don't. Mrs. Curl and her five children have also left today. An empty eastbound stagecoach came through here from one of the army forts out on the Santa Fe Trail. It was one of Russell Majors and Waddell's rigs. The coach had carried an officer's wife and children, and their belongings, from Leavenworth out to the officer's camp, and after depositing them, was making the return trip east. Howland arranged for Mrs. Curl and her children to travel on that stage, at least as far as Lawrence. I wonder what's to become of her. She is an Irish immigrant. Her traveling companions are still camped on the other side of the creek.

Sam and Jerry Jordan struggle to recover Sam's oxen, stolen
by Mr. Hildebrand. They are in a wagon train headed for the
Kansas Gold Strike (Rocky Mountains)...spring, 1858.
Illustration by Alan Reingold

21.

HILDEBRAND STEALS OUR OXEN
May 22 to early June 1858

About midmorning we noticed that our oxen were missing. Our first suspicion was that Hildebrand had stolen them. Adda said, "I'll bet he hitched them up to his wagon and joined that party headed for the Kansas gold fields that rested here a day or two, picked up a few more recruits, including Chase and pulled out late this morning."

Father said, "That makes sense to me."

At noon, Father and Jerry went chasing after them. Well, they won't have far to ride to find out if we are right.

Late in the day, Father and Jerry returned with our oxen. The wagon train had only gotten a few miles west of here. Father said it was a very unpleasant episode with Hildebrand promising revenge as a result of being apprehended and embarrassed in front of all those people when Father and Jerry proved that the oxen were ours and repossessed them.

During supper, I asked Father what happened out there, but he was so cranky about his confrontation with Hildebrand he didn't want to discuss it. So, towards sundown I went outside, found Jerry down by the mill and asked him to tell me about it.

Jerry said that within five or six miles northwest of here on the old California Trail they saw dust from the gray line of schooners stretched out ahead of them. "We immediately spotted Hildebrand's wagon hitched up to your ox team, right in the middle of the train. Hildebrand wasn't with his wagon but his kids were. He was walking a few hundred feet behind it, talking. So we simply rode up to his wagon, led the oxen off the trail and unhitched them. By the time Hildebrand caught up to us and saw us leading your oxen away he assumed a blustery, righteous indignation, swearing loudly, calling us 'horse thieves,' exconvicts, etc., and gathering quite a crowd. The wagon train slowed down and the train boss rode up with one of his lieutenants.

Jerry said, "Hildebrand continued to yell profanities at him and your father. It was hot. I was standing next to Hildebrand and he smelled worse than the rear end of a horse. The wagon boss seemed willing to listen both to your father and to Hildebrand, who claimed we were liars, jailbirds and made explanations about how the oxen were his. Your father seemed to be biding his time. I knew he had the bill of sale for the oxen, 'cause he told me that on the way over. Finally your father unfolded the bill of sale and showed it to the wagon boss and two other men, who were part of the original Lawrence group. Jerry said, "As you know, the bill of sale, included a note that the right ears of both oxen had been deeply nicked to produce the letter "W" for Wickham, the name of the man who sold your father the oxen over in Iowa.

Just then Chase stepped up and explained to the train boss that your father represented this district in the Territorial Legislature and was Eldorado's president.

"The boss and his two lieutenants quickly walked over to the oxen to see if they had those marks. The wagon train had now stopped and quite a crowd had gathered. Two ladies from the wagon directly behind Hildebrand's came over from their wagon. As they approached us the crowd made an opening for them, so I assumed they enjoyed some special status.

"They listened to Hildebrand rant and rave for a few minutes, then one of them, who was standing close to both me and him, nodded in his direction, and I overheard her say to the other lady, 'I don't know which is worse, his foul smell or his foul language.' Chase was standing nearby and I asked him who the ladies were. He said one was a nurse from Ohio and had been invited along for her medical services. She was the only paid member of the train.

"The nurse explained to her friend that Hildebrand's problem was much more complicated than just needing a bath. It was her opinion that Mr. Hildebrand has anal incontinence. She said it could be cured by a surgical procedure but that it was difficult to perform and was mostly done in Philadelphia and Boston. A bath could make him smell better but only for a short time. And then I heard her say, 'Harriet, he is more to be pitied than bathed. I suspect, his problem is the source of his misbehavior.' Nodding toward your father and me, she said she felt sorry for the two gentlemen who would have to walk the oxen back to Eldorado.

The train boss and the other two did verify that your oxen both had their ears notched according to the bill of sale, so they concluded that the oxen didn't belong to Hildebrand, Jerry added, "Then some of the people in the crowd began whispering that they didn't want to be associated with somebody like him, which caused him to start aiming some of his nastiness at them. Then he turned and faced your father and said he knew where the three of you lived, telling your father that he would rue the day he had embarrassed him like this. We had to restrain your father from horse whipping Hildebrand; he was so aggravated by the rascal. I said to the officers of the train that this wasn't the first time that he had attempted to steal the oxen, and I told them about the incident last month when he when took the liberty of unyoking them while I was up at the mill site.

"As we started to walk the oxen and our horses back home Hildebrand began ranting at us that now he had no way to pull his wagon. Hildebrand followed us on foot for a half mile or so, yelling and swearing vengeance on us both."

Today, May 24 is Howland's birthday and we are going to have a surprise party for him this evening. Adda and I have planned it for several days, though when we began I didn't realize that Chase would not be here for it. His train left two days ago and already I miss him very much.

Our guests will include David Upham. His finger that had the felon is looking much better now that I've persuaded him that it was the greasy food he was eating that was causing the trouble. Though he seems to be staying in Little Walnut, we try to include him in social events hoping he'll take a claim down here. When we invited him several days ago, we suggested that he bring along Miss Macintyre from Little Walnut. He tried but she must not have been available because he brought Glennis Bemis instead, a delightful substitute. Enjoying the conspiracy of not revealing anything about the party, Adda went up to Howland's in late afternoon to tell him casually that if he wasn't otherwise occupied, he was invited to supper. Of course part of her enjoyment was knowing that Glennis had unexpectedly arrived and would be attending his party.

Before Adda left for the store, she and Glennis had put the finishing touches on a huge overstuffed raspberry pie with a fancy latticework crust and put it in the oven. Adda asked Glennis to take it out in exactly thirty minutes. She did and the results could have been served in the finest hotels in the land. Aggie Rourke would have been proud of us.

Though father and Jerry Jordan were here all afternoon planning their plowing for the next few days, Jerry became annoyed when first Adda then I interrupted them to ask him to please get the cows out of the corn and bring them into the barn. We were polite with the request but he is the hired hand. Normally we'd do it but we were really busy. We had just done some laundry. I had bread dough rising and a cake yet to bake and there's not enough room in the oven for both, and I also had to get a large roast in the oven in time for it to cook before supper, and tonight we wanted to milk before supper, so we asked Jerry to please bring in the cows. He doesn't mind doing it but he doesn't want two women telling him what to do especially in front of father. He finally agreed and it must have taken him an hour but that was an hour of my time better spent on supper.

When Mr. Howland came in at 6:30 P.M., it was still daylight. I'm sure he was surprised to see such a gathering. What really caught his eye most, though, was Glennis. Her presence was as much of a surprise as the party. They struggled to keep the ardor of their greetings within socially acceptable limits, as we were all watching them.

When we were ready for supper, Adda seated them together. The party was so nice and we had such a good time, including cake with candles, though we couldn't come up with twenty-four of them; singing, oh yes, we had some fine singing, almost as good as on the night of the Bentons' party; and the mandatory paddling, twenty-four swats for Howland. Everybody got in on it, including Glennis.

When we began singing, Glennis asked Father to carry the baritone harmony, but he said he'd rather sit and listen. Glennis led the rest of us in some songs, and we sang for quite a while. Then we gathered around the cake I had made. As we cut it, we called for a speech from Howland. He obliged by reciting some Edgar Allan Poe.

At the end of the evening, David Upham casually said he was going to take his wagon back up to Little Walnut. Though it was a warm mild night, his traveling up there would mean he would have a two- to three-hour ride ahead of him, and it was almost midnight. I found this rather strange, but stranger still when he offered to take Glennis Bemis "home." Glennis doesn't have a home in Little Walnut, or any place else around here for that matter. She's with the Irish outfit camped on the other side of the crick but doesn't like to "camp out." Her folks have staked a claim here and are building a cabin but it's slow going, so Glennis simply spends the night wherever she can find a comfortable roof over her head. There are several Catholic couples between Little Walnut and Chelsea where she's been staying lately when she doesn't stay here, so his offer was somewhat plausible, but it still struck me as odd.

Glennis looked mildly embarrassed by David's offer, but she has such social poise that she was able to deflect his invitation easily and without offense.

Glennis had other plans but was reluctant to divulge them. Neither she nor Howland wanted to explain, in front of all of us, that Howland had invited her to spend the night at his store. Adda and I have known for some time that they have an arrangement whereby, when we have these evening socials, Glennis stays at his store afterwards, which saves her the difficulty of having to negotiate the creek at night. They simply didn't want to discuss this arrangement openly, but I have been aware of it for quite a while, so I wasn't surprised, but what did surprise me is that David Upham seems to know Glennis well enough to offer to escort her home in the moonlight—late-night moonlight.

About midnight, our party came to an end with a so-so

rendering of "Auld Lang Syne." Howland offered to help clean up around the stove. He took the ashes out from the grate. Then he decided to restock our supply of firewood. He went outside, found the woodpile in the dark and brought back a small armful. All of this activity allowed him time to stay here 'til David drove off, then he and Glennis, swinging our old brass-bottomed lantern, left arm in arm toward his store. Seeing them made me miss Chase, and he's only been gone two days.

Father retired to the loft. When he's home, he prefers the privacy of the loft and stays up there, and that way Adda gets his bed.

The next morning, Father and Jerry yoked our oxen up to the breaking plow. This is the heavy plow we use to cut through and turn over virgin prairie sod to prepare the soil for planting. In some areas that has never been plowed, the ground is so hard both Father and Mr. Martin (who's also down here helping) has to control the plow. This deep steel blade turns up the virgin prairie down to a depth of ten to twelve inches, and in the process turning the grassy surface completely over. The newly turned earth shines blue and reflects the morning sun. I wouldn't expect dirt to be reflective, but it is. The fresh ground must then be replowed with a lighter plow, generally at right angles to the travel of the breaking plow. This breaks up the heavy clods. That's what Jerry is doing with his one-horse plow.

Father, Jerry and Mr. Martin have worked out an arrangement such that when they have finished with our acreage (about a hundred acres, twenty of them new prairie), they'll move up and repeat the process for Mr. Martin, who wants to put in more than one hundred acres, though little or none of his is new prairie. He did all his sod last summer with father's plow, within days of their arrival, July 1857. Mr. Martin planted corn and fodder, which he uses to fatten his livestock. He doesn't grow the corn to sell it as grain, but keeps it to feed his animals. I remember his laughing and saying in his English accent, "It was more profitable when his corn walked to market on four legs." When the men are done plowing down here and at the Martin's, they'll start on Jerry's claim.

The three of them came back to the house for the noon meal. At table, father complained, "I don't have time to do all this plowing and planting and be a town promoter and a politician all at the same time." Jerry reminded father that he too planned on putting in at least one hundred acres of corn, all of it on new prairie. He thanked father that he's been making better progress with his cabin now that we've got the sawmill running. "So," he said, in some jest, "don't plan on leaving town for a few days."

I had no idea that Jerry would turn out to be so ambitious. Father doesn't seem to mind that Jerry spends more time at his place than around here lately. We could use more of his help, but I don't say anything to father about this. I never interfere with their business arrangements. In recent days, five new families have arrived, thanks to father's promotional skills. He's invited them all to supper tomorrow. Although I'm glad to see such progress, there won't be room for all of them around the table, but I'm sure we'll manage.

I must finish two letters; one to Frank Swift, before Mr. Benton and another gentleman leave tomorrow, heading for Missouri. I wonder what's over there for them? I can't imagine that they are still involved in freeing some slaves, but I know better than to ask. When I worked in Lawrence, I noticed it was a fairly common practice among the more zealous abolitionists to go over to Missouri to help slaves escape, a dangerous practice and one that I believe serves little purpose, except for aggravating the owners who then find way to retaliate. Anyway, tomorrow early Mr. Benton and his companion will pick up all the eastbound mail from Eldorado that's ready and carry it to Lawrence.

Howland returned late today from his buffalo hunt. He'd gone off with two other gentlemen a few days ago. They had each killed two buffalo and had brought back their hides, which they had been able to skin without damaging them. In the skinning process Howland said it took all three of them, and one of their horses, to roll the buffalo carcass over. They will take the skins to the Osage. The Indians know how to tan and work the leather so that it stays supple. Then we'll sew bolts of soft felt or flannel against the skin side. These skins make excellent lap robes for winter traveling. Some pioneers also spread them as carpets on the floor in front of the fireplace. Most cabins I visit have one or two of these buffalo robes so employed.

Howland and his companions brought Adda and me a present, a young antelope. He's very shy and skittish. We made a soft halter for him but haven't put it on yet. We'll see if we can raise him, though it may be difficult. He refused a small bowl of milk tonight.

Well, I've been appointed zookeeper. I have the antelope with a halter around his neck with a rope tied to a post in our corral. Without the rope, he could easily leap the fence. Mrs. Cordis and Mrs. Rackcliffe, with her baby, came by to visit the antelope, and we took turns feeding him tufts of grass and dry hay.

A few days later, among a small pack of letters brought out by the Fort Riley stage, which comes here from Lawrence, was a letter from Mrs. Gates containing some disturbing news. Enclosed in her letter was a June 4 clipping from the *Herald of Freedom*, which describes a dispute between General Jim Lane and another upstanding abolitionists, Mr. Gaius Jenkins.

On June 3, General Lane killed Mr. Jenkins over a property dispute. They both had filed land claims adjacent to each other in the outskirts of Lawrence. It seems that some of the contested land included a well.

In addition to this quarrel, General Lane accused Mr. Jenkins of defiling and obliterating the gravesite of the general's young daughter, buried on land claimed by the general. After repeated warnings, General Lane shot and killed Mr. Jenkins. During the confrontation the general was also wounded.

Although there was a hearing which acquitted the general of murder, Mrs. Gates seems to feel that the general did murder Mr. Jenkins.

What a shame. I remember hearing stories about Gaius Jenkins being the man responsible for bringing cargo into Lawrence via riverboats. Indeed, Mrs. Gates told me that on one occasion he brought in a hundred tons of merchandise on the little riverboat *Emma Harmon*, and the town fathers didn't know where to store the goods, so Sara Robinson and some of the other ladies in Lawrence formed a ladies auxiliary to help unload and store the cargo.

Mrs. Gates ended her letter on such a nostalgic note that it makes me long to see her again.

Today, about noon, Mrs. Dempsey came by again with our brown-and-tan milk jug with intentions, I'm sure, of refilling it. In the three weeks that the Dempseys have been here we've gotten to know each other so well you might say we're on familiar terms. During this time her husband, with (a little!) help from the boys, has made great progress on the well. They have finally broken through the four or five foot thick crust of hard stone, blasting and drilling the rock until they hit a layer of softer stone, that contained cracks, which made the drilling easier and the blasting more productive. After Chase left for the mountains, we had one less person to work on the well, but Mr. Dempsey, Frank Robinson and Jerry Jordan have continued to dig. A few days ago they hit water. Overnight four or five feet accumulated in the well. They said they had gone down about twenty feet. That seems to be an exaggeration, though they did extend the ladder three or four times.

Mr. Dempsey and the boys quickly lined the well pit with bricks down to the first bedrock ledge, which was only about four or five feet below grade and they have extended that with a three-foot-high circular brick wall around the top of the well. Sometime ago, we acquired an elegant bucket, which we will use for the well. Adda traded with a westbound outfit from the Carolinas some fresh vegetables and berries for it. The bucket is made from staves of white beech wood, which are held together with two encircling shiny brass bands. The bucket has a nicely curved wrought-iron handle, whose looped ends fit over two little "thumbs" forged through holes in opposite sides of the upper brass band. The bucket swings from this handle. Less than a week after hitting water we tried to see if we could lift it out faster than it flowed in but couldn't. The water tastes pretty good, but not as sweet as spring water. We are all proud of ourselves for this accomplishment but we know we couldn't have done it without Mr. Dempsey. And it's so convenient near the mill site. Father is already planning to plumb a pipe from the well down to the boiler. Now we need a cranking winch to raise and lower the bucket. Maybe Chase will build it, when he comes home.

Directly after Mrs. Dempsey arrived, Pete Gilespie came by from Chelsea. He was on a delivery route, one of Pete's part-time jobs. He stopped-by to deliver some mail from the Chelsea post office and a note with twenty-five pounds of yellow cornmeal, a sample for me from Mrs. Hayworth at the mill. Before he left, I introduced him to Mrs. Dempsey and I asked him if he would take a barrel of well water to the Dempsey camp. They don't like to use the river for their water and I don't blame them and it's quite a hike to carry it from the spring.

I offered to share some of the cornmeal with
Mrs. Dempsey, asking her if she was familiar with it. She sifted
a handful of it through her fingers. "Yes, but we call it maize. I
first saw it when I was a girl in 1845. After our potato crop failed
to recover, the British government imported a lot of maize into
Ireland. It was begrudgingly supplied by the British as grits to
people on the dole, she said.

"The problem was, in the West we simply couldn't pay for
the maize and there was insufficient charity. We had always raised
our own potatoes but when the blight hit for several years in a row
we lost those crops, so we had no potatoes to eat and we certainly
didn't have enough money to buy the imported maize. So much
of that grain went to making whiskey. The shame is some of us
seemed to afford whiskey and tobacco but not food, and with
cash in such short supply, more often than not we traded work for
whiskey or food.

"When Francis got so he was able to send us money every
month from Wales, we were a little better off than most," she said
but since I wanted to save most of the money, we became soupers.
We had to go to the parish or sometimes to the union house or
the workhouse to wait in line for soup. Oh that was shameful,
shameful, but the only way to stay alive for most of us was to go
twice a day with our little bucket and stand in line and try not to
be seen, and hope for the courage to avoid having to recognize or
greet anyone we knew in line—and hope they had the courtesy to
do the same."

Her eyes brightened. "I have an uncle now in Baltimore
who became a rather famous souper in the West. He had originally
been a small landlord in Clooney in Sligo. That's up north. He
used to rent out a few small farms up there when I was a girl.
When the potato crop failed, one by one his tenants stopped

paying their rent. Actually, this became a rent game. Everybody in Ireland played it. When a tenant knew a landlord was in trouble, he stopped paying rent and the landlord would soon be in the same boat as everyone else. Then you see, he couldn't pay his taxes. But what happened was that in time, some Englishman would get his property. by paying-up the arrears in taxes.

"Well, my uncle, MacCowley, became a souper like the rest of us, except he became famous for the way he'd get the soup. He loved the church kitchens and the priests who ran them. My uncle would only go to the Catholic charities, of course. He wouldn't stoop to accept soup from Prods. But the priests wanted piety or work, and sometimes both in exchange for their soup. Their policy was, 'Eat my soup. Attend our services.'"

When uncle MacCowley arrived at a new parish, he wouldn't stand in-line like the other soupers. Oh! No! He would go to confession and declare himself to be a terrible sinner, saying that he had strayed from the church but in his current 'fix' he was truly in search of salvation, and then he'd tell the priest that he hadn't eaten in three days. The priest would give him a dispensation, which meant that my uncle didn't need to stand in line. They'd give him soup in the kitchen and solace in the chapel, in exchange for which he'd praise their soup and declare their spiritual guidance had given him the light to see the error of his ways. He became, he'd say, a new man. He started up in Sligo and worked his way south, parish-by-parish, until he got to Galway, where he stayed with us for several weeks. I was still a girl then, and I was still living with my parents. Those were gloomy days for us indeed. We'd lost our home and were resisting eviction when my uncle showed up. His antics provided the only levity we had that year. I still can't understand how he could treat all that misery in such a lighthearted fashion. But he'd often say to me that tragedy; poverty and chronic sadness are humanity's best source of comedy and humor.

"Galway had at least ten parish churches, as well as the cathedral downtown, and he patronized them all. He had so much success he'd occasionally bring his little soup bucket home and feed some of our neighbors, whom none of the charities would feed. The Church and other charities were very snooty about the people they chose to favor. The priests certainly wouldn't feed the Protestants. So, many of the Protestants in Galway, who were too poor to leave, starved by the dozens. Uncle MacCowley claimed his biggest fear wasn't starving. No, he was afraid his newly developed sense of piety was proving so successful that he would gain weight, and he wouldn't be able to claim he was a starving sinner anymore. So he needed to control his passions, both for soup and salvation.

"After he had gone to all of the parish kitchens in Galway, he left for Cork, stopping at every parish church on the way. When finally arriving in Cork, he surprised us all by having enough money to take himself and my two older sisters to Liverpool, then to Baltimore. He paid for most of their fare, though they did contribute the pittance they had from their dowries. He even sent both of my sisters some money so they could take the coach down to Cork, plying his 'trade' while he waited for them."

Mrs. Dempsey said that the parish church schools in the southwest of Ireland had over the years provided a supply of well-educated Irish priests to Baltimore, where there was already a large Catholic diocese. "You know we have a school for Irish priests in county Cork in a town called Baltimore." Neither of her two older sisters had married, she said, and they both still lived in Baltimore with her uncle MacCowley, who now spelled his name MacCaulley.

"The younger of my two sisters is four years older than I am, but due to the terrible diet we had back home she gradually developed a stoop. After two or three years she couldn't stand up straight. When we saw her last year in Baltimore she had become hunchback. As a girl of sixteen or seventeen she was the most beautiful thing you ever laid eyes on but now you wouldn't know it. My other sister, who is eight years older than I am, Meagan, another wasted beauty, and all for the want of proper food." She paused, and tears welled up in her eyes, but she seemed compelled to finish her story. "When women don't get enough food for three or four years and especially if they're young as we were, their bodies start to change. All of us Irish women knew about this, but the subject was too shameful to be discussed openly. First the women lose weight, then the hair gets gray and stringy, their skin takes on a pallor and their bellies start to stick out. When women get this thin, their eyes seem to sink back in their sockets. That, and their exposed cheekbones make them look skeletal, frightening! They are hungry all the time and they begin to lose the one thing that sets them apart from men—you know, Mrs. Stewart, the moon thing, the monthlies. They become irregular. Gradually they stop and that's the end of their womanhood. One old priest I knew said it was God's way to lessen the mouths to feed. Well, I hope it's not, lest the Irish race die out entirely. Of course, the English would love that!

"I don't know if women start getting their monthlies again once they have good food and can eat regularly again. Neither of my sisters has gotten hers back again. When that begins to happen, they lose interest in their beau, and vice versa. Francis tells me the same thing happens to a man who is starving. He gradually loses his manhood. His two 'things' just get smaller and smaller until they couldn't function." She raised her eyebrows and allowed herself a small smile, "If they had the opportunity."

This information was entirely new to me and was slightly embarrassing. To change the subject I asked, "Since you were in

Ireland and Mr. Dempsey was in Wales, how did the two of you manage to get to America?"

"Well, I had saved and hidden away most of the money Francis had sent me, so I decided to take our girls and go join him in Wales. We didn't leave for America until three years later.

"I used the money to pay for our stagecoach fares to Cork and then for our boat tickets from there to Cardiff.

"The coaches in Ireland are much like the coaches that come through here. I took day coaches with my two babes to Cork, stopping each night with relatives along the way. We couldn't afford to stay in hotels. Ireland has no hotels or boarding houses inexpensive enough for people like us. I planned to stay with one of my uncles in Killarney, but when we got to his house, it was just a little stone shack with a missing door. All of the windows were gone, and not a stick of furniture was left. He'd left a note, stuck on a little cracked mirror, saying that he, too, had gone to Baltimore. But we stayed there anyway.

"After about ten days we got to Cork, where we took the boat to Cardiff. Most of the people on the boat were men. Many of them were craftsmen but there were also landlords, who like my Uncle MacCowley, had lost their properties because their tenants wouldn't pay rent. Some of the men on the ship died before we got to Cardiff. The trip was too hard on those who were sick from starving before we left.

"Many of those who leave Ireland get their passage paid through money sent by relatives who have already emigrated to England and America. Our relatives work and save up money so they can send it to us. Thanks to their most Christian effort, some of us were able to escape. But many of those who were too poor to leave, gradually starved.

"We lived in Wales three years. We stayed there that long, partly to save up money for the boat fare to America, but also to see if things would improve back home, but they never did. Some of the men who were with us in Wales became involved in political movements to free Ireland. Sometimes small groups of them would steal back into Ireland to even up a political score. And some of them never came back. It was dangerous activity.

"Mr. Dempsey worked in the mines. It was hard, dirty work, but he never liked farming," she said. I recalled his having said that to me the first day we met.

"In Wales the miners had singing clubs that competed regularly with clubs from other mines and with miners of other nationalities. Mr. Dempsey belonged to the Irish Club.

"On one occasion his Irish club won a singing trip to Cardiff which was some distance from where we lived. Francis said singing with that choir was almost as good for him as the church. In Wales the authorities tried to suppress our church and our church schools, though we did have a few Irish priests. Confession and communion are both important to us, but they were in short supply in Wales."

At the end of three years they had saved enough to book their passage to America, she said. "So one fine day we took a small boat to Liverpool, and then a much bigger one from there to New York."

"Why didn't you leave from Wales?"

"It was much cheaper to go to America from Liverpool. We went to New York because Francis had relatives there and hoped to find work through them. But when we arrived at Immigration, the officers told us that there was no work in New York. They advised us to go to Pennsylvania or Ohio, which had work for miners. "Instead," said Mrs. Dempsey, "We got permission to visit Francis's relatives for a day.

"They all live in a neighborhood called the Sixth Ward, which was a short hack ride up Broadway from the docks.

"The narrow streets seemed so familiar. They were crowded with various-sized carts pulled either by men or by horses. The cooking smells and the sounds of singing and quarreling all reminded me of home. We asked directions of some girls who were skipping rope on the sidewalk. In rhythm they were all singing the same Irish ditty I sang as a girl when I'd skip rope."

"You're from Galway, aren't you," I asked.

She laughed and said that she was from a little north of there. Her father worked in the marble quarries. He was a Ribbon man * and they transported him for it, but the rest of her family now lived in New York. "She asked me how I knew she was from Galway and I sang her another verse of the skip-rope song. "There must have been twelve people not counting our family in that cramped little apartment. All of those men had found work digging a tunnel that was being built to bring water into New York. And there were lots of others from Galway and County Clare who were working on that tunnel. Even their foreman was Irish. He was from county Clare. So there was plenty of work for us Irish in New York, but not enough living space."

Mrs. Dempsey explained that the New York Democrats encouraged immigration and had made citizenship easy to get for all of the Irish immigrants because they knew that the Irish would vote as a block for the Democrats. President Buchanan also favored this policy, but some of the Irish, she said disliked him because he had earlier served as the American ambassador to the Court of St. James. They didn't trust anyone who had dealt with the British, and believed Buchanan was a cynical politician who only supported the policy because it would increase the number of Democratic voters in the country.

*A member of the Ribbon Society, one of several secret societies in Ireland that fought against the English occupation of Ireland. Other such groups included Terryalts, Rockites, Blackfeet, and Whiteboys.

"At supper the men talked politics, off and on, all night long. But they didn't talk just about New York politics, they discussed schemes to raise money for small groups back home that are doing local battle with the English authorities. Francis's relative bragged about the power of these secret societies. I tried to keep him from getting involved in any of this. I've seen what happened to too many of our patriots who have been swept up in this business. They are either executed or transported to New South Wales. Those they consider the most dangerous are imprisoned on Van Diemen's Land. *

"We slept on the floor that night and there were so many of us that there was hardly any room. We left the next morning for Baltimore to see my sisters, and I'm glad we did. Knowing my husband's political leanings, staying in New York could have been dangerous."

Mrs. Dempsey said that they took the ferry to New Jersey, then boarded a train for Baltimore. "Even with stops," she said, "The train ride took less than five hours, and it was an exciting ride. I'd never been on a train before. My but Baltimore was beautiful. It was hot and muggy, but a lovely city, and it wasn't crowded like New York, though there were plenty of Irish and plenty of Catholics. My older sister, who is a saint, works for a middle-class Catholic family and takes care of Mary, my sister the hunchback. It was wonderful to be able to go to church openly. The day after we arrived we all went to confession, and the next day, a Saturday, I made a novena and on Sunday we all took communion together, the first for us in our new country."

I hope the Dempseys will stay in Eldorado. I've asked Mr. Dempsey to consider working in our sawmill. Though he is most polite, I can tell that prospect doesn't interest him. Occasionally, if they stay for supper, and some of the boys are here, we'll have

*A notorious penal colony; Van Diemen's Land is now known as Tasmania

an evening of fine singing, certainly the best singing we ever have. They both have nice voices and know so many songs. They are friendly, but somewhat reserved. Whenever I invite them to spend the night after we have had an evening of singing, they always decline. They are rather clannish and a little "touchy" about their ways. The train from Lawrence arrived in town that morning but the advance man, who had arrived a day or two earlier, picked up a few more recruits including Chase, and pulled out ahead of it.

The party reached Cherry Creek * June 17, 1858. Though some immediately panned for gold that was not the main intent of this group. Their mission was to form a town and prosper by selling lots. They were very well equipped to do so with surveyors and provisions to last six months.

On July 3, 1858 the group surveyed north-south and an east-west boundaries, consisting of 640 acres, a section. (The land laws at the time allowed two sections or 320 acres per "town site.") Temporarily they called it "Mountain City."

"Within a week a committee of ten held a meeting to consider a permanent name for this community, Chase later told me. "Here are some proposed names that were put to vote: 'Eldorado,' 'Eureka,' 'Excelsior,' 'Marshall,' 'Jefferson,' 'Columbia,' 'Mineral' and 'Mountain City.' Note the absence of 'Denver'! It was agreed that it would take six votes (out of ten) on one town name to secure it," said Chase. "It was important to establish priority and to hold the claim," he continued. "To do so they dispatched some of our party back to the territorial land office in Lecompton to file our city claim. I decided to come back with them. The voting continued without resolution all the way back to Lecompton. No single name on any ballot secured six votes.

"Upon returning to Lecompton we invited (the then new) Governor James W. Denver to a camp dinner. At the age of forty-

* Now called Denver

one, Governor Denver had already accomplished a lifetime of heroic experience. A lawyer from Ohio, Captain of Infantry in the Mexican War, a State Senator (California), killed a man in a duel, represented California in Congress, President Pierce appointed him Commissioner of Indian Affairs, and on May 12th 1858 (two days after our party left for the Gold Fields) he was appointed Governor of the (Kansas) Territory.

"Since we had failed," Chase said, "vote after vote, to arrive at a majority to name the new mining town, when the Governor joined us for dinner, we took another vote and 500 miles from the town site, named it 'Denver' after our guest of honor," *

Chase said he learned later that one of the groups of gold seekers who left Eldorado with the May 22nd party was called "'Gregory and Green Russell.' They knew more about prospecting and as a result hit pay dirt in September (1858)." But by August 15th, Chase had returned with the committee to file the Land Office information at Lecompton. He did find a few gold nuggets out there and I have some of them now in a small vial of water.

* Named after James Denver, Governor of Kansas Territory

**Sara Robinson, the wife of Dr. Charles Robinson, the first
elected governor of Kansas Territory. Both were abolitionists.**

Augusta met Mrs. Robinson in Lawrence and learned she was an author,
having written a journal on the early politics of the territory. Her book was
published in 1857 in Boston, Cincinnati and London, "Kansas, Its Interior
and Exterior Life". In 1857 Adda worked in the home of the governor's
brother and saw both families frequently. Sara Robinson was a proponent of
Phrenology. She was a POW with her husband in 1856 for their anti-slavery
views.

22.

HOWLAND'S HEART IS BROKEN
Mid June 1858

Two newcomers, Mr. and Mrs. Barrett, came by this morning, a couple of days after Mrs. Dempsey's visit, to make inquiry about locating here. I like the appearance of Mrs. Barrett. She seems to be about my age. They are camped a bit south of us on the spot of ground where we first located our tents last November. I attempted with some delicacy to inquire about Mr. Barrett's purple fingers. He smiled and said the stains were from mulberries, telling me that half a mile or so south of their camp they had found several mulberry trees in a creek bed. "By standing on our wagon we were able to pick a small bucket of them." He went back out to their wagon and returned with the evidence. I volunteered to wash the berries with some spring water and offered to exchange some of our cream and sugar for some of their berries. We had a little midmorning berry party.

That afternoon Father, Adda, Frank, Mrs. Barrett and I all went to find the grove of mulberries. I don't think I've ever noticed what a mulberry tree looks like before. Mrs. Barrett pointed out that the tree has two differently shaped leaves, both large. Compared with the other trees around here, it is rather short, though still tall enough that we couldn't just reach up and pluck the berries. Father drove our wagon next to one of the trees. Standing up on the wagon seat, he could shake the branches, the ripe mulberries came raining down on to the wagon bed. In the style of Mrs. Strong and her fruit cobblers in western Iowa, I think I will make a big mulberry fruit cobbler for supper tonight. It won't take much sugar, for the berries are so sweet.

June 15 father's fortieth birthday. Among the several things we have to celebrate today is the possibility that the "Mulberry Barretts" might stake a claim here, at least that's what they told Howland yesterday. They seem to be quite curious about the countryside. They told him that they'd gone west some distance along the Arkansas River looking for possible claim sites. They showed Howland a large bucket of small purple plums that they'd picked west of here. And that gave me an idea about getting up a plum-picking expedition. Why not? The men keep going off on two- or three-day Buffalo Hunts. Why can't we go off on a two day plum hunt? When we get back with buckets of plums we'll get the necessary sugar and other ingredients and "put up" several pints of plum preserves.

It's really hot today. The heat seems to encourage the musquitoes. * They visit us in swarms. A the...A single Kansas musquito makes as much noise as a bumblebee and are so tough they pick fights with the sparrows! Staying inside the house is no refuge from them, nor is darkness: putting out the light only seems to heighten their ability to locate human flesh and extract its juices. They must have a well-developed sense of smell. They certainly know how to find me in the dark. I have become their favorite body-juice supplier. They must have passed the word along about how delicious they find me. Yesterday, Mr. Beerop reported that he'd had two mules stolen. Father and two others went off looking for them. It was father's opinion that a small

* Augusta's spelling for the word "mosquitoes"

hunting party of Osages south of us probably had them.

Four days later, about noon, father returned with Mr. Beerop's mules. He said he was glad he'd had two armed men with him. When they located the Osage camp, they found most of the braves gone, and assumed they were out hunting. Father said that the Indians had been there for some time because an accumulated pile of hides had already developed that putrid stink peculiar to buffalo hides after they've been removed a few weeks from their owners and the little adhering shreds of meat and fat on them have begun to rot in the summer heat. The squaws, using stakes, had stretched out a dozen skins on the prairie, and were scraping the hides free of the remaining bits of fat and meat, which attracted swarms of blowflies.

There are buyers out here from St. Louis offering to pay up to $4 per hide, depending on the hide's quality—the average price is $2.50.

Father said that the two mules were hobbled in the way the Indians do it, which allows them to graze, without getting away. "We simply went out, untied the hobbles and brought the ropes back to the squaws. We made temporary halters for the mules and led them home."

Last night the men camped along the Arkansas where like the Barretts, they found several clumps of ripe wild plums, which they picked before bedtime, so they have returned this morning with plums and mules. Well, we had another pleasant surprise this morning. It turns out that Mr. Barrett is a doctor.

Mr. Cunningham, a newcomer, told Mr. Howland that Dr. Barrett was treating him for something. Frank Robinson and father are both seriously constipated and they are considering asking Dr. Barrett to come by. Frank didn't lose his thumb but his thumbnail has dropped off and a new one has yet to appear. They are both skeptical that Dr. Weibley can be sober enough, long enough to treat their illnesses.

I told Frank and father I would fetch Dr. Barrett after breakfast. I did and he said he'd come by midafternoon. Before he left, I offered him some ripe raspberries in a small crockery jar and joshed with him, saying that if my patients got better, I'd show him where I had found the raspberries. The doctor also said we should eat as much of fruit as we can, like these berries. He said it would reduce the number of boils and carbuncles he is seeing out here. I didn't say so, but that was old news to me.

For my constipated patients he prescribed they each eat a dozen wild ripe plums and gave me a small bottle of a liquid laxative with instructions. Dr. Barrett said he was taught in medical school how to make laxatives from parts of certain plants growing locally. He was sure that this "physic" would quickly help father and Frank—and it did.

It rained hard throughout the night. This morning the creek is "up" higher than I've ever seen it. I thought I would ride Puss over to Cave Springs and get a jug of spring water but Frank Gordy, a new settler, has our big saddle and he's on the other side of the creek. I can't get used to the luxury that we have a well, so the notion to go to the spring is really a little outing. Don't know if Puss will "put up with me" bareback. I'll be like a circus performer, but without the scanty costume!

In the afternoon, there was a big swap at our cabin. While father and Frank Robinson were putting in part of our floor using nice flat boards from our sawmill, a Mr. Trask, who needs to make a trip to Texas, came by to say he wants to buy or trade for our little wagon. I'm not sure the trading is over, but so far father has ten dollars cash, a mustang pony, a saddle and bridle (for the pony) and an old flat-bottomed wagon with pretty good wheels, which father says he will convert to a utility wagon for hauling and delivering lumber.

On June 29, a few days later, father and Chase took an order from Mr. and Mrs. Watts for a substantial purchase of timber. They plan to build the largest dwelling in Eldorado, a big two story boarding house. I'm looking forward to the day they have this building finished. Perhaps I'll then be able to send them my occasional "overflow" business.

Howland came to supper this evening. Unlike most nights, we won't have a crowd for supper it will be just Adda, Howland and me. Howland was carrying a medium-sized box and wore a look on his face that said, "You will be pleasantly surprised by the contents of this box." I asked what was in the box. He was very mysterious and said the answer would have to wait until after supper. During supper, he sat where Frank usually sits, that is, next to my sister, and in that spot I could see his broad, clean-shaven face in full view. He was unusually quiet and serious.

"How's business at your store?" I asked him.

"It could be better. The McWhorters are planning to open a general store that will sell whiskey by the glass. The rumor is that they are also trying to get freighters to commit to making regular deliveries of beer made by the Germans over in St. Louis."

"Humph, that's not a store the McWhorters are planning; it's a saloon."

After some more conversation, Howland paused, then put his knife and fork down. We were eating a nice shoulder roast of deer, thanks to Mr. Benton. Howland looked at me and said, "Ladies, you were right. 'Blood is thicker than water.'"

Adda turned to me with her best "puzzlement" written on her face. Worried that something really serious was bothering our best and oldest friend in Eldorado, I said, "Erastus (I seldom address him in such familiar terms), "what's disturbing you? What's happened for you to come to that conclusion and to look so doleful about it?"

Here is what he said: "A week or so ago, the Irish outfit camped on the other side of the creek, including the Dempseys, all left for the gold fields, all except the senior Mr. and Mrs. Bemis. They have stayed and want to buy a town lot, on credit I suppose, but their daughter, Glennis, has gone west with them. So, blood is thicker than water, at least Irish blood."

I knew the Dempseys and the others from the Irish camp were planning on leaving because Mrs. Dempsey had come to say goodbye and to return our one-gallon jug. Tom Cordis reported that they had paid him in full for his services hours of blacksmithing. Attempting to lighten Howland's mood I said, "Did you have a serious interest in Glennis?"

There was a long pause. His eyes searched among the items on our table, as though the sugar bowl or the saltshaker could provide some answers.

I think my question was embarrassing, but we are old friends and, among friends, a question motivated by concern should not be taken as prying.

"Well, Augusta, it's hard for me to explain. Men think of these things as options or opportunities."

I thought to myself, "Well, opportunity is not an exclusive God-given gift to men. Women are as sensitive to their options as men.

Howland added, "That doesn't mean I was going to rush things, but in retrospect, I probably didn't pay enough attention to her. I didn't express how much affection I felt for her—no, what I did wrong was that I did not tell her those things. She was very verbal, you remember. Yes, she had great presence. She was so pleasantly social. I think this trait must be peculiarly Irish.

"She brought springtime to this valley and when she came into my store, it was as if it had just been lit up by a hundred candles. When she asked me about my accounts or what an item had cost me or how I kept track of my suppliers, what she really wanted was to talk about me. She asked me so many questions about the store, but I see now that was her way to get to know me better. I didn't get this through my head until I realized she had left. Glennis communicated her feelings by talking and by being so pleasantly social. She was curious about my customers and all of you, and I was happy to let her do the talking for the both of us. I loved her accent, but what I loved even more was her voice, which could make small talk sound like a poem. On occasion, when I was filling out an order for someone, she would wait on another customer and I'd hear her burst out with her delightful, explosive laughter and I could see that the customer was captivated by her accent, which is so rare around here and which made us all pay attention to whatever she said. It was my notion that customers would rather have her take care of them than me, and that was all right with me. In fact, I took pleasure in anticipating that this would continue because that would be another reason for her to settle here, and I felt some pride in thinking that she would stay with me.

"I'm so sorry she left. Now I wish I'd spent sometime in their camp to learn their ways, and I'm sorry I didn't simply ask her to stay."

Since I suffer the same occasional affliction, I realized that Howland was dejected. I became concerned for him, for what seemed to me could become excessive melancholy.

Trying to be sympathetic, I said, "You know, she was very Catholic. The Dempseys referred to themselves as 'Galway Catholics.' The Galway Irish are much more orthodox, and ceremonial, than most Roman Catholics, or any of us Protestants. Mrs. Dempsey told me that they got that way because of the restraints imposed by the English who tried to stamp out their language, they couldn't own guns, they couldn't vote and they couldn't have a government of their own. The British closed their schools, and "looked down their nose" at their customs. They limited the amount of rent an Irishman who owned a tenant could charge. So they turned more and more to their religion for comfort. Their only hope was to flee, if they could scrape up the means to do it. Flee not just Galway but the English and the Protestants and the poverty and the opportunity to starve."

I was trying to point out to Howland how profoundly different their thinking was from ours.

"Did you ever talk to them about the abolitionist cause? They were almost oblivious to it. When I tried to discuss the slavery issue with Mr. Dempsey, he certainly sympathized with the Negroes but said that if they thought they had troubles here, they should go to Ireland where they could exchange slavery for starvation. His attitude was that we all have to find our own salvation, Negroe, Irish, all of us. Each group, he said, had to escape bondage and pursue happiness. It was his impression that the Northern Yankees had come out here only to pursue their own ambition, particularly for free (almost free) land, and more political and economic opportunity. And it was also his feeling that the Irish in Wales, the Irish in England and, to some extent, and now the Irish in New England continue to be oppressed and were only different from the Negroes because they had the ability to move, if they could afford it.

Howland seemed to agree in general with the philosophical points I was making, but where he and Miss Bemis were concerned, he took exception and felt that love between two people could overcome such cultural differences.

Her departure was a bitter disappointment to him. "She didn't even come over to the store to tell me, in her own lilting way say, that she was leaving." Looking forlorn, he said with yearning, "Do you know that they were gone two days before I knew they'd left? Mr. and Mrs. Bemis came into the store asking for a gallon of coal oil. As I filled up their old chipped-up terra-cotta jug, I inquired about Glennis and Mrs. Bemis said, 'Oh, they've gone, she left last Wednesday.'

"I almost dropped their jug. 'Gone? Gone where?'"

'To the gold fields, son. She's goin' to the Rockies with the rest of them. They figured now the grass would be good all the way to the mountains, so it was time to go.'

Howland started to eat again, signaling that he wanted to put an end to this conversation. Adda and I brought up some other topics. By the time the meal was over, he had become our usual, friendly Howland, and began flirting with Adda, which she enjoys; well, any woman enjoys. And I suspect if Frank had been with us, and he usually is, she would have been in heaven with attention from two gentlemen!

"Supper's over. Didn't you say that you would open the box after we had finished eating?" I asked him. Howland reached over and turned up the wick on the coal oil lamp. He wanted plenty of light for what he was about to do. With the same ceremonial gestures he uses whenever he lifts the lid off his cast-iron roasting pan he stood up and presented Adda with the box.

Adda removed the lid with feigned pomp and gravity. Resting in the middle of the cloth was a small cut glass bottle with a cork-lined lead stopper, the surface prisms of the glass reflecting the lamplight. A little tag on a string announced "eau du cologne" and was from Germany via a fancy store in Chicago.

The toilet water was resting on top of a beautiful dress. To say that Adda was impressed would be a terrible understatement. She daubed a touch of the eau du cologne behind each ear and did a little flounce alongside Howland, then she unfolded the dress and showed it off with a bit of the delightful girlish glee that only Adda possesses. She held the dress up against her well-developed body—it was a long, evening gown that looked very European, cut low in the front and without sleeves exposing the shoulders and arms.

I knew—but there was no need to say so—that this dress had been intended as a gift for Glennis Bemis. He must have had it in his store for the last few days, a constant reminder of "loves Labor's lost."

23.

ELDORADO AN EVENING OF PHRENOLOGY
July 1858

Today July 1 is Jerry Jordan's twenty-eighth birthday, which we will celebrate this evening. Adda will make the cake. And we have other plans for the evening.

We have a wild chicken out here that we didn't see in Iowa that seems to travel in large flocks. It is much smaller than a barnyard chicken, has speckled gray feathers and flies faster than a wild turkey, low to the ground. The meat tastes like chicken all right, but has a hint of sage, which I suppose derives from its diet. When cleaned, the bird weighs about a pound. They are best plucked "dry," which is tedious, since their thin skin tears easily and is almost without fat.

Yesterday afternoon, Howland and Frank presented Adda and me with six plucked prairie chickens, arranged in a deep cake pan and proposed that we have a dinner party of fried chicken. Howland, who thinks of everything, also brought two or three pounds of salt pork, saying that he doubted that I would have enough fat in my cupboard to fry up so many chickens. He was right and I was grateful! Adda said she'd bake a fresh wild raspberry (or is it a wild blackberry?) cobbler in addition to the birthday cake for Jerry. I thanked the boys for the larder and said we'd have a late supper since it doesn't get dark now 'til about 7:30 and then we have a long twilight lasting at least an hour. By eating later, I thought it would be a little cooler and a bit more fashionable, though the musquitoes are a nuisance.

Well, the dinner couldn't have been nicer, particularly with father home. Even without Chase, we had a full table. I thought of how much Chase would enjoy this dinner knowing how he likes fried chicken.

After supper, in a mood of anticipated humor and mischievousness, stimulated by some recent reading, I got up from the table and walked over behind Frank, who was finishing his tea. I began to feel the top of Frank's head to see if I could locate certain bumps, or "prominents" or maybe a small cavity or two on his skull. Frank has a thick, healthy head of brown hair the color of tanned leather. He wriggled free of my grasp, stood up and confronted me, demanding with a big toothy grin the meaning of this "unseemly conduct." Howland was watching me with curiosity and amusement.

Father was curiously amused. Only Adda knew what I was up to since we had both been reading the same books and pamphlets that were about to lead to the evenings' entertainment.

Stimulated by two or three articles from Eastern newspapers, I had sent off to Boston some weeks ago, for two books and two or three pamphlets mentioned in the newspaper articles. They had described a relatively new branch of medicine imported from Europe that's gaining popularity and credibility in the states. Its called phrenology and it claims to predict character from irregularities on the skull. Even Reverend Henry Ward Beecher, the famous antislavery preacher, has made favorable comments on the subject, and I had never forgotten Sara Robinson's reference to phrenology during a party at the Cincinnati house, when the subject of General Jim Lane as a politician was being discussed.

One of the originators calls it the "Science of the Mind."

When the books and pamphlets arrived, Adda and I had read them with such curiosity and fascination, and in the case of one of the pamphlets, with disbelief and skeptical humor. That pamphlet, with its various advertisements, for snake oil, other potions guaranteed to grow hair on bald pates, physics, written by Dr. Fowler, an American, suggests he is more of an entertainer than a medical doctor. Included with all this was a large folded diagram of a skull with arrows pointing here and there to designated areas. Adda and I decided that we'd put our newfound knowledge to use by conducting some experiments. We'd show everybody how modern and up-to-date we were, hundreds of miles from Eastern centers of learning and culture. One of the books was written by a German doctor, Johann Spurzheim, who has studied personalities, temperament, intelligence, and claims to have discovered from a lifetime of examining what he calls "Cranial Pathology," that the lumps, cavities, protrusions, etc., on people's skulls are indications of their character.

The newspaper articles I mentioned lead me to believe that this is a popular parlor subject in our more cultured centers, such as Philadelphia, Boston and New York. Everybody is talking about this new science. Traveling lyceum speakers have been packing auditoriums in the States for some time.

With a mischievous smile, Howland, asked, "Well, did you find any bumps or cavities on Frank's cranium that correspond with what we know to be features of his sterling character and unsurpassed intelligence?"

I didn't want to say so—out loud—but my cursory examination of Frank's head revealed exactly what I'd expected to find: a smooth skull, no bumps, two or three cavities. I would send my findings to Doctor Spurzheim in Germany but he's been dead since 1832!

Dr. Fowler claims in his pamphlet, which is really a lecture he's given on a lyceum circuit arranged by a Boston agency, * that he was a student of Dr. Spurzheim. After his lecture, he asks for volunteers from the audience and performs an analysis of their skulls, using outlandishly artificial medical terms to describe the meaning of their cranial bumps, irregularities and cavities. And, I might add, his "Latin" is so contrived it could be used for cartoon captions.

I told father and our dinner guests about his pamphlet and about Dr. Spurzheim's book. Adda and I also have a book by another European expert, Doctor Franz Josef Gall, who speaks about the "Science of Phrenology" and is also given to a rather generous use of Latin, though none of the phrases used by him are to be found in my Latin dictionary.

"Well, I'm waiting for an example," said Father.

I was still standing next to Frank. Pointing to an area on his forehead, I replied, "A depression or slight cavity here, according to Dr. Fowler's charts, is called 'Proclivitas Mendacium,' and it suggests that the subject can't always be counted on to tell the truth." Frank was mum. "A bony protrusion here above the eyes indicates vision, farsightedness—a good planner, someone who makes things happen."

That's me!" Frank shouted. Ferry in the fall of 1859. It is my belief Redpath, Richard Hinton and John H. Cagi, who were with Father and Chase at Lecompton, met with Brown at the Whitney House in Lawrence to plan the raid on Harper's Ferry. Well, I'm relieved to hear James Redpath lived through all that and the Civil War." (This journal entry has been condensed and

*In 1902 Augusta added this note to her journal: "Twenty or thirty years after we removed from Kansas I learned that James Redpath, our old English friend and insurrectionist from Plymouth and a close associate of John Brown's turned up in Boston running one of these lyceum agencies. For all those years I had believed that James Redpath had died with John Brown at Harper's Ferry

edited.) "Dr. Fowler calls these bumps luminosities. I couldn't tell whether the chuckles were about the name or that Frank might possess those virtues.

"Dr. Fowler says little indentations above either ear which he calls 'Amorvitas Adoramus,' means the person is unusually affectionate and all the more so if the cavities are on both sides."

My sister jumped up and examined Frank above the ears. With a hoot she pronounced him to be blessed with "Amorvitas Adoramus."

"These little depressions here, at the back of Frank's head, are called 'Cavinosities' and they account for incessant talking." Frank became mum again.

I picked up the diagram of the skull and unfolded it on the table, and began to read some more of Dr. Fowler's delightfully humorous pseudo-Latin phrases such as, "Polaritis" and "Cacoethes Carpendi," which means someone with strong urges and passions.

I pointed to some cranial bumps behind Frank's ears, " Those are called, 'Cuniculorium Inhonestus'—sure signs of deceit and dishonesty."

By now my audience was howling with laughter. Frank leaned over to examine Howland's head, and Howland was more than happy to accommodate. Then Frank broke free of my grasp and walked over behind Adda to feel for any protrusions on her head. He discovered a bump on my sister's head a few inches back from her hairline and demanded to see the chart so as to compare Adda's bump with the chart.

"Aha!" he exclaimed. "Adda has a big lump of 'Amorone Vitas' right here," and he insisted that Adda demonstrate with him this rare and outstanding feminine virtue.

Howland, pretending to be solemn, asked me, "Well, Dr. Stewart, what does Dr. Gall have to say about our brains? You said that this new branch of medicine is also called "The Science of the Mind." I knew he was putting me on because the two of us had discussed the other book.

"He proposes that our intelligence can be measured—after the fact, I'm afraid by a close examination of the surface of our brains, which he says contains thousands of little grooves, or 'infoldings.' He says that their depth and location can explain a person's particular interests. A musician, for instance, will have more pronounced grooves in the area of the brain that's relegated to that branch of art. Dr. Gall studied brains of famous generals, mathematicians, composers and other accomplished individuals, to confirm his theory."

"George Washington's brain must have been deeply wrinkled all over," said Howland pensively. "He had such varied interests and distinguished himself in all of them. Washington was a surveyor, a military engineer, a general and an outstanding leader." Howland, looking mischievous again, stood up and said, "I move that Frank O. Robinson volunteer to have the lid of his cranium lifted and exposed to this august group of prairie scientists. I have a saw in my store that will do minimal harm. And, Frank, if you have an ounce of scientific curiosity, you'll agree to cooperate in this noble experiment."

I thought to myself, "When we get in there, all we'll see is a gray surface, as smooth as a billiard ball."

But, I knew that wasn't nice, so I refrained from saying so and simply said, "I second the motion."

Frank, pleased with the unsolicited attention he was getting, didn't seem aware of why we'd chosen him as the subject for our scientific inquiry, and wasn't even mildly indignant about it—and that's because his "infoldings," the little grooves that deal with perception, aren't very deep I'm afraid.

Howland spoke up. "I wouldn't want to cut short this

high-minded inquiry, but as I recall, I was invited to a birthday party for Jerry. I hope you ladies haven't decided to postpone it. Father grunted an agreement and so Adda got up and brought the cake to the table. We didn't have twenty-eight candles. She turned the coal oil lamp down and lit the three candles on Jerry's cake."

Today, July 3 it cooled down after supper. We had our regular breeze but it was more refreshing than usual, and the evening was comfortably cool. Howland came by before it got dark, claiming credit for the pleasant weather and made several complimentary remarks about how sociable Adda and I make life for him and that he appreciates it. As I made us a pot of tea he said, "I have a gift for Adda." It was another new dress. That's two new dresses in less than a week. Adda wasn't home but I'm sure she will be pleased and grateful when she gets back.

Howland speculated as to the size of the celebrating party when the Wattses open the doors of their "mansion" tomorrow with some Fourth of July fanfare. "But the ceremony will be just for show," he said laughing. "The building isn't half finished. The Wattses simply want to use the Fourth of July as a reason to get some publicity for their boarding house."

Of course, most of the lumber for that building was sawed right here by our mill. Some of it has been paid for, but not all— "Not by a long shot," as father would say.

Just as Howland was leaving, father and Adda drove up. Father asked Howland if there were any deliveries he wanted made in Chelsea. "I'm going up there early Monday morning to arrange for the election," said father. He is in charge of supervising the election here, and in Chelsea, when the proslavery Lecompton Constitution comes up for a vote, on August 2. Before Howland left, I was surprised that he didn't mention the dress. But after he left, pointing to the box, I told Adda about its contents.

The day after the Fourth of July, Sammy Freeman, who

lives on Little Walnut, came by midmorning with a note from Mrs. Weibley.

In the note she asked us to send back with Sammy on his return to Little Walnut two or three quarts of milk. Her note also included another request. She rather casually asked if we could send Daguerreotypes of ourselves, "so that her "memory may fondly be refreshed thereby" and she asked that her memory be further refreshed by a lock of our hair. Of course, she is such a sweet lady we'd be glad to oblige, except between Adda and me we have a shortage of Daguerreotypes—but a surplus of hair.

Adda asked Sammy what was new in Little Walnut. "Not much—unless you know the Widow MacIntyre."

"We know Miss MacIntyre," I said, "but that's the first we've heard that she was a widow."

"Well, whether she's a widow or not I don't know for sure. But in any case she was to be married yesterday, a real Fourth of July celebration. The preacher was ready, and so was the wedding party. Everybody was ready but the bridegroom.

Sammy told us that this gentleman, who trades in horses locally, never showed up."

Tuesday, July 6, two newcomers visited us this morning asking about available land and the usual set of questions. One of them, Mr. J. D. Conner, a very outgoing Irishman, who said he was born in County Kerry and had come to the United States with his parents in 1846, at the height of the potato famine, when he was nine years old. They landed in Boston, which they found not to be hospitable to either Catholics or Irish, so they moved up the coast to Portsmouth, New Hampshire. Since he came here at nine, I'd put Mr. Conner at twenty-one to twenty-two years old. He's rather tall and rather handsome, and very mature for his age. He said he was thinking about opening a store hereabouts. Mr. Conner's traveling companion, Mr. Smith, is a fellow countryman.

They joshed about the fact that they are both bachelors and would be more inclined to settle here if I could assure them of a supply of unmarried ladies. Adda, hearing this comment, decided to join in the conversation. She offered to show the pair around our settlement.

They already seemed to have some acquaintance with Eldorado, as they spoke to us about the McWhorters, who are also Irish. Maybe they'd stopped over there first.

On July 14, Mr. Cruze, a fairly young man, came in from Wyandotte * with a package containing the printer's first draft of the sections of the Territorial

Constitution that father's committee has been working on. Mr. Cruze gave Father the package and began a conversation with him in the presence of Adda and me, but seemed concerned that we were both in the room. Father led him outside. The weather was nice and hot and they took a long walk. But before they went outside, I heard Mr. Cruze warn father about bringing the corrected manuscript when he returns to Lawrence in early August: "Don't reveal your route and don't tell anyone when you'll leave here or when you expect to arrive in Lawrence. The proslavers are getting active again, and they are out to get all of our leaders, and your name is on their list."

His message didn't seem to particularly concern father. I suspect that he took Mr. Cruze outside so as not to upset us.

Mr. Rackliffe came by Sunday morning, while it was still cool, to say that he expected a "rush" down on the Youngs' claim, which has acres of blackberry bushes, all with ripe berries.

"I'm not well enough to go pick berries," said father, "but I'm well enough to eat them."

*Wyandotte no longer exists as a separate town. In 1886, it was consolidated with Kansas City

Actually, he's getting ready for his trip to Lawrence, but after Mr. Cruze's visit he's reluctant to talk about it.

Mrs. Rackliffe was with her husband, so the three of us went looking for berries, but we stopped first at the Youngs' cabin to ask for permission and they decided to come with us. This is the first time I've met Mrs. Young, who's about my age. She's a very attractive lady, "pleasantly plump," as Charles Dickens would say. We had such a fine time of it that we didn't get home 'til after dark, with enough blackberries to make lots of jellies or jams, if I can find containers. Howland has some half-pint glazed terra-cotta jars, though they might be a little expensive. (I'll need to find some wax to top off the jelly.)

Adda and I had planned on visiting Mrs. Martin and her little daughter last week but things kept coming up. So, today we went up and had a nice visit. Though they live in a small cabin, which they intend to enlarge, they seem to be a family with a taste for nice things.

Many of their household effects are from England. Mrs. Martin served us tea, using a beautiful English silver strainer that she said was a wedding present. Everybody I know simply pours tea directly from the pot, which, of course, includes some tealeaves. When the tea is consumed, occasionally some one will offer to tell a fortune by reading the tealeaves in the bottom of the cup.

Mr. Martin came into the house only briefly. We reminisced about their arrival a year ago with the Jacob Careys, the Bemis family and, of course, Erastus Howland. About fifteen families came in that month, though not all of them have stayed.

Henry Martin is almost thirty years old and is quite a gentleman. Their family is certainly a fine addition to our community. **August 2** Election Day for the Lecompton Constitution; election held here, the men in town voted twenty-three against it. I later heard that when this Territorial vote * was tallied, it was 1,788 for the Lecompton Constitution, 11,300 against. I guess that old proslavery "bill" is dead.

On August 5, father left early in the morning for Lawrence with a comment that if strangers come looking for him, that we should not reveal his whereabouts. We know he is going to work on the Free State Constitution and he's carrying one of the "drafts" with him.

August 8, my nineteenth birthday, and I miss Chase who is still in the Rockies. Two years ago today, we first saw Kansas.

*Confirmed: Kansas State Historical Society, Vol. 5 pgs. 540-541.

Jacob Eastman Chase from New Hampshire

In vol. I: he fought with Sam's company and was captured. He was released from the POW camp on promise that he'd leave the territory. On the way to Nebraska passing through Plymouth he informed the girls as to their father's whereabouts and health.

In this volume he follows the girls to Lawrence, then out to Eldorado, becoming one of Eldorado's first builders.

Chase was Augusta's first love. They have a troubled romance but do marry... in volume III.

24.

ELDORADO
The Mule Skinners Adopt Adda

August 1858 About noon a train of ten wagons, each pulled by six mules, forded the river and made camp west of us within walking distance. In a half hour the wagon boss and his lieutenant, two rather colorful visitors, came by inquiring of father. I told them he was gone, but didn't say where or why, (he's off at the Free State convention in Lawrence). The boss said they are with Russell, Majors and Waddle. I know that freight-hauling outfit. It's run by Southerners and they usually hire their own kind, so I was a little guarded about where father was. The boss asked if this is the same Stewart who owns a sawmill. I said it was. "Well, I have a bill of material for 2,500 board feet of lumber sawed to various sizes for one of the forts between here and Utah. According to the order it will fill my only empty wagon, a sixteen-footer," he said.

"I've got sixty mules," he added, "and a few of them need their shoes looked at. You got a blacksmith here in Eldorado?"

Oh, I was so pleased to hear him use the name Eldorado. We haven't even been here a year, yet some of the wagon trains made up in Leavenworth that pass through here now expect to stop in Eldorado to get repairs. Apparently Fort Leavenworth knows we have a sawmill. I can't imagine we're on any maps yet.

The gentlemen said they'd recently moved their freight operations to Nebraska City, which when we went through there two years ago, already had a big enough proslavery element that we were warned to be cautious. That this train is escorted by a cavalry squad probably from one of Colonel Cooke's companies tells me they must be carrying freight for the military. Hum, I wonder if Captain Henry is with them.

Howland was planning on having supper here and we invited these two to join us and spend the night. They knew our rates. The boss is about father's age. His assistant seems to be a little younger than Howland and is called Davenport. It's also his job to look after the welfare of the mules. When Adda asked if that was his name, the boss interrupted and said "Nah, he's got a girlfriend there. So when we're on the trail, we hear a lot about Davenport." Within ten minutes Adda was calling him Davenport and they became "boon" companions. Adda teased Davenport that it only took two oxen to pull our load from Iowa City and she asked him, in her friendly, provocative fashion, why it takes six mules to pull each of theirs, adding that we crossed the Mississippi into Iowa at Davenport.

"Whatever you paid for those two, you certainly got your money's worth," he commented, adding, "but I suppose your wagon was a twelve-foot Schooner. Your load was probably a ton to a ton and a half. Ours are all sixteen-footers, except two that are eighteen-footers and our freight loads are double or triple yours. Where did you get your wagon?"

"Michigan," said Adda, with some pride,

"Smart move! It's probably a Studebaker. They are made in Jackson, Michigan. The best wagons come from that area, because the best wagon makers in the country are German and a lot of them settled up there."

"We're from Michigan," Adda commented. "We owned a sawmill on Lake Erie, a little south of Detroit."

The boss said eight of his wagons, the sixteen-footers, were all Studebakers or Fifty-fivers. "They can carry over 5,000 pounds each, but we overload them, maybe by 10%.

"We also have two Murphys. They are our eighteen-footers made by an Irishman over in St. Louis, He uses Northern, kiln-dried hardwood brought down on the riverboats.

I said, "I'll let Mr. Jordan, our sawmill foreman, know about the lumber order. We might have some sizes in stock, but for the rest we have plenty of logs on hand. It won't take long to fill this order."

The boss had given me the two-page bill-of- material. I asked him how he planned to pay for it. He said with Army script and he handed me a little coupon and a note signed by an Army paymaster addressed to Sam Stewart. "We're not allowed to carry cash, the Territory is so lawless." Scribbled on the script was "2,500 board feet @ $30.00 per M = $75.00." So, this order is worth $75.00. Won't father be pleased to hear about this?

Adda volunteered to walk them up to Tom Cordis' Blacksmith shop. Davenport thanked her and said in exchange he would teach her how to "pop the whip."

"I already know how to snap a whip," said Adda. "We have one for our oxen, though it's probably not as long as those you fellows use, but thank you. What I'd really like to have though, is one of those fancy shirts you freighters wear."

"These plaid shirts, a red or a yellow neck bandanna, and large-brimmed hats are the skinners' uniform! We have to buy this stuff when we sign on and it's deducted from our pay."

The two teamsters with Adda left for Tom Cordis' shop. It was late in the afternoon before she got back. She said first they walked over to their camp, where they haltered twelve mules. Several skinners walked with them up to Tom's place. "Davenport assigned two of the mules to me and made me put on their halters," Adda said. "I asked him if these were the two most stubborn birds in the outfit. He laughed," she said, "and told me I was being too polite, that I was new to these mules and they were taking advantage of me. He cussed them using pretty salty language and told me that if they balk or misbehave on the way to the blacksmith's, he would be busy with his own mules, so I'd have to manage those two and the best way to begin, he said, was to use language more persuasive than he suspects I normally use. I did and it worked. On the way over two of their mules got loose and ran off up the river because their skinners weren't paying attention. I'll bet they are still chasing those mules. Want to hear some of my new salty vocabulary?" she asked. "I invited them to breakfast tomorrow."

The next day, early, Davenport and his boss came by again. Adda asked if they ever caught up with the two runaways. The boss said the mules finally stopped to socialize with some mules at a claim north of here owned by a family with an English accent. I said, "Oh, that's the Martins."

Davenport reported that Adda showed promise as a teamster, "After I taught her some language that mules understand," he said with a grin. After breakfast the three of them went back up to Tom's to supervise the shoeing job. I invited them to supper.

At supper, Adda said to Davenport, "You owe me something for all this help I'm providing an' I'll settle for your yellow bandanna."

Adda walked over and untied Davenport's yellow bandanna and put it around her neck. "Now don't I look better than he does?" she asked, turning towards the wagon boss and me. She paused behind Davenport and whispered something in his ear. Later I asked her what was it that she said. She said she asked him if he ever washed his hair.

The boss smiled. "Your sister will talk the shirt right off Davenport's back," he said to me rather jovially. A day later Adda came home with one of the teamster's shirt, saying she agreed to wash it and she did.

It wasn't until noon the following day that it was dry. When she left for their camp, she took a gallon of milk. Late that day Adda came home wearing the shirt. She didn't say who had owned it.

The sleeves on her "new" plaid red-and-white heavy cotton shirt are about two inches longer than they need to be, which she handles by neatly folded back cuffs. The collar is also a little large, but she handles that with Davenport's yellow bandanna tied loosely around her neck. I'm really surprised she hasn't talked one of those freighters out of his large hat.

Tonight, when Frank discovered the source of her new costume, he put on a little jealousy act, to which Adda responded that after the freighters make their delivery, she might join them on their way back to Leavenworth, not only as camp "cook and bottle washer." But I want to cash-in that $75.00 script we'll get when their lumber order is ready. Frank asked me if she was serious!

The freighters will need to stay here long enough to get their mules attended. Tom Cordis appreciates the work and father will be pleased to know we are getting some lumber business from the freighters by being where we are, though this is not much of an order.

Adda finds an excuse to spend some time with them every day. She's picked up more of their slang than I think is necessary, and a few other terms I might add, which I overheard her use in telling Jerry about their mules, when the two of them discussed their lumber order. She has sold (or traded) them a gallon of milk every day and says she really enjoys their company.

One day while the wagon boss was visiting, Howland came by and joined in our conversation. The boss was telling us about mule trains. "There are at least eight freight hauling companies similar to ours operating west of the Mississippi, but ours is the best if not the largest," he said, claiming that Russell and Majors had 3,500 wagons and 4,000 employees."

"I occasionally get supplies hauled in by Ben Holladay's outfit," said Howland. "His posters say he has 15,000 men and 20,000 wagons."

Howland's comment provoked a good-humored guffaw. "Shoot, Holladay can't read or write," said the boss, "so I doubt he can count much above 100. But I agree he is a worthy competitor—even though he hires the greenest haulers and pays the least of all the freight companies. Holladay only hires 'bull-whackers' and he uses mainly Texas longhorn cattle to pull the wagons. When his men reach their destination, they sell the cattle as beef, often to the Army, so the drivers have to walk home or find employment elsewhere.

"My boys are all mule skinners and more experienced. We are faster, our rates are higher and our boys are better paid—and we dress better."

He told us that his wagon train had loaded up in Leavenworth with cargo that had come off the riverboats there.

"We're working for Major Sibley, the quartermaster at Fort Leavenworth and this haul is part of a two year contract. My company is charging the Army about twelve dollars per hundredweight to haul goods from Fort Leavenworth to the military camps beyond here, but our days of hauling freight are numbered. The railroads will soon replace us. Railway freight rates back East are already one tenth the rates we are getting on this job." The boss said he was trying to decide whether he should get a claim out here in the Territory or just go to work for the railroad. I suggested he consider purchasing a city lot in Toronto, the town Chase and Dave Upham founded. "Toronto is near here. You can buy a city lot there for one hundred dollars or file a claim for a quarter section of first-rate farmland for about two dollars per acre, which includes the surveying and filing with the Territorial Land Office."

But the wagon boss said he thought he might do better working for the railroad instead. "For the next few years, there will be plenty of work building them."

He said that Major Sibley, as well as the Federal Government, wanted to see the railroads extended west from both Iowa City and St. Louis. "Most of the Army's forts are out here west of the Mississippi in the new territories and it needs to supply about a million and one half pounds of freight a year to them. The savings the Government would get by using the railroads instead of us would soon pay for the cost of construction." The wagon boss said that two summers ago there was a big discussion about linking Leavenworth with Lawrence via a railroad line that would continue west to Fort Riley. He said someone from his company attended that meeting where they considered a plan to link rail service between Lawrence, which is Free State, and Leavenworth, which favors slavery. The boss didn't hide his opinions. He said the Government was willing to back the railroads but that the shareholders could only be induced to invest in the Territory if the abolitionists started showing more moderation in their "attitude." The boss said that it was "common knowledge" that Governor Robinson favored an armed insurrection to establish a state free of slavery. (Since I had met the Governor and his wife when Adda and I were working in Lawrence last year, this observation surprised me. Of course, since Lawrence was almost devastated two years ago, and he was charged with treason and jailed more than once, I can understand the Governor's sentiments.)

The boss said that the plan to build a railway line between Lawrence and Leavenworth resulted in the Big Springs Convention. "It took place two years ago in September near Lecompton on the Santa Fe Trail. There were 125 or so in attendance. Governor Robinson must have gotten religion since he managed to get himself appointed the chairman of the convention, and that other abolitionist, Jim Lane, was one of the organizers. The crowd was about fifty-fifty proslavery and Free Stators. I figure the prospect of prosperity that the railroads are sure to bring to the Territory is reason for both parties to put aside their differences."

Adda asked him, "What are you carrying that requires so many mules?"

"I don't recall the exact manifest but I know we have one wagon that's completely loaded with bacon—6,000 pounds of it. Another is carrying about 6,000 pounds of ham. Each of my wagons can average about 6,000 pounds, so after we've loaded your lumber, we'll be carrying about 60,000 pounds of freight in total, and this is a fairly small train." He said that one of his Murphys is full of flour, packed in 100-pound bags. "That's probably our heaviest load. Our other Murphy is loaded with beans, which are also packed in 100-pound bags."

He listed the inventory for his seven Studebakers. Some of them carried 100-pound bags of oats, corn, barley, and "green" coffee beans.

Two of his Studebakers were full of general hardware: hand tools, ax handles and shovels, as well as some leather goods. "And in one of the Studebakers," he said "all we have is barrels—barrels of sugar, barrels of vinegar, barrels of sorghum and several barrels of ale, which we mustn't get into. We have three Quaker drivers who act as our conscience where alcohol is concerned. Our outfit allows absolutely no drinking when we're on the trail and we take a pledge not to use profanity but I'm afraid that the only way to manage mules is to cuss 'em."

Adda laughed and said, "Well, I can attest to that. I've never heard such a variety but Davenport sure convinced me that the only thing that melts a mules stubbornness is salty language."

"We eat out of wagon number four. It's also full of cargo and is carrying a little bit of everything. We call that one Empress Josephine." Looking at Adda with a twinkle in his eye, he asked, "Do you have any idea who Empress Josephine was." Just as quickly, Adda replied, "She was Napoleon's first wife. She was born on one of the French sugar islands in the Caribbean."

"Well, I asked for it, didn't I?" he said, smiling at me. "She's as full of information as a mail-order catalog."

The day before the teamsters left, Adda and I showed Davenport where, at the springs to get the best water. He used our wagon and a helper to transport several barrels and Adda made the trip with him. It was almost sundown when Adda got home. She reported that their wagons are so loaded that they strapped a barrel of water on each side of several of their Studebakers, which has a metal straphanger and belt on each side just for that purpose.

I needed help with supper and the cows needed milking, which we both attended to. In the shed Adda was unusually quiet. As we walked up to the house, Adda said, "You know, they are leaving tomorrow and I will really miss those fellows, in their rough but jovial way they were really interesting."

"You mean Davenport. He was the one you spent the most time with," I said.

"Ya, he wants me to help him harness-up his mules tomorrow."

"Are you going to?" I asked.

"You betcha wouldn't miss it. Guess I'll have to get up

early."

The next morning after Adda left, two of the drivers brought their empty wagon over to the mill and they and Jerry loaded up their lumber order.

Midmorning Adda returned. "Well how did the harnessing go?" I asked.

She laughed and said, "It was a lot of fun and takes a lot of cussing to get sixty mules harnessed. When we finished several of the skinners came around and said they didn't know what they'd miss most, our fresh milk or me, and they joshed about my coming with them.

"You know, Augusta, I was at their camp nearly every day, including this morning, and I probably wouldn't want to say this in public, but one of the fun things with the skinners is the way they cuss, particularly the way they cuss their mules. My vocabulary has grown by a dozen of the filthiest and funniest words, I'd ever heard, but they are just words. They don't mean a thing. Those muleskinners get a lot of enjoyment yelling and cussing those mules. Seems to me the biggest chore they had was to get the individual mules to move out of their group and into their harness to make-up a team of six. That's when their language became the most 'salty.' The skinners try to out-do each other in saltiness.

"I had visited the camp several times you'll recall. Some of the older men said they missed fresh milk on the trail, so whenever we had a gallon to spare, I would take it over to them. One day I mixed a gallon of milk with some of that sweet malted chocolate that Howland sold in those one half-pound red tins. That's the day I came by my shirt. Want to hear some of my new salty language?" she laughed.

"No." Looking at her I said, "I'm going to the store for some stuff for Frank's birthday."

"Oh, that had slipped my mind."

"Well, it's next week." and I left for the store. Today, August 11th is Frank's birthday. He's been jealous of the time Adda was spending with the teamsters, particularly Davenport, and he told me he was glad they were gone. He announced his birthday to get my sister to throw a little party for him, which, of course, must include the customary cake with candles, and she has duly complied. He remembered the fine time we had a few weeks ago at Jerry Jordan's birthday party and wants the same kind of festivity. The party was attended by Howland, his new competitor, J. D. Conner, Jerry Jordan and myself. Father hasn't come back yet from the convention in Lawrence and Chase is still in the mountains seeking gold. I'd put down in my journal how much I miss him, except that everybody who can read seems to use my journal as a means of "keeping-up" on our romance.

After the cake ceremony, Howland suggested that it was time to spank the "birthday boy," and inquired as to the number of spanks he was entitled to. Frank hesitated. Ignoring his unwillingness to answer, the men and Adda surrounded him in gleeful preparation, rolling up their sleeves, etc. Finally Frank said, "Well, I was born in 1833." There was a moment of silence.

Howland spoke up, "Thirty-three from fifty-eight makes twenty-five. You, sir, get twenty-five swats for good luck and many returns of the day. Bend over."

But I had other thoughts. I had assumed that Frank was about my age, maybe a year older, but not six years older, which would make him seven years older than Adda, who won't be eighteen until December. All eyes for a moment were on Adda but she deflected the stares with a small, indulgent smile.

(It's just dawned on me: Frank must have lied to the officials at Lecompton who released him and Chase, thinking they were both eighteen-year-old "boys." Well, maybe they didn't ask. Chase was born on November 29, 1837. He won't be twenty-one until November, so that makes Frank four years older than Chase, even though they both look physically to be about the same age.)

After our guests had left, Adda and I finished off what was left of Frank's birthday cake, with some milk. She looked up from her plate, "You know, I'd never really figured out the difference in age between Frank and me."

I asked her, "Well, didn't you know what year he was born?"

"No, I just knew he was a little older—but not by that much! He did seem to want to take certain liberties with me that I suppose older men would ..."—and her voice tapered off and she became silent. I thought it best to let silence do its work.

25.

ELDORADO - CHASE RETURNS:
Frank and Howland Depart

Mid-August and September 1858 Doctor Weibley dropped in for a few minutes on August 15th. He said he was making a nearby call. He invited Frank Robinson, Adda and myself to come up to his place to spend the afternoon. We all crowded into his little shay and drove up to his cabin. When we arrived, Sammy Freeman was there, together with Mr. and Mrs. Stewart (we have the same last name but are no relation), Tom Muzzel and, of course, Mrs. Weibley, who had made a little lunch for everybody. We had hardly arrived when Dr. Weibley announced that he'd learned from Sammy, (the local gossip) that Jacob Chase was back from the mountains and would soon be here with David Upham. There was polite clapping and smiles aimed at me; I realized then that this was supposed to be a surprise party for me and a welcome home party for Chase. The rush of anticipation to see Chase caused such a sensation that I needed to grasp the top of a chair to steady myself, but I don't think anybody noticed this. I had thought that this affair was just going to be a casual Sunday afternoon social, a rather common occurrence in our little community.

Well, I was happy to hear the news but embarrassed and a

little aggravated that I was getting it last (but I guess that's what a surprise is.)

After the applause, everyone asked me how soon could Eldorado expect a wedding as though it fell on me to announce a schedule, as if one existed.

Before long my sweetheart appeared with David Upham. But this was not the place for a proper reunion of two people in love and engaged to be married, so we were both shy and reserved in our greetings. Apparently those gathered here lacked the optical apparatus to detect our true feelings because before the party broke up, Mrs. Weibley took me aside and, with a motherly smile of both approval and forbearance, told me, "Augusta, I'm really a little put out by you this afternoon. Why didn't you show a little more romance and affection? We arranged this reunion for the two of you." I didn't know how to respond, so I just smiled, patted her on the cheek and told her how much I appreciated her surprise party for me and Chase.

Dr. Weibly spoke up and said, "Mr. Chase, we're certainly glad to see you've returned, but what happened? A fellow named Cantrell came through Leavenworth maybe two weeks ago showing off a pouch of gold, claiming that some prospectors from Georgia simply gave him. They say he's in Lawrence or Westport now. As a result, we have people from the territory and Missouri, even now, in late summer going to the Rocky Mountains through Eldorado."

"I knew some of those Georgia prospectors. They seemed to know which streams or gulches would contain gold. They were the ones who found the gold where the south fork of the Platte River meets a Cherry Creek. Then they went up another gulch called Dry Creek and made a bigger find. That's the Russell party. There are three Russell brothers and a partner, John Gregory. They are really experienced miners. They had learned prospecting in Georgia. When that mine gave out, they all went to California and prospered.

(Author's comments: Cantrell's news of the Pike's Peak gold discovery was in the St Louis Dispatch September 10th followed by the same article in the September 20th edition of the New York Times.)

We got home in time for a hasty supper, and then Chase and I took a long twilight walk on the prairie together. I asked him if he knew how many days there were between May 22nd and today, August 15th.

"Eighty-five," he replied, answering in the blink of an eye.

"Well, that's correct but to me it felt more like 850 days. Now I know how the wives of sailors feel when their husbands finally come home safe and sound. "

I asked Chase how things went during those days.

"Well, our party reached Cherry Creek * June 17th" he replied. "Though some immediately panned for gold, that was not the main intent of our group. Our intent was to form a town and prosper by selling lots. We were very well equipped to do so with surveyors and provisions to last six months. Between June17th and July 2nd we scouted the area, looking for a good town site.

Chase gave me a little sealed glass vial. It was smaller in diameter and length than my little finger and was full of water. It contained two small nuggets of gold, not quite the size of a kernel of corn, and not as thick. I left them in the vial and have them now. The sun, rapidly dropping off the edge of the distant prairie allowed just enough light to cause the nuggets to sparkle slightly. Out on the prairie I gave Chase the homecoming that the afternoon welcoming committee had expected to see. By then the sun was long gone, so God was our witness.

On the following day, we learned that Frank has blabbed about his intentions to break off his engagement with Adda. And

I've noticed quite a change in her attitude since we discovered last week that he is so much older than she is. Frank has always badgered and begged Adda for both marriage and the physical gratification that normally comes with marriage. Adda has told me, on more than one occasion, that he was trying to get one before the other. At times, I've envied all of the attention he gives her. How I long for Chase to be one-tenth as affectionate. There are times when I can hardly get Chase to say hello. Frank on the other hand is constantly trying to get Adda off by themselves. Though it seemed to me that Adda appreciated his attention and romancing, she was also apprehensive about it. In this regard, and in most others, Adda was wiser than Frank. Not only is Adda healthy and beautiful, she is a very bright, inquisitive girl, who has far greater intellectual talents than Frank. Whether it was she or Frank, who broke the engagement, doesn't really matter; she would have come to make the same decision herself, as she's been increasingly troubled by his demands for physical attention and by their difference in ages, and would have surely backed away from marrying him, if indeed she ever entertained such notions.

Since Chase's return, he has told me some very interesting information about the well-organized and well-financed outfit he joined. He said that the Colorado Town Site Association had formed up in Lecompton with the intention of founding a town site out in the Rockies. The group also planned to do some prospecting while there, but its main purpose was to start a settlement and prosper by selling lots.

On August 19th, father got home late in the evening. Mr. George Nye and Mr. Spaulding were with him.

When we heard them come in, Adda and I were already in bed, but we were more than happy to get up and fix the men a "midnight" snack and hear the news. The two visitors spent the night at our house. Tomorrow morning they plan to set up a tent near us and stay here. I noticed father didn't eat much, though he drank some milk and softened some cookies in it. "What happened to your appetite?" I asked him. He said he had a mild throat infection and it hurt him to swallow.

Father told us that the Free State Constitution session in Lawrence had gone well, but that the Territory's economy is not good and immigration has dropped way off. "We need more settlers—thousands more—to have economic growth, but the people from back east don't want to come here because of all the civil strife."

We have had some disturbing news from Mrs. Rackliffe. She stopped by today to report that Mrs. Smith has delivered her baby. The way she described the birth, it sounded like she had been there to help. Mrs. Rackliffe said that, "Little Smith weighed only four pounds." That seems abnormally small. *Gunn's Book of Medicine* agrees with me. I hope mother and son make it.

Mr. Smith is away in Lawrence. He had gone there because he didn't think his wife was ready to deliver yet, said Mrs. Rackliffe, who added that she had helped move Mrs. Smith over to the Careys' place.

I would go help but I've got my hands full here with father. He has been sick with fever and a very sore throat and mouth since he's been home. His throat is so infected that he can't talk, so he writes instructions. He spits out greenish-yellow sputum and the surface of his lower throat shows the same color. His tonsils are swollen. Gunn's Book of Medicine identifies this disease as Quinsy, an advanced form of Tonsillitis.

Sensing father could spare me for an hour or two, the next day I went down to the Careys' to see how Mrs. Smith and her little fellow are getting along. I planned to take them some syrup. Just as I was leaving, Mrs. Cordis came in to check on father.

Riding along the creek, I came across Chase. I told him

where I was going and he decided to go with me.

Mr. Smith had just returned and was at the Careys'. Throughout the afternoon he kept asking Mrs. Carey, then me, how we thought his wife was. We tried to be encouraging, but Mrs. Smith is quite ill, so unwell it appears she can't produce milk for the baby, who needs it because he is so small. Late in the day I came home to take care of my own patient. He really wasn't much better.

A couple of days later, Mr. Smith came by after borrowing a horse from Tom Cordis and reported that the baby had died sometime Thursday night and that his wife is so sick that she's unaware of it. The poor child must have died Thursday after I left.

This afternoon Mrs. Rackliffe asked if either Adda or I could come over to the Careys' to help. Adda volunteered, even though she had another felon on her thumb, which Doctor Weibley lanced when he was here earlier. I continually plague her to eat more raw fruit. Land! Even though it's late summer, there's still plenty of good fruit around including melons, blackberries, wild plums, wild grapes and a variety of apples that are coming in from Missouri. Howland even had ripe pears a few days ago. But to get Adda to change how she eats—well, I might as well talk to the wall.

For months now, Frank Robinson has spent a considerable amount of time talking with the gold seekers who pass through here. They stop in Eldorado to buy their last-minute needs, knowing we are the last commercial outpost for 500 miles before they get to the Rockies. The lure of gold must be irresistible for people to come this far from home. For the past several months Frank has gone back and forth about whether to go to the gold fields. He uses his, "Maybe I'll go, or maybe I'll stay" as a romantic threat to my sister.

This morning, Frank announced with unusual finality that he had made-up his mind (considering what little there is of it, it should not have been a formidable task.) Anyway, he's leaving. Before he broke off with Adda more than a week ago, he'd told others in town he'd stay if Adelaide Stewart would marry him. But Adda isn't ready for marriage and she knows it. It's my opinion that even if she were, it would not be to Frank. So, that seems to be the deciding factor in Frank's departure.

After breakfast he said, "Good-bye, all hands." With his arm around my sister, but his eyes addressing me, he declared, "When I strike it rich, I'll get properly tutored in grammar and Latin. I'll improve my table manners by taking all my meals in first-rate hotels. Then I'll send for your sister. We'll build a castle in Denver and, live like 'Boston Swells.'" He joined a small outfit that had been camped here for a few days. They left yesterday. He's been in the territory two years. He has staked a good claim here and in Arizona. He owes money on both. Other than that and a little mule, that's all he has to show for it. He's taking the mule. If Adda is sorry to see him go she has a strange way of showing it.

If I were sure he was leaving for good, I'd get out our tablecloths and would start using them again at supper, particularly when we have paying boarders. I discontinued that bit of pleasant etiquette while Frank was boarding with us. I simply got tired of washing and ironing the tablecloths to accommodate Frank's sloppy eating habits. When I'd put down a newspaper at his place at the table, so I could protect my tablecloth, he would pick up the paper and read it—and soil the tablecloth anyway. I suppose he thought that paying for his meals entitled him to soil one tablecloth per meal.

Finally I resorted to using "oilcloths" for the table, which I resented having to do. In my opinion, people who use "oilcloths" resign themselves to being uncouth. We should at least once or twice a day try to be better, and one way to do that is at mealtime. There should be pleasant and intelligent conversation and good manners, even if we are on the frontier. I should have made Frank take his meals outside on the tailboard of the wagon. I told him on more than one occasion that in my house we should not behave as though we are camping out. I may as well have talked to the wall.

Frank knew he did certain things that annoyed me. In reading a newspaper he couldn't quietly turn a magazine or a newspaper page. He had learned somewhere to flip up the newspaper page in a way that produced an attention-getting pop, like the snap of Spanish dancer's castanets, as he turned to the next page. Then he would look over the edge of the paper to see if anyone had noticed, and then grin. He didn't make this noise regularly, which added to my irritation, particularly if I was sewing or knitting or writing, as I'd be waiting for Frank to do it again. But still, despite all of his faults, I'm sure I'll miss him, rather like one misses a rash of poison ivy. Father has been mostly in bed since the Thursday he came home. That's five or six days ago and I don't see any improvement.

Jerry went up two days ago for Dr. Weibley but the doctor was out. Yesterday Adda took Kate, one of our horses, and said she'd find the doctor and bring him down. She didn't get back last night but came home Wednesday morning with the doctor.

Father wrote on a note to Dr. Weibley that he's feeling worse each day. The doctor hemmed and hawed, looked at me and declared, "He's been on the wrong medicine." He "salivated" Father and gave him a dose of morphine.

Father has slept for the last two days. When he woke up today, Friday, he wrote on a note that his "morale" was good but his throat was still too sore for him to talk. The doctor came by so early we invited him to have breakfast with us. After he finished examining father's throat and tonsils, he pronounced that Father is going to be all right. I know father is getting better because he's starting to get cranky with us, which means he's attentive to what's going on in the house.

We have a new horse, Charley. That fact is not particularly important, and I'm only noting it in the journal because Mrs. Smith's baby died and I wanted to ride him over to the Smiths' place to pay my condolences. I thought maybe I could be of help around their house, as Mrs. Smith is still sick.

As I prepared to go out and saddle Charley, leaving Adda as head nurse, father made a tapping noise to get my attention. He handed me a note, which read, "Don't let him go to sleep." I wondered who "him" was but I didn't want to ask. That would oblige father to write me another note. I managed to get a saddle on Charley, and we set off for the Smiths'. As we went down into a little muddy draw Charley stopped. I humored him. I didn't give him a kick to get him moving, as I thought he might be bothered by the soft, swampy ground. That was a mistake. Some animals, horses in particular, will take advantage of any kindness shown to them, and that was certainly the case with Charley. I thought he was just a little cautious about the soft ground, so I let him rest. He lowered his head—and went to sleep. So now I know whom the "him" was on Father's note. Charley's behavior was a new frustrating experience for me. I didn't want to dismount, get down into the mud, to wake Charley up and then walk him apiece. So I popped the whip, and it worked: Charley woke up.

Normally, I don't like to whip a horse, but I swear the only way to keep a contrary horse like Charley awake is to give him a "pop" now and then. I did. He stayed awake but we rode on to a very disturbing problem.

Charley and I finally made it to the Smiths'. Doctor

Weibley had followed me there. Since we are old friends, he came over, placed his hand on my arm and said in a soft voice, out of Mr. Smith's hearing, that he'd appreciate it if I'd stay with the Smiths for a few hours, as he had to make another call (is it to the store for a little whiskey?) He added that he didn't think Mrs. Smith would make it through the night. He was right, I'm sorry to say.

Mr. Rackcliffe came in about noon and told us the news that Mrs. Smith is dead. She died last night, just as Dr. Weibley predicted. He said some of us should get over there if we could. (I thought, "I hope I can keep Charley awake long enough for the ride.") Adda and I both rode over to the Smiths' cabin. She had been moved back to their place from the Careys' after her baby died. Mrs. Cordis and old Mrs. Bemis arrived just as I did. Glennis' mother seems to be so unaffected by death, perhaps it's because she saw so much of it in Ireland. The Smiths' cabin is pitiful: a small, disorderly one-room cabin with a dirt floor, insects, (particularly Musquitoes, and other bugs are as thick as the dust)—and a dead woman on the bed, but Mrs. Bemis made herself useful in cleaning up, constantly humming little Irish tunes, as though she were practicing some hymns to be sung at next Sunday's service.

Mr. Smith refuses to believe his wife is dead. (Poor soul, only a few days ago he also lost his baby son.)

We cleaned up the body and laid her out in one of her better dresses, which we found in a musty old trunk. I must say she looked very natural. We are about the same age. She might even be a year younger. Her father lives in Lawrence. They are abolitionists from Massachusetts, but he was born in England. He was opposed to her marrying Mr. Smith, an Irishman, and worse than that, a Catholic. On more than one occasion, I understand, her father threatened to kill him. That's why they left

Lawrence and came out here, to escape Mrs. Smith's father. Well, she's dead now and, when he hears about it, he will surely blame Mr. Smith.

Mr. Spaulding and Mr. Nye, who came here from Lawrence with father, have been living in a small, dirty old Army tent on our claim since the day after their arrival. This morning, Mr. Nye came in to say that Chase had been hurt by a wagon. Mr. Nye said that Chase had been walking beside a wagon, which was carrying a large log over to the sawmill. Somehow the wagon had accidentally run over his leg. Adda and I anxiously rode down to Careys' only to find Chase walking around and joking. I asked him about Mr. Nye's report.

"Well, it's true the wagon ran over me," he said, pointing to his leg, "but the ground under it was so soft, no harm was done." I noticed, however, that he had a decided limp, so I suspect he'll have a sore leg for a few days.

The next afternoon I was so tired, just exhausted from missing so much sleep two nights in a row, that I took a little nap. In midafternoon, Chase and Tom Cordis came by with Tom's wagon and woke me up to get my opinion about Mrs. Smith's burial.

We decided it would be best all around if we buried Mrs. Smith before sundown, so we made plans to go up to the cemetery, which was the area we had set aside for burials when Mr. Curl died. As it's quite warm today, I didn't need to wear a coat. I had a choice about how to get there: I could ride with Tom on that stiff old wagon of his, or I could ride my somnambulist friend, Charley. I chose Charley.

There was no preacher. I was disappointed that Tom Cordis couldn't repeat the service he had performed so nicely for Mr. Curl, but he has not been well lately. He stayed throughout her burial but was listless. I must not have been totally awake either. Hours later it dawned on me that someone had dug her a proper grave and nailed together a coffin.

I had planned to ride Charley home after her funeral but Chase said he wanted to talk a little, so Chase, Charley and I all walked home. And, lo and behold, Charley stayed awake!

Chase said the Bentons are going to leave the area and he wanted my opinion about his taking over their claim after they go. I was so happy to have a discussion with my sweetheart, particularly where he wanted my opinion; in fact, I'm happy to have any kind of talk with Chase. Usually I can't get two words out of him. His behavior is so incongruent for a man who is supposed to be in love or at least my expectations of a man in love.

A few days later, on Saturday morning, Chase stopped by the house but didn't come in. He rummaged around in the shed, probably looking for a tool of some sort. I stood in the doorway so as to be conspicuous. He walked past me twice, never looked up. In response to my greeting he gave me a half wave of his hand but nothing audible came from his lips. I just don't understand the man. Why, if he followed me from Archer to Lawrence and from Lawrence out here, why can't he spare me a word or two? Never mind a whole sentence, I couldn't cope with that prosperity. Perhaps he believes that he only has a fixed and finite supply of words and once he depletes this skinny larder his stock of words will be diminished never to be replenished—like teeth, when they're gone, they're gone. All right, if he's so parsimonious with his words, I'll settle for a smile, a wave, and any kind of acknowledgment that he's noticing me.

The next day, late in the afternoon, Howland came by with a bundle of books and magazines, which was not unusual, except his manner was unusually serious.

As he put the bundle down on the table, he said, somberly,

that he would miss our literary discussions. Before I could respond, he added he'd decided to leave Eldorado, as he thought his chances were better in the Cherokee Nation, which he referred to as Neutral Country. His demeanor seemed to foreclose that I should question why in the world he would go down there. I'm sure he realizes that to the extent that any white people live there, they are all Southerners…and pro slavery. Now that I recall, I should have had some concern about his intentions. One or two of our neighbors had made recent comments to me that Howland had been around to collect on their grocery bill. For him that's an unusual practice since he rarely pesters anyone to pay up.

Howland began to unbundle the books and magazines, which were held together with a new, rather nice thin brown belt and a shiny metal buckle, arranging the books on the table as though he intended to present and discuss each one of them with me, which he did. Most of them were used books, a few were new. This was not the first time my friend Howland and I had discussed books, but I sensed that it was going to be the last. On similar occasions, Adda and I had speculated about the quality and the source of Howland's education but he preferred to be mysterious about it. He's always been concerned about what I'm reading, even critical of it, as well as of the library I'm accumulating. He favors reading several books by the same author or on the same subject by different authors.

In the pile he brought are two books by Daniel Defoe: *Robinson Crusoe* and *Moll Flanders*; I've read neither, though I've seen scathing but intriguing reports in some Boston newspapers about *Moll Flanders*. I believe it was, and maybe still is, illegal to print or sell this book in Massachusetts. The Defoe books were printed in London, Paternoster Row. This volume of *Moll Flanders* claims to be the second edition. Howland likes English history, particularly biographies of Henry VIII. Three of these books are about Henry's first wife, Catherine of Aragon. One is by a Spaniard, H. Bernaldes, who explains the Spanish side of the dynastically useful alliance, but a mutually frustrating marriage. The second book, by an English author, gives the English side. The third book, a volume by W. H. Prescott, deals with Ferdinand and Isabella, Catherine's parents. Prescott is a very popular author just now. I'm really quite flattered that Howland wants me to have these books. I know they are from his personal library.

Howland's package also includes a small well-used leather-bound dictionary of English to Latin, and vice versa. In the pile there is also a rather thick, nicely bound new volume that contains two English novels by the Brontë sisters: *Jane Eyre* and *Wuthering Heights*. I've loaned my old copy of *Jane Eyre*, which isn't of as good quality to Elizabeth Cordis. I think I'll make her a gift of it.

In the package are several recent issues of *Graham's Magazines*. I like that magazine for its poetry. Occasionally *Graham's* publishes Poe's "stuff," which I read even though it depresses me. Howland says these seven or eight issues of the magazine; carry all the installments of a new Dickens novel, which he's read. Dickens' work is also quite popular right now and is held in very high regard in the States.

Finally, we got around to another of Howland's favorite subjects, second only to politics, and that's Napoleon. There are no books in this pile on Napoleon but there are two books by Stendhal (that's not his real name), who was a great admirer of Napoleon. One of the books was Stendhal's, *The Charter House of Parma*, which Stendhal wrote during the Napoleonic Wars. Howland says if you want to know how people thought and behaved at the time of Napoleon, as well as know what the real social structure was like in France after the failure of the French revolution and after Napoleon was exiled, read Stendhal. I haven't but I will.

The other Stendhal book is titled, *The Scarlet and the Black*. He said earlier editions call it, *The Red and the Black* and refers to the choice Stendhal's hero may have had between Napoleon's Grand Armee (Red) and the influence on French society by the church (their black robes). "It is a tragic love story," said Howland, "but not as tragic as this one," and he handed me a thin little book, which he had obviously read many times as it was well-thumbed through. "This book is called, *Manon Lescaut* and it's by Antoine-Francois Prévost. The story begins in France during the time of Louis XIV and ends tragically a few years later in New Orleans, when Louisiana was still a French colony.

Howland was so impressed with *Manon Lescaut* that he'd collected other editions of it, as well as other translations, and he gave me two more copies, both in rather poor condition, but readable. (One refers to the author as simply Abbé Prévost. He was trained as a Benedictine monk, but gave it up to be a writer.)

Toward the end of this discussion I asked Howland how it was that he was so scholarly. He said, "Before I was a grocer, I was, or wanted to be, a teacher," but he didn't finish the sentence and I didn't press him.

I thanked him for the books and told him I looked forward to reading them. As he prepared to leave, I asked him just where and how big the Cherokee Nation was. "I know it is generally south of us but that's about all I know of it," I said. He told me that he'd just received a map that included the Cherokee territory. "I'll bring it by tomorrow," he said.

The next day, September 6, Howland came by after breakfast and unrolled a large cloth map on our kitchen table, which displayed most of North America. It was printed in color by Jacob Monk in Baltimore and was dated 1852. Howland pointed to a very long, narrow rectangular strip of land directly south of Kansas Territory. "That's the Cherokee Nation." An east-west centerline seemed to bisect this territory. The northern half of its eastern border is against Missouri, the southern half against Arkansas. The Cherokee Nation extends west to the northern finger of Texas, and doesn't appear to be more than seventy-five miles wide from north to south, though from east to west it is about as long as Kansas Territory. A note on Mr. Monk's map implies that this land had been set-aside for 25,911 Indians, who had been moved there from Georgia. The name on the map for the area depicting the Cherokee Nation is Thah-Lah-Kee. That must be the Indian word for "Cherokee."

I will certainly miss Howland—his frequent visits, his fine companionship and everything else about him. I don't think he's ever gotten over his loss of Glennis Bemis, when she went west with the Irish outfit and I suppose since he was here first, he resented the competition from the new storekeepers in town. Although it's just a tent, the McWhorters' store is "up" and selling whiskey by the glass; and occasionally the McWhorters sponsor sporting events, mostly outdoor prizefights, with Irish boxers. Howland also has competition from Mr. Conner, whose store offers about the same goods as his but has become the town's gathering place for men who want to talk politics. Mr. Conner also leaves an open bottle of whiskey on a back counter for those who want a sample but don't want to bother asking.

I've since discovered that Chase knew all about Howland's leaving. Why didn't he mention this to me?

Beyond what I said here, Howland didn't tell me a great deal about his plans to leave, but he did say this: He's going with Mr. Spaulding and Mr. Nye.

Today it rained all day. Well, it hailed some, too. Adda is quite sick. I think she has what father had. That doesn't surprise me, as most of these diseases are contagious, but what does surprise me is that my sister is "down" with it. Except for a felon or a boil or two she is always so healthy.

Chase has been here most of the day and he took supper with us. He said Mr. Smith refuses to believe his wife is dead, though he has visited her grave every day for the past four or five days, ever since we buried her last Friday.

We talked about some disquieting news that we had heard about Mr. Smith. He left sometime today, in the rain, for the plains, no coat or vest, no provisions. Some boys coming back from the Mountains said they saw him eight miles west of here going in that direction as fast as his horse could carry him. It's Chase's opinion that the death of the baby, followed by the death of his wife, only a year after their marriage, has "unhinged" him (that's carpenter talk.)

Maybe Mr. Smith has come to his senses. He returned here today, and will stay with us tonight.

Mrs. Benton came by to confirm that they are leaving. There is not enough business in Eldorado to provide a "living," she says. She offered us a nice kitchen table and a long straight-back bench, or "settee," as she calls it. They will be welcome additions to our furnishings. I've already decided to put my writing materials on one end of the settee, for it's so long.

Adda's journal is missing. She noticed it a few days ago but said, since she wasn't feeling well lately, she thought she had mislaid it. Now she's sure it's gone and she's very upset. We discussed who might have an interest in taking it, and of course Frank's name was the first to come up. I reminded her that Frank might have been concerned that she had included in her journal certain personal items, intimacies that he didn't want to see in writing. It's a shame since she has been "at it," almost as long as I have and has distilled some of her entries into articles that's she's submitted to Eastern newspapers with some success.

It's September 18th and I haven't felt well, myself. I had a fever Monday night and all day and night Tuesday. Father's home with the chills. Adda is the only one among us who is getting better.

The doctor was here this morning. He seems pessimistic about Tom Cordis' health and that's not like him. So, from the doctor's gloomy words, I've concluded that Tom is pretty sick.

After supper father and Chase discussed another episode involving Hildebrand and his violent inclinations. Chase said that on Monday he happened to come up on Mr. Hildebrand holding a revolver on Mr. Carey. They were having an argument. We don't know what grudge Hildebrand has against Mr. Carey. Chase said he forcibly took the gun from Hildebrand, whereupon Mr. Carey gave Hildebrand such a whipping that Chase had to summon help to get him onto a wagon, so he could take him home. Mr. Carey refused to help. Chase said he understood. Chase said that he and the man he had found to help him finally got Hildebrand home.

"Hildebrand was in no condition to get up on a horse," said Chase. "I'm beginning to understand Hildebrand a little better. Over and above his being a Southerner, he was here ahead of us, which I think is his main reason to resent our being here. But since my trek to the Mountains, I've come to see another reason for his strange social aggressiveness. Addressing father, Chase said, "This May, when you and Jerry repossessed your oxen from Hildebrand, you'll recall it was the same wagon train I'd joined. One of the few women in the train was a nurse, an abolitionist who had come out from Ohio to Lawrence at the height of the hostilities in the spring of 1855. She saw the quarrel you and Jerry had with Hildebrand, and I told her I was also from Eldorado and planned to be your son-in-law.

"She was a very experienced woman, a widow, probably in her early fifties, and she was the only paid member of the party. On the way to the Mountains we struck up several conversations. She claimed she had seen some of Hildebrand's symptoms before in her long nursing career and she was pretty open about discussing them with me.

"She said it was her opinion that he has little or no control over his bowels. That's why he smells so badly all the time, and it was her belief that that fact contributes to his social problems. I told her that everyone here in town that knew he's from Mississippi and is rabidly proslavery, though he owns no slaves and has probably never owned any."

The discussion became lighthearted, and we started to debate whether excessive personal odor is enough reason to cause criminal behavior.

Adda said the old Roman lawyers had a phrase for this situation: "res ipse loquitur." "The thing speaks for itself." But she added that the situation is much more complicated. "The fact that Hildebrand was here first, only gives him an excuse to be resentful, which in turn, as we've seen provokes acts of violence against us. He keeps to himself. He has children but since his wife is not here, they have no mother to look after them, if she were here; it would provide a socializing effect on him. I think he is a vile, treacherous man, one that bears watching!"

Chase said, "As usual, Adda was just being haughty with her Latin and big words." It was Chase's contention that this assumed superiority of hers is what unraveled her romance with Frank Robinson and drove him away. "Well, I'm surprised to hear you use such big words ... those words by the way all have roots in Latin." Little does Chase know! He seems upset that he's been deprived of Frank's companionship. Of course, he's only heard Frank's side of it. Frank was Chase's best friend.

Father said, "All right, you two," then he asked Chase, "What happened to the Ohio lady?"

"She stayed in Denver. She wasn't part of our small group that came back to Lecompton to file the land claim for the new town out there."

Adda got up from the table, walked behind Father and tousled his hair, putting her face next to his. "You wouldn't have an interest in her, would you?"

"Well, I'm a widower with two bright, attractive daughters who are my housekeepers, laundry maids, farm hands, bookkeepers, milkmaids, cooks—oh yes, also my nurses, but one of these days I will lose all those services so I must look out for my own interests— even if this lady is a little older than I am."

Father asked Chase if she was good-looking.

"Well, she won't win any beauty prizes at the county fair, Mr. Stewart, but you might like her. I don't know. She was always neat and well dressed, even on the trail. And she was smart, though a little domineering."

I said, "I will not be a party to such a discussion, even if it's in humor," as I bade the debaters goodnight. The discussion about the reasons for Hildebrand's criminal behavior and whether the Ohio nurse would make a suitable companion for father continued into the night, but without me.

26.

HILDEBRAND, THE SOCIAL MISFIT
September 19 to October 19, 1858

Early this morning I heard what sounded like trumpets, or bugles, nearby. I rushed to the window (oh yes, we have windows now but that's another story). Looking a little south of us, I saw a large body of U.S. troops that appeared to be stopped and making camp here. While the wagon masters were organizing their wagons into a camp, others of them on horseback continued to come in. Some of the soldiers seemed to be milling around but I knew they would soon be putting up their tents. Quickly dismounting, the new arrivals saw to their horses and joined the soldiers who were making camp.

My first thought was of how much this scene reminded me of Colonel Cooke's neat but oppressive camp near us in Plymouth two years ago. These soldiers began putting up tents, here and there sticking poles in the ground for the Army's little blue flags that were soon fluttering in the breeze. It was a beautiful, early fall day. The sun shining on the small tents made them appear much cleaner than I knew they would be up close. I hope their presence doesn't mean they expect trouble. I'm curious to find out if we know any of those soldiers. I wonder if any of them are from the Plymouth camp. If so, they will mostly be Southerners.

When we finished our morning chores, Adda and I moseyed down to the new camp and struck-up some conversations. We discovered that there are two separate companies here, and both had returned from service in Utah. The soldiers jokingly called themselves the Utah Veterans. I asked them what war they had fought in Utah. I hadn't heard about any serious Indian wars out there, though I'm sure there have been dozens of "incidents."

"It was mainly a wild good chase," volunteered one of the corporals, "but I guess we had to do it. The Utah Mormons had planned to secede and make their own nation. Our two companies went out there with four other companies. Our combined forces in Utah represented about twenty percent of the whole Army of the West."

Remembering the group of Mormon settlers we had seen while crossing Iowa, I thought to myself, "How could people so poor they were pulling handcarts all the way to Utah, form an army big enough to try to secede from the United States?"

Out of curiosity, I asked one of the sergeants, "Who was in charge of your forces in Utah?" He replied that their leader was Colonel Albert Sidney Johnston, and his second in command was Colonel St. George Cooke. I began to say that I'd met that officer up in Plymouth, but thought better of it. Instead, I asked them if Captain J. A. Henry was involved in the Utah campaign, telling the soldiers that two years ago Captain Henry was a cavalry office at a camp up at Plymouth under Colonel Cooke. Nobody had heard of him.

As I had some tasks to do at home, I came back but Adda stayed.

When Adda returned, she told me that she thought these cavalry officers were as friendly as the teamsters, but not colorful. Adda reported that the soldiers had spent some time talking to her about the Utah campaign. "The soldiers spoke of the Mormons, with a mixture of respect and resentment," she said. "Apparently the Mormons were very clever in finding a way to protect themselves from the superior force of the U.S.

Army. It seems that some weeks after the soldiers arrived and set up a winter camp several miles east of the Mormon settlement in the Salt Lake Valley, one of their major provision trains was 'mysteriously' intercepted forty or fifty miles east of their camp. Though the supply train carried the Army's winter provisions and was operated by commercial freighters, it was so poorly guarded that most, if not all, of the wagons were set on fire and the train's draft mules were turned loose in the Wasatch Mountains.

"The soldiers couldn't be sure that the troublemakers were Mormons, since the attack had taken place so far from their camp. But then a few weeks later Brigham Young sent word that he was "so" distressed to learn that the U. S. Army might be short on rations, particularly now with winter coming on. Old Brigham said he would be more than willing to share their own ample bounty and look after any sick soldiers as well if Colonel Johnston promised not to interfere with their peaceful settlement. Colonel Johnston agreed to the deal, and by spring the army broke camp and moved out of the area."

Adda said she teased one of the corporals about his old Army issue muzzleloader and asked him why the Army hadn't issued them Sharps carbines. The corporal said every soldier he knew asked the same question, but he thought the Army quartermaster was afraid that since the Sharps can load and fire ten times faster than a muzzle loader, it would use up ammunition too fast.

Well, apparently the Army doesn't like our valley either. This morning, at about 8 o'clock, I heard bugles again and went outside. The troops, after barely spending a day here, are already leaving: all of their tents are down, their wagons are loaded and the two cavalry troops are riding in formation through town, followed by their supply wagons. Miss MacIntyre has once again provided us with an unusual and interesting incident. A couple of days ago, she came down for supper from Little Walnut and stayed with us for the night. I wouldn't include her visit in the journal except that she had visited us in April, her Fourth of July wedding failed to come off and events surrounding this visit have all caused me to make this entry.

Chase also came down though well before supper and after a little small talk volunteered to restock our woodpile, which he had noticed was getting low. He chopped wood until I called him in for supper. That must have been 6:30 or 7 o'clock. I couldn't believe the size of the woodpile, he'd accumulated, in just an hour or so.

After supper, Chase, Adda, myself and Miss MacIntyre, who is so attractive and charming, enjoyed a nice tea. Then we played cards until we used up all of the coal oil in the lamp. I'm afraid we lost track of time, not necessarily because of the card game but because of the interesting running conversation we had with our talkative friend, "Miss" MacIntyre. Sammy Freeman had speculated that she was a widow, but we still haven't found that out. She never speaks about having had a husband, which I suppose she would if she'd had one.

Her story goes something like this. She's from Ohio but didn't come out with any abolitionist outfit that I know of, not that I know them all. Nor is she an "Oberlin" Congregationalist. She has a gentleman admirer who is from Missouri and believes rabidly that this territory should be a slave state and is bitter that it will not be. They fight over this and several other issues. Her comments and hints during the card game led me to believe that, while they are not married, they are already living together as husband and wife. She said in many respects he's a fine man but in some ways he frightens her. That's why she had come down here, she said…adding that she had needed to get away from him for a few hours, and that wasn't the first time it had happened, she told us. Adda asked her if she could find someone more suitable. Miss MacIntyre replied that at her age she couldn't be as choosy as Adda or I could be, since we are both younger, and she brought up the subject of her Fourth-of-July wedding, which we had not mentioned out of tact. It was common knowledge, up and down the valley, that the wedding had all the ingredients except the bridegroom, who simply failed to appear the day of the wedding. Miss MacIntyre said that he was a horse dealer, though she suspected that sometimes those horses didn't belong to him. After that disappointment, she told us, she had taken up with her new gentleman suitor, a friend of the intended bridegroom and who was also a Missourian.

When Chase looked at his "turnip," it was 11 PM and too dark for either of them to try to find their way home, so they stayed the night.

Directly after breakfast, Chase left to go to work. No sooner had Chase left than a very handsome man, about Miss MacIntyre's age, opened the door and walked in uninvited. Startled, Adda jumped up. "Who are you?" she asked him.

The stranger pointed to Miss MacIntyre, "She knows who I am." He took Miss MacIntyre by the arm and brusquely insisted that she come with him. Adda and I guessed that he must be her new gentleman. Obviously embarrassed to have him act like this towards her in front of us, she made a snippy remark to him and he went outside, muttering that he'd wait, but not for long.

She then moved close to the open door next to Adda, I guess to make sure he wouldn't leave without her.

Miss MacIntyre put her arm around Adda and in a voice low enough that the fellow outside couldn't hear confided that when the horse trader hadn't shown up for the wedding, she had been really concerned because she was afraid she had been in the "family way." "Well, that turned out to be just a case of nerves," she said, telling us what a relief that was. "If you're ever in that fix," she added, "You'll know what I'm talking about." She gave Adda a hug, waved good-bye to me and told us how much she appreciated being able to come down here and associate with real ladies every once in a while and she hoped she hadn't used up our hospitality this time.

After she rode off with her "companion," Adda looked at me, "And we think we have romantic problems!"

We discussed how old she was. In April, when we first met her, we figured she was a little older than David Upham, who was paying her so much attention, while she was here. David is twenty-seven or twenty-eight, but I think she may be older, perhaps by three or four years.

Adda broached the topic that I had hoped would not come up, asking me if I supposed that Miss MacIntyre, due to misfortune beyond her control, had become a lady of dubious virtue. If she is, Adda said, she didn't fit the image she had always had of such women: coarse-talking, poorly dressed chippy with body odor they tried to mask with cheap Egyptian or Spanish perfume. If she had been widowed young, at nineteen or twenty, she probably could have been having gentlemen friends for the past ten years or so. "I've observed one thing out here on the frontier," Adda said, "most things are never quite as they appear."

How's that?" I asked

She pointed out that Mr. Buchanan, the fellow she debated at the Lyceum, had posed as a bachelor, and then all of a sudden a Mrs. Buchanan materialized. And Frank Robinson, she said, was a lot older than he seemed, which in hindsight explained why he had been so forward with her. He regularly accused her of not being as "generous" as other girls he'd known but now she realized that he'd simply had more experience in such matters than she'd had. Adda had always had some doubts about his sincerity and whether or not he's had her best interests at heart. Yet when he left, she missed him she said, and the flattering, intimate things he used to say to her.

I was glad that Adda was getting some of this off her chest, but after a while I steered the conversation back to Miss

MacIntyre, as I wanted to tell Adda how much Miss MacIntyre reminded me of *Moll Flanders.*

I got up and pulled Defoe's book, which I had recently finished, from the shelf. I handed the book to my sister and told her to look for the similarities between our lady friend from Little Walnut and the heroine of this popular and spicy novel. Adda seemed unimpressed until she finished reading the title page, which informed her that Miss Flanders had been born in Newgate, * was twelve years a whore, five times a wife, once to her own brother, twelve years a thief, was transported to Virginia as a felon. Miss MacIntyre may have been around the Mulberry bush a few times, Adda commented, but in no way could she hold a candle to this Moll Flanders.

Adda stepped outside, closed the door behind her, carrying Moll Flanders with her. She likes to read down by the boiler shed when the saw's not working. Saturday, September 25, we saw the comet * again last night. It was more visible than on any of the previous evenings that we've been watching out for it.

During the next two days, Chase was sick. Doc Weibley was here but too drunk to doctor. I notice that when Chase gets a little under the weather he seems to surrender some of his aloofness, his New England sense of independence. He comes to our place and gets very domestic. He very much enjoys my coddling, and asking me when I put my hand on his brow, if I think he has a fever. He wants to know why he is dizzy, what can be done for his shakes, etc. I'm certainly glad to be of help, but it offends me that he seems to use me as a last resort, as a nurse, rather than as a future married companion. After all, we are engaged. I do the best I can to doctor him. I now have about ten remedies in my medicine chest.

The doctor came by again this morning to inquire if

*Newgate was a notorious prison in London.
*Augusta doesn't identify the comet, but it was probably the Great Comet of 1868, also known as Donati's Comet.

father or Chase could survey a land claim of his. Father isn't home and Chase is still sick. Doctor Weibley had hardly arrived, when Hildebrand suddenly rode up on that beautiful horse of his (probably stolen) and yelled into our cabin. I went over and opened the door, though I didn't want him to come in.

Hildebrand had stopped just fifteen or so feet from our kitchen door, reining in his horse alongside the doctor's wagon. He remained on his horse, so I pulled the door to, but didn't close it. In a mean, truculent voice, he accused the doctor of something. As I resumed clearing the dishes from the kitchen table, I didn't catch what he said. The doctor got up and opened the door just enough to hear better what the old rascal was saying. I sensed that Hildebrand was getting more agitated, which caused the doctor to become more angry with Hildebrand and they began to exchange words.

It seemed to me that the doctor couldn't make up his mind about where he was going to continue this dispute. First he took an agitated step into the doorway, and then he'd step back into the kitchen, though all this time his body was close to or in our doorway.

Doctor Weibley asked Hildebrand, "How did you know where to find me?"

"I followed you."

"You've followed me before, haven't you?" "Yes."

"Well, let's have it, what do you want?" asked the doctor angrily.

But I couldn't hear the answer.

They continued to argue. The doctor was wearing that long old waistcoat of his, even though it was fairly warm. With his right hand, he suddenly, but casually brushed his coat back. From the side, I could see that he had a revolver with a long barrel, very unusual for Doctor Weibley. I've known him almost a year now and I've never seen him carry a gun. Perhaps, because he had suspected Hildebrand had previously followed him, he'd anticipated a confrontation. Slowly, with studied deliberateness, he withdrew the pistol from its holster and ordered Hildebrand to be gone. He gave Hildy five seconds to leave…or else.

"Or else what?"

I could hear that.

The doctor remained standing in our doorway. I heard a loud click. I looked at his revolver. He had pulled the hammer back with his thumb. The gun was ready to fire. He began to count. "One…"

I thought to myself, "Hildebrand is either very brave or very stupid. I figured that Doctor Weibley had imbibed enough whiskey to give him adequate courage to shoot the town bully." Doctor Weibley was in such control, and had such a rapt audience, that I was suddenly fearful that I was about to witness my first murder. In fact, it didn't take much imagination to foresee what might happen. Hildebrand would either be dead on the ground in front of our claim or he would remain on the horse but the shot would so startle the horse that it would gallop off with Hildebrand dead or wounded, riding on the horse's back.

I wanted to put a stop to this fighting, but wasn't sure how to go about it. I was also concerned that all this squabbling would wake up Chase, who is here sick and had slept through breakfast. Doctor Weibley's right hand was very steady and I could see his fingers begin to tighten around the pistol grip. "Two…"

Hildebrand spit out a curse or two, though he had raised his voice, I still couldn't make out his words.

When all of this started, Adda had been sitting at the kitchen table, writing. She became annoyed, "I can't hear myself think with all this bickering going on." She walked over to the doctor and in one smooth deft motion took hold of his collar and rather gently, almost affectionately, put her arm around his neck and pulled him sideways, just enough so she could also get into the doorway.

The doctor was nevertheless able to keep his gun leveled at Hildebrand. "Three!" Adda's maneuver had caused the doctor to take a half step back into the kitchen, but he was still in the doorway.

Still facing Hildebrand, he muttered to Adda,

"Dearie, you'll have to pull a lot harder than that to spoil my aim."

Adda stepped through the open doorway and reached out for the door handle, making sure to duck under his gun. As she began to close the door, she lowered her forehead, which is her trait when she gets a little bossy...and looked up at Hildebrand sideway. Lowering her voice, the way Mrs. Strong did, my sister assumed her best teamster accent, said, "Now you listen good, ah jes saved yore bacon, peeler, now scoot," and with a delicate flick of her wrist and a little smile of forbearance, dismissed the town roughneck.

Now reduced to viewing his quarry through the door's small opening, Doctor Weibley announced, "That's four, Mr. Hildebrand." I heard a grunt from the horse. I couldn't see what was happening outside but I assumed that Hildy had spurred his horse.

Just as the doctor finished his "Five" count, Adda closed the door behind her. She looked at Doctor Weibley. Actually she looked at his gun, staring at it with such disapproval that he carefully uncocked it and slid it back into its holster. Doctor Weibley seemed relieved that the dispute had ended without bloodshed. With a grin so big not even his mustache could conceal it, said to Adda, "Now look what you've done. I had the drop on him. I had adequate provocation to shoot him but you just spoiled everything." Adda squeezed her left arm around his neck. They were both grinning and laughing at each other, like two old vaudeville actors, who knew that the act they have just put on was the best on the bill.

"For heaven's sakes," said Adda, "if you'd shot him, we'd have had just an awful time getting his stinking body up onto your wagon. And you, better than the rest of us, know how he smells. My, his clothes smell like he just finished cleaning out a three-hole outhouse."

Hearing all the commotion, Chase had gotten up and began to join in on the humor, "Doctor Weibley, if you really wanted to shoot him, why did you give him a count of five? You could have shot him at the three count and if you had only wounded him," he said, "you'd have had him for a patient. Then when he got well again, he would add your name to the list of people he likes to pester."

"Son, I'm already on his list."

Then the relief Doctor Weibley felt because the episode had ended well…together with the whiskey he had drunk earlier… took effect and he got very paternal and affectionate towards Adda. He and his missus had lost a little girl back in Baltimore, he disclosed for the first time and had she lived, he said, he was certain she would be just like Adda. He repeated his job offer, that Adda come and live with them, telling her that he would add two rooms to his cabin: one, a bedroom for her, and the other for a clinic. "Adda, you will be the nurse. Well, that is, after you have served the usual apprenticeship. With Eldorado growing the way it is, I need help preparing prescriptions and ready-made poultices." He said he could also use her help to deliver babies, especially the difficult ones, like Mrs. Smith's little boy (the one who died), and he offered up many more reasons.

My attitude is if the good doctor doesn't stop his incessant

223

drinking, particularly now with Doctor Barrett on the scene, he won't have a practice and he sure won't need a nurse. I suspect that's the reason he and Mrs. Weibley have moved so often.

On October 1, a little after dawn, Mr. Rackliffe arrived at our cabin in his buggy, and walked in the back door unannounced. I was making breakfast. Father was outside, harnessing our old utility wagon to his black Canadian and the Trask pony, the pony we had gotten in exchange for our little wagon. Father was doing all this in preparation for another trip east. Is it to Topeka this time…a session of the Territorial Legislature?

I'm afraid my rattling of the pots and pans to make breakfast woke Chase, but he seems better today. He was sitting at the table when Mr. Rackliffe came in.

"Good morning, Augusta, " Mr. Rackliffe called out cheerfully. "What smells so good in here?"

"Buckwheat cakes! I've made them from a sample of shorts * from that new gristmill up in Chelsea. Mr. Conner has just begun stocking it.

Their shorts are an improvement over the brown flour Howland used to sell. Actually, Howland's flour wasn't hard to beat. The worst bread I ever made was from that flour…I actually found weevils in it. 'Course they weren't hard to sift out, but even without the bugs, that was bad flour and bad flour makes bad bread. If flour is not milled fine enough, the grist left in the flour produces coarse bread. The bran must be cut well enough to get most of the 'germ' out or it will turn rancid.

By late September, all of Howland's flour had gone bad. The flour was so rancid even baking didn't help.

I found this out in a most unfortunate way over the summer, when I tried to bake some bread for Doctor Weibley.

*Shorts is term for a type of brown wheat or barley flour. Shorts are a byproduct of milling consisting of bran, wheat germ and coarse meal.

In July, he and Mrs. Weibley had a little gathering for some new arrivals, and the doctor asked me to bake them a couple of loaves of bread. (It seems I have the best oven in town. At least that's the excuse everyone uses to get me to be the town baker.) Well, of course, I tried to oblige the Weibleys, but I just couldn't get that dough to rise. Even with Mr. Howland's new Yeast the bread wouldn't rise.

You asked me what smells so good. "Yes, I've had a pan of syrup on the stove for some time. I'm trying to boil it down a little. It does add a nice aroma to the place, doesn't it? I suppose you are also smelling the Mexican vanilla. I just added a few drops of it to the syrup and that's also in the air." I told Mr. Rackliffe that we had just received our first supply of sorghum cane. Our sorghum mill has been up and running since this spring but we didn't have any cane to produce the syrup until now.

"Father hasn't had his breakfast. Why don't you join us?" I said to Mr. Rackliffe. "I'm anxious to get your opinion on this syrup. It's not the first batch we've made."

"Sure," said Mr. Rackliffe. "By the way, my wife sent along a small crock of butter. I know you girls make butter but she thought with all the people you feed, you can always use a little more butter."

I was eager to hear what Mr. Rackliffe thought of the syrup. In my opinion, it's still a little sharp, and it's still not as clear as the syrup we used to have back in Michigan. I think the boys will need to find a finer strainer. I hope our syrup is better than the Leavenworth syrup Howland used to complain about, even though he said that every grocer from Missouri to Fort Riley was selling it. * That syrup tasted of sulfur. We'll need to find a

*Augusta is referring to the syrup mill owned by Charles Stearns of Leavenworth. Set up in 1856, it was the only syrup mill in the Territory until 1858. He reported selling 5,000 gallons of sorghum syrup for $1.25 a gallon, according to D.W. Wilder The Annals of Kansas, 1841-1885, new ed. (Topeka: Kansas Publishing House, 1886) p. 124.

way to take the sulfur out of our syrup. Sugarcane has sulfur in it and when the cane is squeezed and cooked, those sulfurs remain in it. I think that's also true of sorghum.

A few weeks ago, Chase brought over someone who had worked in sugar mills in the Caribbean Islands. He was now a freight hauler and was stopping here for a day or so. Chase invited him to come by to give us some advice on how to run the mill.

This gentleman was rather amused by our operation. He thought we must be very wealthy, since we are using a steam-driven mill instead of one driven by the wind…and he's got a good point there, considering the constant wind out here in Kansas. He told Father that if molasses were reacted with sulfur dioxide, which is a gas, it would remove the "sulfurosity."

Father made him a bargain: if the freight hauler could locate some of that sulfur gas in St. Louis and bring it out here, Father would give him a job that would pay better than freighting. Our type of mill leaves plenty of sugar in the pulp after it has been squeezed. The French call that residue "bagasse" and when allowed to ferment and is distilled, you get rum. He said it was a shame to waste all that sugar, particularly since there is no Territorial law against making alcohol. I hadn't given much thought to that opportunity. Father said that he knew making rum was legal here but with all the whiskey coming into the Territory, we didn't need another alcohol producer.

During this conversation, Chase remarked that he thought we use more wood for the sorghum mill, boiling off the water to thicken the syrup, than we do making steam that drives the crushing mill. That fact came as a surprise to me. Thank goodness wood is plentiful.

While Mr. Rackliffe seated himself for breakfast, father came in from the outside, having put his surveying equipment in the wagon. Although a territorial legislator draws no pay, father often "drums" up some surveying work while attending these meetings, so he regularly takes his equipment with him.

Chase, who had already finished his breakfast, stood up to leave and said to me rather formally that if I had any quinine left, he'd like to take another dose of the powder tonight, but before I could respond, he put on his jacket and slipped out...no thank you, no lingering touch on my arm or shoulder, nothing. He just left!

Father nodded to Mr. Rackliffe.

Mr. Rackliffe, said, "Good morning there, Landslide! *His greeting provoked a guffaw from father. I asked Mr. Rackliffe why he called father "Landslide."

He replied, "Well, district 17, which includes Hunter and Butler counties, has about 224 people eligible to vote in this election and 221 of them voted for your father, with two or three voting for Mr. Herd, the proslavery candid. That, Augusta, constitutes a landslide."

As soon as Chase had gone, Mr. Rackliffe started to tease me, "Tell me, Augusta, rumor has it that we're about to celebrate a big wedding here at the town president's house. Any truth to that?

I smiled but avoided giving him a direct answer. "Well, that certainly does seem to be the big topic of conversation around here," I said. "Not a day goes by that Doctor Weibley or his charming wife or people at Mr. Conner's store plague me with the same question. You would think that Adda and I are the only

*D. W. Wilder *The Annals of Kansas, new ed. (Topeka: T. Dwight* Thatcher, KS Publishing House, 1886) p. 174.

eligible women in the county the way everyone is always after us about our marriage plans. In fact, there hasn't been a wedding in the county yet. All the eligible bachelors around here are either running off to the Kansas gold fields or are trying to make up their minds about going there. The gold fever is certainly a big deterrent to romance. Chase has come back, unlike some of the other eligible men. I'm glad for that but wish we could start making some specific wedding plans."

"These pancakes are just dandy, Augusta, especially with your syrup," remarked Mr. Rackliffe. "I'd appreciate it if you could spare a quart of it."

I told him I'd be glad to give him a quart if he brings the container, for we are short of containers of any size.

"Augusta, where is the sorghum cane coming from?"

"You know, I don't know."

Father spoke up. "I told several haulers on my trips to Lawrence that we had a mill out here and that I'd buy all they can locate and haul in. We've had two loads so far. I'm hoping they can keep this supply going until the cane gives out for the year. By the way, I think it's coming from Missouri."

"Augusta," said Mr. Rackliffe, "may I impose on you or Adda to do me a favor? I would like one of you to drop off my horse and buggy at my place sometime today, as I'm going up to Leavenworth with you father as soon as we finish breakfast. We are still tinkering with that danged Constitution."

So that's where father is going this time.

After breakfast, Mr. Rackliffe gave father a hearty slap on the back as the two of them left the cabin to head for Leavenworth.

October 4, the so-called Leavenworth Constitution, which Father had worked on, was adopted and changed in Wyandotte. The reworked Constitution was put to a vote: 10,500 for it and 5,530 against it.

Saturday, October 9 we've got the sawmill running again, cutting logs for an extension to the Watts' place. It opened officially on the Fourth of July but that was just ceremonial. The construction is still going on. The Wattses have placed an order for more timber, so they can continue the project. Chase and Dave Upham have been working pretty hard on their order all week. Even though the mill is some distance from the house, I can tell by the sound if the mill is running. "When that saw whines," says father, "we're makin' money!" (The first time he said this, I thought to myself, "Well, yes, the money is 'on the books' but collecting it is another matter."

Mrs. Young, who lives quite south of us, has sent up a large basket of apples, which probably came from Missouri. I want all the people who have felons or boils etc., to eat two raw apples a day and I will, as well. *Gunn's Book of Medicine* recommends it. I have asked Mr. Conner to order some citric acid. I've heard if you add it to food, you can avoid scurvy. Lemons and many other fruits have that beneficial property. The British Navy has discovered this: all of their sailors are required to eat limes.

Recently, we've had our first incidence of impudence by the Indians. This week some of them came into town secretly and stole ten of our horses, taking them two or three at a time, and each time the Indians succeeded…undetected!

The owners went after them, figuring where the Osages most likely would be. When they located the Indian camp, our men saw their horses but the Indians cheekily ordered them to leave, telling them: "Go back where you came from or we will scalp you." So they returned here without their horses, but as soon as they got back, they came to our house to "file a complaint," with father, the Territorial representative.

They told father everything that had happened. "The bad news is," said father, "you fellows should have recovered your horses, even if it meant using force. In their culture, that you didn't fight back will be interpreted as weakness. You should at least have fired a rifle or two in the air, or near the feet of the Indian who was doing all the talking. Now they will be back."

After the horses' owners had gone, father said to me, "Those fellows should have taken along someone with some military experience. During the Mexican War, our boys all learned just how limited negotiation could be when you are dealing with the Mexicans. If our boys didn't make it abundantly apparent to the Mexicans that they were willing to use force, the Mexicans would win. The same is true for the Indians. If you don't fight back, you'll lose."

This afternoon I went to visit my old "undertaker" friend, Mrs. Weibley, for the afternoon, hoping to get some matrimonial advice about Chase. On the way over there I saw several Osages hanging around. One of them looked like Paul, Adda's friend. I yelled a greeting out to him, but it turns out I was mistaken. I suppose, now that they have had success stealing ten horses, they're here looking for more.

Knowing how gracefully she has managed the terrible burden of her husband's drinking, I thought with her strength, good humor and wisdom, she would be a good source of marital advice. I need a companion to talk to. Father is helpful but, in this matter, far from satisfactory. Adda is more than willing to give advice but is so young, she lacks the experience to form useful judgments.

Mrs. Weibley's advice to me was to be patient and willing to listen to Chase, but to be sparing in using my female charms. According to her, it sets a bad example. She also advised me to make sure Chase had good character traits before I married him, being alert for any signs of dishonesty, laziness, bad manners, profanity or drunkenness.

On October 17th Father came home with a bleeding nose. Adda rode Charley up to fetch Doc Weibley, but even with her help, he was too drunk to get into the wagon. In fact, while trying to get up into the wagon... Adda said, he fell, skinned his forehead on the wheel rim and blamed her for it.

Since Doctor Weibley was going to be of no use, I looked up the treatment for nosebleeds in Gunn's book. He advised dusting some alum powder into some cotton and stuffing the cotton into the patient's nose, and make the patient lie down. I followed those instructions and it worked.

Later in the day, Dr. Weibley came by. He was not friendly and I suspect he'd been drinking. He came in and sat down at the table. Adda and I were at home, but father and Chase were outside, working at the sorghum mill.

Doctor Weibley claimed we owed him money for his services, and I suppose he is right, as he has come by to treat father and Chase on several occasions recently, though whether his services were effective is debatable...more often he was too drunk to attend to them properly.

Rather than press us for payment, he said he wondered if I would bake him some bread. He said he had some men working on the road going up to his claim and his missus would need to feed them tonight but she didn't have any bread. Doctor Weibley offered to trade what we owe him if I would bake him as many loaves of bread as possible from the flour he had brought along. When I agreed, he excused himself, went out to his wagon and returned with a cloth bag that held about five pounds of flour. I told him I would start baking the bread right away and that he should return in midafternoon for it.

I had some yeast, but I didn't know how long it would take for the bread to rise. The flour didn't look very good to me.

Well I was right about the flour. I made all the bread my

oven could hold, filling the oven up twice, but for each batch, the dough rose about halfway up the greased pan.

Doctor Weibley sent someone to fetch the bread late in the afternoon just as the last batch came out of the oven. I packed up the loaves and sent along a little note to Mrs. Weibley, blaming the quality of the bread on the flour. I have learned a lot about bread, and a few other things as well, from this dear lady, so I'm sure she will understand.

I am glad I baked the bread. It has cleared up our medical bill. I think we got the better of the deal. Even though the medical care he gives us is often impaired by his drinking, we did owe him for his services.

The next day father woke up with some blood clots in his throat, but at least his nose bleeding has stopped,

The following night, we all had trouble sleeping. The wolves are serenading us again. I miss my friend Howland, the wolf slayer.

Howland has already been gone almost two months. I half expected him back by now, but it seems I've been wrong. I am now starting to believe that he won't ever return to Eldorado.

Whenever the wolves come around, I stand in the doorway of our cabin, with our Sharps half-cocked waiting for them to come into view, but they are too smart for me. I hold the gun up against the doorjamb, and even though only an inch or two of the gun's barrel protrudes out the door, the wolves seem to know they are in danger and they go behind the cabin, where I can't see them, but where I can still hear them…and they continue to howl all though the night.

Standing there in the doorway, I always feel like such a fool, waiting for the wolves to come within rifle sight. I wonder if this is a contest. These wolves have some reason in circling our cabin, yelping and howling. Could they be lonely and want companionship, or do they resent our being here? Although their purpose is unknown to me, my purpose is to put a stop to this irritating annoyance. I could use another skin, but I have yet to slay any of them. Actually, I have never even seen this adversary, not once. With exasperation, after waiting patiently and for a long time, I'm always forced to give up. I close the door and put the gun up. The wolves know they are out of danger and in less than five minutes they resume their circling and their serenade. Having thought about it from the wolf's point of view, the noise is not so annoying.

27.

CHASE KEEPS ME GUESSING
October and November 1858

Chase was around most of the day, working with father on the rollers for the sorghum mill. We are anxious to keep the mill in good running order, so that when more cane is available, we'll be able to make syrup, and lots of it. One of the lessons we learned when we squeezed the last load of cane was that we should cut the cane stalks in much smaller pieces. For our last batch, we chopped the stalks in half, then thirds. I'm thinking, from the way the rollers just pushed the longer stalks to one side, in spite of the pan's corrugated bottom, that we should cut the cane to lengths of a foot, or maybe even just six inches. And a pest we never gave a thought to was the honeybee. They come down the valley in swarms, when they smell the syrup boiling off. The upper rim of the juice pan, where the cane is squeezed, gets sticky from the juice and the bees feed on this. We all learned the hard way to be cautious in that area and to wear enough protection. Someone suggested that we could put up with their annoyance in exchange for their honey by building them some hives nearby. I know I can't keep them away from the big pan and its sticky edges when we are running the mill. And the strainers take care of those unlucky few that venture into the hot plenum, where the syrup is boiling off. I've sent to Chicago for some wax combs and have sketched what a hive should look like based on a drawing in one of our "pioneer" books.

For a week now, Chase has been very distant. Even when he's here, he's remote. He won't explain himself. In fact, he doesn't want to talk about "us." Perhaps his being withdrawn is really a measure of just how much he cares for me. My fear is that he doesn't give a fig for me and that I'm wasting my affection, as well as my hopes and expectations on this reluctant carpenter. I must not allow his rebuffs to bother me, or to create in me a feeling of self-depreciation, since I'm already inclined to melancholy. Yet I love him. Since well before last March when we became engaged, I've loved him. He knows that Jerry Jordan proposed. In fact, he said it pleased him that I didn't accept Jerry's proposal, but what has Chase done with that opportunity? He doesn't court me with any more ardor than if I'd never had any other suitor. He's become very friendly with Mr. Conner, who seems to like my company—and perhaps may think of himself as a rival with Chase for my affections. But Chase doesn't appear to be jealous of him either.

I've never discussed with Chase my very first proposal from my Army friend from our Plymouth days, Captain J. A. Henry. I was flattered by his proposal, though it was most impractical, but I've often thought about him and wondered whether he ever deserted.

Lately I seem to be bothered by a case of chills. Sometimes they end up by my having the shakes. I wish I could determine the cause. Mrs. Benton, while she was still here in Eldorado, used to blame the sickness in our valley on the air. With two cricks and the river, there was too much moisture in the air, she said, and moist air carries diseases; that was her opinion.

After a few more days of feeling ill, I've begun keeping a

medical "log." I've had a chill or two every day since Friday, but I can't seem to get at the "bottom" of these chills and occasional shakes.

This morning, father, Adda and her new friend, Dick and I had a big discussion on the architecture for the addition we are going to make to the house. I'm wondering if Adda has some romantic intentions for Dick—a replacement for Frank Robinson?

Now that we have some good lumber, we are planning to build a loft. It will be good to have more room—it gets tiresome, and it's not dignified, when I get up to begin breakfast, for me to step over the bodies of our boarders, who are still sleeping on the floor. Adda and father want to extend the walls of our house upward so we can have a two-story house: a real "upstairs." Father says having an upstairs is fine with him now that we have some proper lumber, but he doesn't know where to put the stairs, since they take so much space. I will be satisfied with just having a loft, rather than an entire new story. Our roof, in my opinion, is already high enough to accommodate a loft. And our boarders could get to the loft by using a ladder, which would solve the stair problem. After some debate we agreed on a loft whose floor will stretch from one wall to the other and be a little over six feet off the floor, but will only cover about half our living space.

After Dick and Adda went down to the shed to locate and measure the timbers we will need, I mentioned to father, in a way I hoped would not come over as a complaint, that it would be nice if Chase were to come down and participate in this construction. We could use his carpentry and I'd like to see more of the man I've promised to marry. This seemed to provoke father's curiosity, but he tried to avoid offending me by appearing to pry. Father said, "You and Chase have been engaged since March. That was eight months ago. When's the big day? If you have fixed a date, I should know about it, so I won't be away politicking or filing land claims."

Father was teasing me a bit. I appreciated that he wasn't asking me too directly about my wedding plans with Chase. I told him that I didn't know yet when Chase and I would get married.

I've never heard of a more on-again, off-again romance than ours. There are times when Chase is around here working on the mill, when with great warmth and expectations, I'll prepare a little lunch as an excuse to say hello. With a song in my heart, I'll take the basket down to the mill, but often find him so formal, uninterested in a bit of conversation that I'll simply settle for a grunt of acknowledgment. I consider myself fortunate if he invites me to share the picnic. Usually he just says, "I'm too busy to eat. Put the basket over there." So then we play a little game: I wait around to eat with him, but he delays, then I leave and return to the house to take care of my work. Later I'll either retrieve the basket or he'll bring it back, but the food is always eaten. No thank-yous; in fact, no comments at all about how good (or how bad) the food was.

Father told me that some men don't like to give up their independence. "Some find it easier to make a commitment to a job or to a military hitch than to matrimony because that is not forever. They view committing to wedding vows as final—for ever." Father quoted Napoleon, who said that for a battle to be a success the first requirement was to get a commitment from his officers to the plan. Marriage following an engagement is one of the most serious commitments a man can make.

Father seemed to appreciate my frustration.

"Why don't I suggest to Chase that he clarify his intentions?" he asked. I wanted father's opinion but not his intervention.

"No, heavens, no!" I said. "If you push him, he will impute your question to me, and your inquiry will offend his sense of independence."

By October 29th, we had all the lumber we needed for the loft. Mid morning, Dick began putting up an overhead scaffold. Actually it's just a big flat plank, which he put at a diagonal between the two adjacent right-angle walls. He placed it a foot or so above our heads, jamming the ends of the plank between the logs that make up the walls.

The ten-or eleven-foot-long plank fit snugly enough between two logs that he didn't need to nail it down. Dick, who is well built and rather athletic, placed his hands on the plank and in one catlike motion hopped up onto the plank, and that's a six-foot hop. He must be exceedingly strong to do that.

Pretending to be a circus performer, he tilted the plank back and forth under his feet while standing on it. He took a little bow, drawing applause from Adda and me. His performance worked just fine, as long as he was paying attention only to the task of balancing himself on the plank. His purpose for going up there was to nail two purlins, one of on each opposite wall. The horizontal purlins one of which Adda was holding for him will support the loft floor. As he began some serious pounding, nailing the purlin to the wall log, the unanchored plank rotated enough under his feet to unbalance him and the whole contraption came crashing down. His body, or the plank, broke a picture frame and scattered things all over. To his utter embarrassment he landed smack on the table in the pan full of water in which we were washing the dishes. Nothing important broke but his dignity. I noticed Adda's reaction. She had put her hand over her mouth, either to stifle her amazement or to stifle her laughter. That was quite a show Dick had put on.

Father said he thought if someone held the purlin against the log, Dick could simply nail each of them in place by standing on a stool. Adda held the purlin up against the log; Dick tried it and was successful. Once he got the horizontal supports well nailed onto two opposite wall logs, all he and Adda had to do after that was to place each end of the cut loft planks on top of two purlins. To keep the planks from sagging in the middle when the loft is occupied, father and Dick had decided to use two-inch thick planks. Except for the first one, Dick didn't need to nail them down since the planks are going to stretch from wall to wall with their ends resting on the purlins. When Dick had finished putting up the planks, he and father built a ladder and nailed it in place. Adda and Dick had a little friendly wrestling match to see who would be the first to get up the ladder and occupy the loft. There wasn't room enough for both of them on the ladder but they tried. As they tussled on the third or fourth rung of the ladder, Adda used the motion of her hips to dislodge him and quickly gained enough rungs to put her body above his. Just as he was losing his footing he managed to grab Adda's ankle with his left hand, which was now above his head. Again exhibiting his strength, he pulled her leg down and began biting her calf just above the ankle, which produced a shriek. But I know my sister. That shriek contained less alarm for her safety than a girlish delight with the struggle, which was far from over. As Adda tried to kick at Dick's head to get him to stop biting her leg, she lost her hold on the ladder but Dick had not lost his hold on her leg. Her body rotated and landed on him, straddling his shoulders. I remember as little girls enjoying riding on Father's shoulders and that's exactly the position that Adda was in now, except Adda wasn't six years old anymore. Thank heavens she was wearing bloomers, which is a recent addition to women's wardrobe.

Adda still had one hand on the upper plank of the loft. With the other, she had a firm grip on Dick's ample brown hair. Both of her legs were dangling down in front of Dick's chest. In this fashion, and with shrieks of hilarity from my sister, who was enjoying this horseplay enormously, Dick proceeded to climb up the ladder with Adda on his shoulders. As his head and shoulders approached the loft floor, he bent his head down and dumped Adda off onto the loft floor. From a kneeling position she declared herself to be both the "Queen of the Mountain" and the first person to occupy the loft. In mock surrender, Dick descended the ladder, looked at me and winked. Adda seems to have a talent for these spontaneous shenanigans. And although I envy her blithe spirit, I couldn't possibly provoke, never mind allow, such familiarities.

The loft is fairly sizable. Two or three people, maybe four, will be able to sleep quite comfortably up there. The loft is high enough to allow them to stand up, though not at the sides. And there is enough space between the loft and the ground floor so that we can walk comfortably under it without stooping over or bumping our heads.

On October 30th, Chase came down and worked all day at the sawmill. I went down there mid morning with a small jug of hot chocolate and biscuits. We had an unusually friendly chat, unusual in that it's been difficult in recent weeks for me to get Chase even to say "hello." In addition, it's hard for me to predict how "friendly" each encounter will be. I can't believe I'm writing the word friendly about the man I've promised to marry.

During our chat, he acknowledged that we should try to be more sociable with one other. I said that would suit me fine.

Another load of cane came in today. I don't know from where, maybe southern Missouri. I think we will celebrate the Sabbath by making syrup. I look forward to this whole process of milling the sorghum and producing syrup, and it gives me a chance to work side by side with Chase. I've decided to chop the cane in six-inch lengths. I hope it's too late in the season for the bees to bother, but we will see.

It's the last day of October, and I'm wondering if it is normal for a man who intends to marry a woman to take advantage of the engagement by intermittently but deliberately ignoring her? Who can I turn to, to confirm that it's normal? Certainly not a woman my age. Since the question deals with male behavior, what good would come from another woman's opinion anyway? And if I did ask Elizabeth Cordis or Mary Rackliffe, both of whom are slightly older than I am, my question might reveal more than I care to about my toleration of this strange arrangement Chase calls an engagement. His behavior towards me is so far from the expectations I've formed about love, mainly from my reading of novels, (mostly English novels and French translations), that it seems to me that I must be misinformed or that I'm simply expecting too much. I've finished Stendhal's *Charter House of Parma* and I'm halfway through his *The Red and The Black*, which Howland called a poignant and unrequited love story, and there is nothing about my engagement with Chase that resembles the romance described in those two novels.

I've gone back into the entries of my journal since our arrival here last November and counted the number of times, before and after our engagement when Chase could have acknowledged my presence or said something nice, given me a smile or even allowed me a thin grin, but didn't. Occasionally he's within a few feet of me. Why can't he spare me a pat on the arm or a touch on the shoulder? Would extending such physical generosity offend this image he seems to possess of himself as a taciturn, independent Yankee?

It's been cloudy and cold since Tuesday. It's snowing lightly now. Chase came down this morning, but went directly to work at the sorghum mill. He is preparing to mill the syrup. The water in the boiler was hot from being heated last night, but not hot enough to make steam. Chase threw several sticks of wood into the firebox and busied himself with cleaning out the moist pulp from the cane we'd crushed yesterday. In an hour or so I could hear the rhythmic clank of the rollers as they were being driven by the little steam engine. I went out to carry some chopped cane over to the mill, thinking I could provoke a discussion with him. No luck!

By noon, I could smell the aroma that comes from condensing the syrup. Gallons of water from the squeezings must be evaporated to produce one gallon of useful syrup. In the process the whole neighborhood fills up with a pleasant aroma of sweet caramel.

A little after noon, I took a picnic lunch consisting of thin slices of sage hen on light bread down to the mill.

Though Chase was preoccupied with the syrup press, I invited him to supper and he accepted the invitation. Adda and Dick were not at the house tonight, and directly after supper father excused himself, saying there was something he needed at the store.

Having the house to ourselves allowed Chase and me some privacy, and we had a talk.

Someone, I told him, had teased me at Mr. Conner's store, appearing pleased to tell me that he thought Mr. Chase had some "interest" in a young Irish lady who was staying at a claim between Dr. Weibley's cabin and Little Walnut. I asked Chase about this, wondering aloud if that might be the reason for his remoteness these recent weeks. I brought the subject up, because of my concern over that person's comment. I was curious as to whether Chase somehow met or was involved with our friend Miss MacIntyre.

Without reciting here all the details, Chase gave me a plausible explanation. My suspicions were all a mistake. Though I was mildly embarrassed about having revealed so much of my personal anxieties, I was greatly relieved, and Chase and I shared a few pleasant moments until we heard father at the door.

On November 5th, with the help of Tom Cordis, who was attending to the sorghum mill's engine and little steam boiler, we made several more gallons of syrup, and, I must say, I like the taste of this batch very much. Cutting the stalks into shorter sections allowed the rollers to work better and increased the yield, and we have had no bees to contend with.

Our sorghum mill is the first mill of its kind in this area. We are having a hard time finding containers for all the syrup we're making.

Monday, November 8th, a year ago today we arrived at Eldorado.

A week has passed. Today, the 16th, it's been unusually warm particularly for November. Before bedtime, I stepped outside and saw a beautiful full moon. What a contrast to a year ago when we arrived in Eldorado in that raging snowstorm.

Chase started for Burlington, Iowa, this morning, though I haven't seen him or spoken to him since last Saturday, so I don't know much about it. When we last talked, he didn't say when he'd return or what's in Burlington for him.

On November 23, Mr. Rackliffe, who's just a few years older than myself and who has the loveliest wife (twenty-two years old), Mr. Carey and father all have been making big plans for a hunt. I presume it is for buffalo, but it would sure be nice if they brought back some deer meat. Venison is so much nicer than buffalo, more tender. Three or four days ago, Mr. Carey gave me the front shoulder and leg, (he called it a joint from a young deer he had shot within a few yards of his claim. It made a delicious roast.

At dinner we spoke about how much we missed Howland's company. We had a fine time recalling the many dinners at the

Stewart "manse," where Howland often provided the supper.

In addition to the venison, we had a large pot of white beans baked in some of our syrup. I had soaked the little hard beans overnight. Then I had cooked the beans with the syrup, flavored with some onion and strips of bacon rind for several hours and it was delicious.

28.

FATHER PURSUES THE HORSE THIEF
November 24 to December 13, 1858

It was early morning and father and I were both up. I had started breakfast. He had gone outside. Suddenly he burst in through the back door. "Augusta, Puss and Jerry's mare are gone, stolen from our corral. They left us Kate and old Charley."

He told me that the wire gate for the corral was open and lying on the ground. "I've got to go after those thieves and get those horses back. I'm no tracker but with this light snow it will be easy to follow them. I can ride twice as fast as those thieves trailing two reluctant horses."

"Father, do you think the Indians did it?"

"No. Indians out here are still wearing moccasins. I can tell from the footprints that there were two thieves. One of them wore boots, and the other, shoes. And the one wearing shoes is heavy. These thieves each had a horse and both of their horses were shoed. From prints in the snow, I know exactly how they stole the horses."

Father quickly explained that they had tied up their two horses to the outer corner of our fence posts, walked along the fence to the corral, and undid our wire gate, then they stole two bridles that he had left on the wood railing near the cabin, and put them over the horses' heads and walked Puss and Jerry's horse out of the corral.

One of the thieves walked the horses several yards south, followed by the other thief, who was leading their own two horses. "The thieves' footprints stop where they mounted and rode off south."

While father talked, he rummaged around the cabin for something. "Tell me what you're looking for," I said. "Maybe I know where it is."

"I'm looking for my gun, holster and belt, my heavy mackinaw, and my old soft winter hat with ear flaps." By the time he'd finished the sentence, he had located his gun and belt, but he hadn't found his mackinaw and cap. "I can't spend the time looking for them now. With those two horses gone I've got to get a horse somewhere—and fast," he said. I knew he wouldn't consider Kate or Charley.

"I'm sure Tom Cordis will loan you a horse, but shouldn't someone go with you, particularly if you think there are two thieves?"

"Damn, I wish Jerry were here. Where is he anyway? The one night he chooses to leave his horse at our place, it gets stolen."

"Father, you'll need to eat a little something. I've cooked some cornmeal mush. The coffee's ready. Eat a little before you go to the Cordises. I'll bet they will let you borrow their black horse."

While father wolfed down the mush, I ventured my guess about who was behind the theft. "Father, I'll bet anything Hildebrand is in on this. He's never forgiven you for embarrassing him when you caught him with our ox team."

"You may be right. I think I'll follow those tracks south to the crick. If they turn east, I'll ride over to Brother Hildebrand's." Father took another gulp of hot coffee. But I don't think he would be stupid enough to keep the horses at his place. If all the tracks go south at the crick, I'll come back and pack up."

"Do you think they stole them during the night?"

"No, it didn't start snowing until a few hours ago, so it was an early-morning theft."

Father had another cup of coffee. While he finished it, I put two thick slices of hot bacon on a piece of coarse wheat bread I had baked yesterday, folded the bread over the bacon, dripped a little bacon fat on it the way he likes it and handed it to him. "I'll take the sandwich with me while I run up to the Cordis place."

"Come back here before you ride off. I'll pack a lunch and roll a blanket for you, and I'll put some grain in a feed bag for the horses, in case you are gone overnight."

Not long after, I saw father ride by our place on Tom Cordis' big black horse, but father didn't stop by the house and come in. I yelled out, "Be sure to pick up your lunch and blanket before you go." He waved to signal that he had heard me, but he kept on going.

Father had someone with him. I could see it wasn't Tom Cordis, they rode off too quickly for me to tell who it was.

Less than an hour later, father and his companion returned. It was snowing lightly. Father was carrying a lace-up men's shoe that reached up to the ankle. Reuben Palmer was the man who was with him. I had met "Billy" only a few days ago. He's new here and is working at Tom Cordis' blacksmith shop. He was carrying a side arm. He's so young. I hope if he's put to the test, he can prove himself useful. After all, they are not going out to shoot rabbits.

"Well, what did you find?" I asked. "Well, at the crick one set of tracks turned east, but all the other tracks, including the stolen horses went south. I hadn't expected that. Billy and I followed the tracks east directly to Hildebrand's cabin, that old buffalo hunter's lean-to where he moved to. I surprised him and used my gun to force him to remove his shoes. I brought this one back to our corral, so I could compare the shoe's prints with some of the prints in our corral. And, as I expected, they were made by his shoe. The two of them came here together. He helped with the theft 'cause he knew where we lived." Before he left, father hung Hildy's old shoe on a fence post out back.

I asked father if he had seen any signs of our horses at Hildebrand's.

"No, he's too clever for that, the other thief has them and he's headed south."

"He claimed that he hadn't stolen the horses."

But father said that what he saw at Hildebrand's cabin had confirmed his suspicion that Hildy was involved, even before he had matched Hildy's shoe with the footprints. "Hildebrand's old checkered red-and-black mackinaw was hanging on a line behind the stove. There were some dark spots on the dirt floor directly under his jacket, which was enough to convince me that he had recently come in from the outside. The water from the snow had dripped off his jacket onto the floor.

Father asked me if I remembered Hildebrand's lean-to, which was on the east side of the crick. He squatted in that cabin with his two youngsters after he sold his claim up here to J. D. Conner.

"Sure," I said. "I remember that there was a huge bleached-out deer skull with enormous antlers hanging under the roof over the doorway.

When Adda and I first saw the cabin last spring, before Hildy moved back into it, a bird had made a nest in one of the skull's eye sockets and the twigs that stuck out looked like an eyebrow. And the cabin's roof had grass and bushes growing on it almost right up to the top."

Billy spoke up, "I walked around to the back of his cabin. His horse with an old quilt over it was in an open shed. A bunch of pigs were eating punkins in his cornfield, but there weren't signs of horses other than his."

"You two were lucky he didn't shoot you in the back when you rode off," I said.

I gave father two rolled-up army blankets, the lunch I'd prepared, and a canvas feed bag full of grain for the horses.

Father found his heavy mackinaw and his cap with ear coverings. To make a little conversation while he put on his coat,

I said to Billy, "Father's horse was a beautiful two year-old black French Canadian. We brought Puss with us all the way from Michigan. Father has been offered over $250 for her a couple of times. Puss is so big and attractive and this territory is so lawless, that she's been stolen three times since we've been here, but thank heaven father's been able to retrieve her each time." I began to tell Billy how father had recovered Puss before but father interrupted me, saying they had to leave. He added that, with luck, they might be back tonight, since he and Billy could ride much faster than the thieves, pulling the two horses.

Father and Billy Palmer rode off. It was a bright day yet snowing lightly, a standard prairie inconsistency.

They had left a little after eight o'clock in the morning. Later in the day I spoke with Mr. Conner, telling him about our stolen horses and that father had matched Hildy's shoe with the prints in the snow. I told him that father and Billy Palmer had gone in pursuit of the thief, heading south after him. I wanted him to know these things since Hildy trades at his store.

A couple of days have passed. Adda and I have had no news of father.

Today, Friday, was anything but a pleasant day. It commenced raining in the middle of the night. It turned cold this morning and there is a very cold, unpleasant mist on the prairie and an unpleasant pall in this household.

Two men came by after supper, making the usual inquiries about available land, what their prospects here might be, etc.— the usual questions all such newcomers have been putting to father since we arrived here a year ago. But there seemed to be something more they wanted to say. It finally came out: They are missing some cattle and have ridden down from Chelsea looking for them. Since we are on two trails west as well as on the north-south Cherokee trail, they figured we might have seen them. Well, outfits go by our front door every day, some with cattle. So we would have no way of telling which cattle had been stolen, and which hadn't. Out of sympathy and as it was getting late, Adda and I invited the gentlemen to stay the night. We had a pleasant cup of tea before retiring. Father has not returned.

On November 27, J.D. Conner, who has built a new store down near Hildebrand's old claim (Chase did the carpentry using timbers and siding from our sawmill), stopped in to inquire about getting his claim surveyed. He asked me if father had done any surveying in that area. I answered that I thought so, but to be sure, I offered to look it up in father's "form" book,—only to remember, when I couldn't find it before, that Tom Cordis had borrowed it for the same purpose.

Mr. Conner is very friendly and seems genuinely interested in our safety and well being in father's absence. His words of encouragement help, though I sometimes have difficulty understanding his strong Irish dialect.

Mr. Conner reported that Hildy is a frequent customer at his new store and always makes disparaging comments about father, his politics, and a few days ago said sarcastically that it was "too bad" about Sam Stewart's horses—that he doubted that this community would ever see Mr. Stewart again.

It's been four days since father rode off to recover our horses. I have confirmed a rumor that Hildebrand bought a new pair of shoes at Conner's store, as well as some indulgences for his children. Prior to that he owed money. I have also heard he is riding around the county pricing claims and dropping hints that he's evened up the score with Sam Stewart. Of course, we all know what trouble Hildy has made for everyone here. He has been violent with Father, Jerry Jordan and Doctor Weibley. Then this September Hildy drew a loaded pistol on Mr. Carey. We've yet to figure out what grudge he's got against the Careys. Chase, who was standing some distance from Hildebrand, saw what was going on. He rushed to Mr. Carey's assistance and knocked the pistol from Hildebrand's hand. Afterwards, Mr. Carey gave Hilly such a beating others had to carry him home.

November 29 Today is my sweetheart's birthday. He is of age today, twenty-one years old, but he is not here to celebrate it with me. He must be celebrating elsewhere, since he's not back from Burlington. No news of father either.

We are now in the first week of December and still have yet to hear anything about father and Billy Palmer.

Hildebrand is becoming more bold in his remarks about father. At J.D. Conner's store, he was so reckless as to venture that Sam Stewart would most certainly never return.

Today, December 11th, I needed something at the store and I wanted to get out of the house for a while. As I walked in I interrupted a conversation between Mr. Conner and Mr. Pogue, a recent arrival. Mr. Pogue was saying that a few days before our horses were stolen, a stranger was standing outside Conner's store and inquired where Mr. Hildebrand lived. Mr. Pogue said he gave the gentleman directions down there. Since nobody else saw this stranger around town, Hildebrand must have secreted him for a few days. He must be the one that took the horses south toward the Cherokee Nation since, when father was in Hildebrand's cabin on November 24th, nobody but Hildebrand and his two children were in the cabin.

This afternoon, December 12th, rather late in the day, Reverend Floyd, a traveling preacher, came in. We struck up a conversation. He is an itinerant abolitionist preacher, rather in the style of old Reverend Moore, who preached up in Plymouth in the fall of '56. I invited Reverend Floyd to stay for supper and who should return but my prodigal sweetheart. I was curious to know what it was in Burlington, Iowa that's kept him away three weeks but it wasn't a good time to ask.

Reverend Floyd agreed to preach an afternoon service tomorrow at our place if we bring in a congregation from the neighborhood.

I told Chase and Adda that they would have to do the rounding, as I was having frequent chills. It's the ague again and I've dosed myself with quinine, which makes me a little dizzy and my ears ring.

The next day, at 3 p.m. we had a real turnout. Reverend

Floyd held us spellbound. He preached a long, beautiful sermon. Some of our neighbors missed it, so he volunteered to do another service that evening. He preached an entirely different sermon for them and for several who had remained. Reverend Floyd says Eldorado is the farthest west he has preached the Gospel of Jesus Christ. During the service we must have sung a dozen old favorite hymns.

After the service, toward the end of the evening in a conversation with Chase, the Rackliffes and the Cordises I enlarged on the reason for father's absence. I thanked Tom Cordis for the loan of a good horse for my father and I thanked him for allowing his new employee to go with father in Jerry Jordan's absence. I explained why to those that didn't know about young Reuben Palmer's going with father.

Reverend Floyd asked some questions about Reuben Palmer that were mostly answered by Tom Cordis since Billy was working for him and it developed that Tom Cordis had also loaned Reuben Palmer a horse for this trip.

During this discussion Reverend Floyd asked, "You say his name is Reuben?"

"Yes, why?"

"Well, the name Reuben has some interesting biblical history. We all know that Reuben was the first born of Leah and Jacob, though Leah was not Jacob's first choice." and he softly chuckled, which assumed we all knew the story of Laban's deception. "But it was Reuben, the first born, who should have gotten a double inheritance, but he didn't. He offended his father by defiling Jacob's maidservant, Bilhah, while she was asleep (apparently Jacob was gone). Some biblical texts I have studied explain that Reuben had previously caught sight of Bilhah in her bath, similar to King David's observation of his general's wife, Bathsheba in her bath. As a consequence, Jacob gave Reuben's birthright to Joseph, the first born of Rachel, the beautiful wife Jacob favored over Leah and for whose hand he had traded fourteen years of labor.

It was Reuben, however, that persuaded his brothers, jealous of Joseph, not to kill him but to sell him to some passing Ishmaelites bound for Egypt. They did, for twenty pieces of silver. Of course, this was not the end of Joseph's problems or temptations, all of which, by dint of an outstanding personality he overcame, to become ruler of all Egypt under the pharaoh."

Chase asked Reverend Floyd whatever happened to Dinah, Jacob and Leah's only daughter and he told an engrossing story I'd never heard in Sunday school, about her rape in the city of Shechem by the prince of that town and the terrible revenge Dinah's brothers took on the city. His story went into more detail than I need to write here but it was fascinating, and it was so nice to have someone so well informed in our midst.

It was close to midnight before our guests left. Reverend Floyd stayed over and occupied the loft. How I wish father could have been here to listen to this very interesting speaker.

The next day I intended to record some parts of Reverend Floyd's two sermons but found that my concern about father caused too much distraction to concentrate.

He's been gone twenty days. The whole community has been worried about him.

Charles Samuel Stewart
1818 – 1858

Father of Augusta and Adda
was murdered in November 1858.

He was an abolitionist pioneer to Kansas Territory, served in Jim Lanes Militia, was a POW, founded Eldorado, Kansas Territory, represented District 17 (new) in Territorial Legislature and worked on the Free-State Constitution.

29.

THE MURDER OF SAM STEWART
*December 14, 1858**

Today was bright but cold. In the middle of the morning we
heard someone "hallooing" from across the creek. Hoping that
it might be father, Adda and I rushed outside without our coats.

We saw three horsemen stopped on the other side of the
creek, which hadn't frozen over yet. "That looks like Puss but father's
not on her," Adda said. "Those are strangers and Mr. Carey."

"No, Adda, that's not Puss. That's Old Bill. That's the horse
father borrowed three weeks ago." When I saw that familiar black
horse with its sweat reflecting in the morning sun ridden by a
stranger, that and the fact that Billy Palmer was not one of them,
I was gripped with a foreboding that whoever this rider was, he
was bearing some very bad news.

Mr. Carey and the two gentlemen followed us into the
cabin. He introduced them as John Freshean and his cousin, Mr.
Riley. They both seem to be about eighteen years old, both were
white men from the Cherokee Nation, which is south of us, a
neutral country, not a territory, just a large reservation set aside
by the Federal

*Sam Stewart was murdered November 28, 1858. It took
about three weeks to get the news to Eldorado Government for

Indians moved there from, of all places, Georgia. Neither stranger spoke or smiled. Mr. Carey said they'd stopped at his place to inquire about us and he had ridden on up the valley with them to our place.

Mr. Freshean seemed nervous. Mr. Carey had just introduced us; nevertheless, as though he hadn't heard the name Stewart the first time, he asked us if we were the Stewart girls. We both nodded yes.

Mr. Freshean and his cousin seemed more than just tired from their trip. There was something stiff and unnatural about the way they shuffled about evasively. They didn't give us the usual smiles young men bestow on young women. In fact, they didn't give us any greeting. It didn't seem like bashfulness.

Adda rustled about trying to put them at ease. When she inquired if they'd like a cup of hot coffee or tea neither of them responded, nor did they sit down when she suggested it.

John Freshean fumbled for something in his clothing. He produced an envelope, which he handed to me, looking away when he did so.

"Well, if you are the Stewart girls," he finally said, "I have some very bad news. Your father is dead. He was murdered down in the Cherokee Nation the night of November 28th."

"What about Billy Palmer?" Adda asked him in a subdued voice.

"Well, he's dead, too. He was also shot, but he lived for two days and was able to tell Mr. Harrison and Judge Lynch what happened."

Adda interrupte+d, "Who are they?"

"Judge Lynch owns the ranch where your father was killed, and Mr. Harrison, who lives on it, leases some land from him and raises cattle. They both took care of Mr. Palmer.

"That letter was written to you by Mr. Jim Bell. He's an

attorney, who lives nearby in Requah where I live. The facts in the letter come mainly from your friend Mr. Palmer and Mr. Harrison. It's his testimony of what happened. Although he was shot in the jaw, he could still talk. Judge Lynch called this letter an affidavit." The three men finally sat down at the table. I was too stunned to open the envelope. It was some time before I could bring myself to read it and weeks before I was able to really comprehend it.

Mr. Freshean went on to explain. "Your father had tracked the horse thief, whose name was Worldy, to to the ranch of Judge Lynch about 160 miles almost due south of here.

Your father saw your two horses in a corral next to a cabin on the Lynch place. The saddle was still on the big black horse, so he hadn't been there long. Your father rode up the hill to Judge Lynch's place to explain the situation to the judge, leaving Mr. Palmer by the corral. It was sundown.

A little after dark your father rejoined Mr. Palmer.

They rushed into the cabin and surprised the horse thief. Your father and Mr. Palmer took two large caliber pistols from him and his gun belt and hung them over the chair that Mr. Palmer was sitting in by a table opposite the horse thief. I guess, they assumed, that he was disarmed. Mr. Harrison told me they failed to find a small Colt repeater that he had hidden in one boot. That night your father and Billy Palmer were keeping guard over the horse thief in the cabin.

About midnight, your father decided to fetch the judge for a game of cards. Directly after he stepped outside Mr. Worldy distracted Mr. Palmer, who was drowsy, drew his small gun and shot Palmer twice. When your father heard the shots, he rushed back with a pistol in his hand. As he opened the door, Worldy shot him twice with one of his big pistols, which he had quickly retrieved. Judge Lynch told me that he was still up, heard the shots and he ran down to the cabin. The judge said your father had walked about thirty steps toward him. Judge Lynch asked him, "Stewart, are you hurt?"

"Yes, he has killed us both." Your father fell in front of the judge. One bullet had opened his jugular
vein. Another bullet went through his neck into his spine. He died instantly, according to the judge.

The judge went into the cabin and found Mr. Palmer on the floor still alive. Between Judge Lynch and Mr. Harrison, they kept your friend alive for two days. As I said before, he was shot in the neck or throat with that small Colt revolver, the bullet didn't even come out, but he could talk. Mr. Harrison said all the facts in Mr. Bell's letter came from talking to Mr. Palmer for two days before he died.

"What happened to father's murderer?" I asked (I hadn't read the letter.)

"Well, in all the excitement of the shooting he escaped on the pony that was saddled. Judge Lynch ran to the bunkhouse where several ranch hands were still up playing cards. By dawn, Mr. Harrison's men had captured him. They chased him for forty miles. I believe they hung him early that morning."

Adda interrupted him, "You believe they hung him? Don't you know for sure?"

"No, I'm sorry, I don't live on the Lynch ranch. About a week after the murder, Judge Lynch asked me to pay him a visit. That's when he spoke to me about delivering that letter. Before I left, I visited around the ranch and asked the old nigger cook what happened to the horse thief. He was the one who told me they hung him.

"I stayed around the Lynch ranch two days, so I had a chance to speak with Judge Lynch and Mr. Harrison. They really felt bad about what happened to your father and Mr. Palmer. They both asked me to tell you that if you want to send someone to fetch your father's things, Mr. Riley and I will guide you down. Most of the way down is the Cherokee Trail."

Freshean said "On the way here I stopped at my cousin's house a little north of Requah. He agreed to come up with me.

Mr. Carey, who was still with us, asked Mr. Freshean how it was that he knew Mr. Bell. He said, "Well, we both live in Requah and my folks know him. He's the local lawyer." I was surprised to hear Mr. Carey say that he knew Mr. Bell.

Word traveled fast about father's death. Everyone in Eldorado and surroundings knew about it within a few hours. Mrs. Rackliffe came down midafternoon. Neither Adda nor I were of a mood to visit and she understood that. Without much talking, she began doing the housework. She made supper for all of us, which included the two Cherokees and Mr. Carey, who said he would stay around to see if he could help. Mrs. Rackliffe churned some butter for dinner. Looking out the window, she said she saw Mrs. Barrett leading our cows in from the pasture to their shed.

"In a little while, Mrs. Barrett brought in a gallon or so of milk, along with a pan of baked goods, some cupcakes and cookies, which Adda passed around as dessert. She picked up a load of laundry and said she would take them to the "new" laundry in town.

After supper, while it was still light, Mr. Carey and the two Cherokees went outside for a breath of fresh air.

Tom Cordis came by. Mrs. Rackliffe answered the door. She asked us if we wanted to visit with Tom. We asked him to come in and he did for a few minutes, but I could tell he was uncomfortable, so he confined himself to a few questions about keeping the sawmill going for the Watts job. I told him that I suppose we can count on Chase to take care of that.

Tom said, "Well the reason I brought it up is that I haven't seen Chase for two or three days." It dawned on me that I hadn't either. Before Tom left, I gave him the old pistol that the Cherokees brought back with them. Tom muttered something to the effect that this is the gun he had loaned to Billy Palmer . . . "Looks like it hadn't been shot," he said.

"You know, one of the Cherokees rode your black horse back up here and he appears to be in good shape."

"Yes I'd heard that. When I go out, I'll settle-up with those youngsters," Tom said and he left.

On Wednesday a messenger brought a small bowl of custard pudding with a little decorated card from Mrs. Weibley. Written in her beautiful calligraphy at the top was the word, "Condolences."

Our neighbors are all so nice. Each in his own way wants to comfort us, but there's not much anyone can do for this kind of suffering. I so much appreciate that we have these friends—but grief is a private matter. For me, no amount of sympathy offsets the agony and sorrow. Adda doesn't seem to mourn or suffer the way I do; she is angry. She makes bitter remarks about Hildebrand, wishes she had known Worldy, and so, as she says, she could put a face on him. Adda seems consolable by others. She can mix socializing and grief, which I find mildly offensive. For me death is too personal. I don't want to hear from others how awful it is. I know it's awful. I just don't want to hear about it. It was that way when mother died and it's that way now.

Mrs. Barrett came again early Wednesday morning with some delicious oatmeal porridge with very thick cream. Adda thanked her for milking the cows yesterday. She brought some eggs, which she offered to cook, but I didn't feel like eating eggs. Adda had two fried eggs with some bacon. Oh yes, Mrs. Barrett had brought that, too.

On Wednesday, Chase came by. He knew about the deaths

and was very shy around us. Adda took him outside and I guess filled him in on all the details. He volunteered to go back with the guides whenever they are ready. Adda wanted to go with them. Freshean had warmed up a bit towards us, but I discouraged her from going.

Well, the two Cherokees stayed with us the rest of Tuesday, all of Wednesday and Thursday. This morning, Friday, the 17th, Chase and Mr. Carey left for the Lynch ranch with the Cherokees. They took our small wagon and an extra mule. Chase went to bring back our horses as well as father and Billy's possessions, particularly the saddles. Mr. Carey, having some business down there, went with them. Suddenly it's very quiet in the cabin.

The morning after the people left for the Lynch ranch, Adda said, "You know what we should do?" and as usual before I could answer, she said, "We should write to that U.S. courthouse in Van Buren, Arkansas and ask if Mr. Worldy or whatever his name is was ever convicted or if he's still in jail. I wonder if the evidence of murder and that he was also a horse thief was enough to get him hung? What I'm getting at is," she said, "what has happened to him? As daughters, we certainly have a right to know. But you should write it. Your penmanship and writing is better than mine." Her question came as a complete surprise.

"What U.S. courthouse? I thought Mr. Freshean said that those ranch hands down there hung him," I said.

"No, no, for heavens sakes, didn't you read Mr. Bell's letter? Two days after the murder Worldy was taken to Van Buren, Arkansas, where a Federal Court is in session."

"Well, to tell you the truth I haven't read the letter. I keep putting it off," I said. What I didn't say was that I had begun to read it two or three times but just couldn't do it.

"Well, I think it's high time you read that letter. It's been lying right there almost under your nose by your journals on the settee."

That night Adda was quietly writing at the table. I was so glad that she was home. I opened the envelope for the first time and read the affidavit/letter.

"The Murder of Stewart and Palmer"

We have been furnished with the following particulars of the murder of Messrs. Samuel Stewart and Reuben Palmer, both from Eldorado, Kansas, which took place in the Cherokee Nation on the night of Nov. 28, 1858.

Requah, Cherokee Nation

December 7, 1858

To the Settlers of Walnut Creek, Gentlemen: - This will recommend to your kind consideration, two young men of Our Nation, who cheerfully undertake the perils of a trip to your remote settlement, for the purpose of bearing you the painful intelligence of the murder on the night of the 28th, of November, about 12 o'clock of Mr. Samuel Stewart, and Reuben Palmer, two of your citizens, by the man they were in pursuit of, whose name was Worldy. The circumstances that resulted in so horrible a scene was as follows: Mr. Stewart and his friend came up with Worldy on the above day in Saline District, Cherokee Nation at the residence of a white man by name of Harrison, living under permit, and raising stock for one of our prominent citizens, J. M. Lynch, and proceeded to the arrest of said Worldy, on the charge of horse stealing. On searching him they unfortunately overlooked a Colt's repeater that he had secreted about his person, and with which he killed them, shooting Mr. Stewart in the neck and killing him instantly. Mr. Palmer was shot in the jaw, ranging down through the neck, the ball lodging. He lived two days and could talk-related all the circumstances attending the case-gave his age, native state, etc. It was impossible to get a physician, but all that sympathizing humanity could do was of no avail. If the desire of those that attended him in his last moments could have been gratified he would more than have lived. It will afford you pleasure to know that Worldy was taken prisoner on the Tuesday following, 30th Nov., and that he was taken on to Van Buren, Arkansas, where the United States Court is in session. Said Court having jurisdiction over the case, where it is generally thought, (there being very strong evidence) that the justice he so richly merits, will be speedily meted out to him.

The promptness of the arrest is attributable to Mr. Lynch and other Cherokees, who also attended to the internment of the remains of Mr. Stewart in as decent a manner as circumstance would admit of. The attentions of Mr. Harrison on Mr. Palmer were unremitting to the last.

The horses that were stolen, as well as those rode out by Mr. Stewart and his friend, are in the possession of Mr. Lynch. One of the young men had to ride one of them back, which is unavoidable. He also takes along with him Mr. Palmer's pistol. There is a schedule of all that they had. It would be advisable for some of their friends to come in immediately, there is not the least danger attending the trip and the young men will act as pilots.

Very respectfully,
James M. Bell.

It was an emotional struggle to comprehend Mr. Bell's letter. * My mind continually wandered away from the page. What's to become of us? What sort of devils would do this? Then I would return to where I was, one sentence at a time. Sometimes I had to read a sentence over and over to comprehend it. Adda had read it immediately because she wanted to discuss details of it with me but I just couldn't accommodate her and she would get a little peeved with me. Without an ongoing discussion of what

*Augusta recorded the entire letter in her journal, as did Adda, whose journal was published under the title *Memories of Addie Stewart Graton* by her daughter Alice Graton Kincaid, p. 11. archived as part of the Kansas Collection, University of Kansas Libraries KHMS 84:5:13 The Bell letter also appeared January 15, 1859 carried in the *Kansas News*, Emporia.

was wrong with me, she understood. No, she didn't understand, she simply tolerated me.

Having read Mr. Bell's letter, I realized that his version of what happened to Worldy was different from the account Mr. Freshean * reported, which meant that father's murderer might still be alive.

I slowly realized it was a very well crafted letter, complete in describing all of the details, as they were known to Mr. Bell, an attorney. Needless to say, he was under no obligation to us, for he didn't know us, so I suppose it was Judge Lynch, who asked him to write it. And so the fact that he did write in such detail added to my understanding. Somehow I felt grateful to this man I'd never met and found some distraction in wondering what he was like.

Everybody in Eldorado wants to get involved in trying to unravel the mystery of father's death. This afternoon two local gentlemen came to our place asking specific questions about the horse thieves. Since they stole father's best horse, the French Canadian, what other horse did they take? What occasioned Reuben Palmer to accompany father in the pursuit? Why didn't Jerry Jordan go instead, since the other stolen horse was his, etc.? Adda said to one of them, "You're getting rather personal aren't you?"

"Well, yes, but the town is getting up a posse and some of them asked us to do this chore," he said. I told them that we should appoint a sheriff to bring some law and order to Eldorado

*During our research for the publication of this journal, we have obtained from the National Archives and Records Administration, Fort Worth, Texas, a microfilm of District Court of Arkansas 12/3/1855 through 12/15/1860, a copy of the formal handwritten Court arraignment for December 15, 1858, of a "Mr. Worley" for murder. We find no court records of the trial. The Van Buren courthouse was burned down during the Civil War and again in 1877.

informing these gentlemen not only about our stolen horses, but also about the two men who had come down from Chelsea looking for their ten head of cattle. They heard rumors that led them to Eldorado. We must have a terrible reputation if the first place people come looking for stolen cattle is our settlement. Of course, we told them to check around Hildebrand's cabin and I'm sure they did. I learned later they had ridden all over the county but hadn't found their cattle, and my guess is that within a fortnight that meat was on the table of some Army fort in the Territory.

Mr. Conner and Mr. Cordis visited Adda and me this afternoon to gather more facts. They are talking about arresting Hildebrand on suspicion of conspiracy for horse theft. They believe that if they put him on trial and he comes under vigorous questioning, he will reveal the details of the theft, where the horses were hidden, who the stranger was who came to his claim a few days before our horses were taken, where he got his recent money, etc. Since after the murder, Hildebrand visited Mr. Conner's store and more than once speculated that he, Hildebrand, doubted that Sam Stewart would ever return, Mr. Conner thinks Hildebrand knows more about the killing than we do.

I should have gone down to the Lynch ranch with Chase. Both Adda and I should have gone down there. That trip might have taken care of the vague empty feeling I have, clearing-up once and for all my nagging uncertainty about whether father is dead, really dead. I continue to hope that father will somehow appear, just walk in, and this will all have been just a big mistake. If we had gone down to the Cherokee Nation with Chase, we could have spoken with Mr. Harrison, met Judge Lynch, seen the cabin where they say Worldy shot father and Billy Palmer. I could have asked the ranch hands, "How do you know you buried Sam Stewart? You fellows didn't know either Worldy or my father.

Perhaps my father killed Worldy and the one you buried is the horse thief. That's always possible." I have so many questions I would like to ask. Where is father buried? Who dug the grave? Is it suitably marked? Is it marked at all? One of these days we should get a tombstone for father. I spent hours choosing the appropriate inscription, finally coming up with these words:

Here Lies Charles Samuel Stewart
Born June 15, 1818   Died November 28, 1858
Father of Laura Augusta Stewart
and
Adelaide Henrietta Stewart
The Founder of Eldorado, Kansas Territory
A Fighter for the Cause of Abolition
A Builder of Cities

But we didn't go, and that's a shame. Chase went—will they do him in, too? Will I ever see my intended again? My God, the fact that I even write these thoughts is an indictment of this place and time.

I know it's my job to write father's obituary and I've made some notes, but when I write and of the details, when I put down the facts that Father, Sam Stewart, no, Charles Samuel Stewart—died November 28, 1858, in the Cherokee Nation— no, was murdered on that date in the Cherokee Nation—and so on, it's like writing a book report. The words don't seem hooked up to the reality. What if all the newspapers in Lawrence and the one in Emporia owned by our friend Mr. Plumb carry the obituary that I'm writing, and then, when Chase comes home, he brings father? Maybe wounded, that's possible. That is entirely possible. So, I'll put off doing this obituary until Chase gets back with the facts. Sunday, December 19,   I suppose I should begin writing all our relatives to tell them that father is dead (or that I believe that father might be dead.) The very notion of this family obligation has brought back vivid memories of the letters I wrote to our relatives, on both sides of the family, when mother died. I remember Aunt Julia writing back, "My, what a nice letter" and I recall thinking at the time, "How could an obituary be 'nice'?" But I was flattered by her letter—her light purple stationery carried a fragrance of violets. When I did all that writing and got a response from every letter, that's when I decided I'd be a writer.

I remember getting a letter from an uncle in Flint, one of father's brothers. He knew mother before she married and remarked not only on what a beauty she was but that every bachelor in Flint had his eyes on her. He, too, said my letter was nicely composed for someone so young.

Midmorning: Adda came in from the outside and went over to the stove to warm up her hands. After throwing a couple sticks of wood into the little firebox, she made us both a cup of hot tea and sat down where father usually sits. For some seconds her eyes seemed to examine my face. Finally she said, "Let's wash your hair."

"I don't think I'm in the mood for that. Anyway we don't have enough soft water."

"I've got some little crystals that Howland gave us last summer that will soften the water." She got up and put the large basin on the stove, the basin we use for washing dishes. She poured into it all the water from the bucket, and then sat down at the table again to wait with me while the water heated up. "Yes," she said, "we're going to wash your hair and dry it. We won't use homemade soap. I've got some special soap. Then after we've washed your hair, we're going to braid it in two braids, and coil them up into two buns over your ears, the way I wore mine when the teamsters were camped here. Davenport said that with my hair like that, I was almost as good-looking as his girl friend in Iowa, but the way he said it, I think he really meant, 'Adda, you are really better looking than my girlfriend in Iowa. You're just a little too young for me.' That, Augusta, is my modest opinion."My sweet sister was trying to cheer me up a little.

While waiting for the water to warm up, we had some more good sisterly chatter. Then Adda got up and rummaged through one of the cabinets until she found a gaily-decorated cylinder and sprinkled some of the little box's contents into the basin. She pulled her sleeves back and immersed her elbow into the water, emitting a little "uh huh" of satisfaction to let me know that the water was now just right. Adda came over behind me and, humming a little tune, began undoing my hair. As she did, some of my hair fell forward toward my face. Adda lifted my hair back off my face. That gentle motion caused me to recall vividly my mother doing the same thing.

I seldom pull my hair back or lift it off the back of my neck without thinking of my mother. In the summer of 1847, a traveling carnival had come to town and Uncle Ransom took us all to it, and I'm afraid we stayed past our bedtime. I ate too much, or ate something that disagreed with me. When we came home, I quietly went to bed with a bellyache and couldn't sleep but was too proud and independent to cry or complain. We are not whiners in our family. In an hour or so, I had to vomit. Everyone in the family had all gone to bed. Uncle Ransom was sleeping on the sofa. I got up to vomit and decided I could quietly do it in the kitchen without having to light a candle or disturb anyone. But it didn't work out that way. I had a big swollen stomach, full of candied apples, roasted peanuts, caramel popcorn, fried chicken, oatmeal cookies, hot salted pork cracklings and sweet lemonade. I was able to get to the kitchen and use the pan where we wash our dishes but when the food I'd eaten all decided to come-up and it did— explosively—my vomiting was followed by a guttural retching over which I had no control. My little stomach continued to heave and squeeze out the last of its offensive contents.

Suddenly, I felt my mother's warm body close behind me in the dark. She was gently pulling my long unbraided hair away from my face. My mother was as proud as I was of my long hair. We used to brush it together, and we had several ways to braid it: the Dutch braid, the Swedish braid and a three-braided bun that Mother said was the way Swiss girls wore their hair.

Mother pulled a kitchen chair over towards us and had me nestle in her lap as she rubbed my stomach. I still had little gritty, sour pieces of popcorn and fried pigskin from the cracklings, in my mouth. Mother seemed to know this.

Mother diluted some maple syrup with water and made me wash out my mouth. Then she showed me how to gargle to clean out my throat. The following summer my mother died. I have never vomited since: ever. And I never pull my hair back or braid it up without thinking of her; what friends we were, what companions.

Adda washed my hair and braided it as promised and things got better between us. Her kindness diminished some of the tension that had arisen between us because of our different responses to father's death. **December 26** A posse of men, calling themselves the Eldorado Vigilantes, rode over to Hildebrand's claim, arrested him and brought him back to J. D. Conner's store, where they setup an impromptu courtroom to hold a the trial. They had appointed Mr. Conner sheriff.

Members of the jury were Tom Cordis, Doctor Weibley, Henry Martin, Jesse Curry, Arthur Keyes and Jerry Jordan. * Of course, Adda and I attended on orders by the posse as potential witnesses. Chase and Mr. Carey were still down in the Cherokee Nation.

It was late in the day when the trial began.

* Confirmed "Kingdom of Butler" by Klintworth & Butler County Historical Society.

Mr. Conner's store was really quite crowded. After Mr. Conner conferred with Doctor Weibley and Mr. Martin, he said the court would allow Mr. Hildebrand to make a statement, which would then be followed by questions from the jury. He said he expected those questions to deal specifically with either the theft of two horses on the night of November 23, 1858 from the Stewart claim or with any involvement Mr. Hildebrand might have had leading to the murder of Sam Stewart on the night of November 28th in the Cherokee Nation. Mr. Conner said, "All right, now, Mr. Hildebrand, you may talk." Mr. Hildebrand stood up and began to speak with remarkable confidence. He said his name was Reverend William Hildebrand. Adda leaned over and whispered to me, "I've never heard that one before." Hildebrand said that he'd been in this area two months before Sam Stewart and his gang of abolitionists had come in June of 1857 to lay out Eldorado, some of it on land, that he had already claimed. He disregarded the fact that he had been paid by the town committee for that claim.

"I've only lived where I live now for a few months. Prior to that my two children and I lived on a claim over on the river.

"I was formerly a missionary with the Cherokee and Chickasaw Indians. My mission was supported by some Baptist churches in the South. I came up here from Mississippi with Colonel Alexander Bingham, a hero of the Mexican War. Some months ago the Colonel departed, leaving the area, but I stayed behind and I'm now carrying on a mission with the Kansas Osages."

Mr. Martin interrupted him "That's strange," he said. "I've never seen any Osages around your place, even though they occasionally come into Eldorado. I've seen them at my place, the Stewarts' place and up at Jacob Carey's. On the other hand I've seen many white men, all strangers in these parts come and go around your place. I've seen horses corralled at your claim down by the creek, then they've disappeared—and the language you used when you attacked Mr. Carey in September, that language, sir, doesn't seem to me to fit the personage of a Baptist Reverend, which you claim to be. What have you got to say about that?"

Hildebrand was defiant. He ignored Mr. Martin's questions and claimed he knew nothing about our horses or father's whereabouts.

Mr. Conner asked him, "How did you know in late November and again in December that Sam Stewart would probably not be returning to Eldorado? Also, please explain how your footprints matched those found in the snow at the Stewart's corral on the morning of November 24th. Mr. Hildebrand offered an evasive explanation.

Questioned about the money, Hildy answered that he has always had money.

"Where did you get the cash for the new shoes you bought?" It was common knowledge that Sam Stewart had, at the point of a gun, made him remove both of his shoes, and had kept one. "I couldn't go around barefoot on the prairie in November, so I bought a new pair.

He continued to be cheeky to everyone who questioned him. He refused to give any details about Worldy except to say that a "Southern boy from Baltimore" had stopped by his place on his way to Pike's Peak.

"But he didn't go to Pike's Peak, did he?" said Mr. Martin. "He went south with the horses the two of you stole. Isn't that right?"

Hildebrand was not to be tricked. "I don't know where he went."

"Well then, "continued Mr. Martin, "tell us what day he left. Wasn't it the morning of November 24?"

"Ah don't recall when he left," shot back Hildebrand.

When the questioning was over, Mr. Henry Martin, one of the older gentlemen on the jury, said he wanted Mr. Hildebrand to be held outside, guarded with a gun, while the jury deliberated. He assigned one of the younger men to do that. The jurymen talked amongst themselves in hushed tones, for maybe fifteen or twenty minutes. Then Mr. Conner said Henry Martin would speak on behalf of the jury. Mr. Hildebrand was ushered back in.

Mr. Martin addressed Hildebrand, "For all the antisocial behavior you have worked upon Mr. Jordan, Mr. Carey, Doctor Weibley, and Mr. Stewart during the ox incident, all citizens of Eldorado, and pursuant to the information brought out at this trial amounting to circumstantial evidence that you were involved in a scheme to steal his horses, get him out of the community and to murder Mr. Sam Stewart, President of Eldorado, you are to be banished from this community.

"In addition, the jury has sentenced you to fifty lashes of the whip."

The jury gave him three days to clear out of Hunter County. Doctor Weibley and Jerry Jordan were assigned to reduce the verdict to writing, which they did.

A committee of five from the jury was appointed, each to administer ten lashes on Hildebrand's bare back. They did the whipping directly after the sentencing, in the woods next to J.D. Conner's store.

Adda and I, and everyone else, remaining in the makeshift courtroom could hear Hildebrand scream as they whipped him. Adda leaned over and said to me, "Let him scream and yell. That won't bring father back and this punishment is not enough. He should suffer like father suffered. I hope the whip cuts deep enough for him to bleed to death and I hope it takes a long time."

I told Adda to hush up with that kind of talk.

Hildebrand was supposed to have fifty lashes, but someone later said that he had kept count and Hildebrand had actually received sixty lashes.

The men who whipped him reported that when they stripped him of his shirt, they saw the scars of a previous whipping all over his back.

December 31st New Year's Eve, Chase has been gone two weeks. Of course, I've been worried ever since he left, but now I'm about out of my mind with worry about what might have happened. I had a terrible dream last night. I dreamed I was Halcyon waiting for her husband's return. In the myth, of course, the husband of the Greek goddess doesn't return. I woke up, no doubt disturbed by the dream, but quickly reasoned that the lady in the dream couldn't have been me. Chase and I aren't married yet.

Several days ago Adda made a very good suggestion. She said we needed a distraction, aside from doing our chores. "Of course, if we were wealthy, we'd travel—we would 'take the waters' in Germany or Switzerland," she said with a flourish, "but since we can't do that, let's begin writing all of the notes we have hidden away about our time over in Plymouth and in Lawrence. If we don't gather them up and put them in chronological order, the mice will get 'em or we'll simply lose them."

Adda was right. We had stashed away dozens of notes in food boxes, clothing, any place where we thought they would escape detection by Colonel Cooke's search parties, which came regularly across Pony Creek looking for cannons, stores of guns, kegs of gunpowder, etc., as though anyone in Plymouth would be stupid enough to hide weapons, which were necessary for our defense, in places that would be easy for a private in the U. S. Army to find!

I had been particularly careful about hiding the letter from Captain J.A. Henry in which he proposed that the two of us go west together and disclosed his intent to desert the army. That revelation could have been dangerous to both of us. I also had hidden all of the notes I'd written about Captain Henry's visits to Plymouth, both his social calls and his inspection tours, looking for weapons or for runaway slaves, and I had included in my hidden notes his long monologue about how the middle and lower classes of the South viewed slavery, as opposed to what the plantation owners thought about the issue.

This wasn't the first time Adda and I had discussed the idea of organizing our notes. Several months before Howland closed his store, I had him order for me four bound ledger books. When they arrived, I began copying into one of them some of the entries from all of my miscellaneous notebooks, loose notes, etc. going back to our leaving Michigan and our trip across Iowa. The entries I had made in Archer and Lawrence, before we came out to Eldorado, were quite orderly but the notebook was of lesser quality than the professional ledgers I am using now.

I started to go over my notes about Plymouth, transferring them into one of the ledgers. Because of the danger we faced when we came into the Territory, I'd never committed those events to the final, bound journal.

I decided that I would also add some of the information I had learned about some of the visitors who had come through Plymouth, some rather mysterious, others more open and seemingly lighthearted, like Preston Plumb, who had tried to appear so casual, when he brought three supply wagons in on September 15th and later that day transferred them to a much larger southbound train, a train of 300 people. I certainly wanted to expand on the events of October 10, 1856 after the Army had established a camp at Plymouth and searched our wagons, tents and found a keg of powder under the floor boards of our own house.

I have also added more about Reverend Moore. I suspected at the time we heard the sermon he gave in Plymouth that he was a man of considerable substance. Adda and I had carried on a correspondence with him afterwards, which had expanded our information about him considerably. While Adda and I were in Archer, we had delved into the background of some of the other abolitionists who had come to Plymouth that fall, people like General Lane, Richard Hinton, John (Old Osawatomie) Brown, James Redpath and many more. It took months for me to comprehend what really happened at Plymouth, and most of this realization began to unfold as Adda and I started to reconstruct those early events.

While we were there, we had been given a copy of the Boston Traveler, which included Richard Hinton's article about the conditions at Lecompton and listed father's name among the 106 antislavery prisoners. Of course, the months we lived in Lawrence had also exposed us to more information about the abolitionist movement, including how important Plymouth, Lexington and our other rough and crude little Free State settlements had been to turning the tide away from the proslavery elements.

In the process of rewriting my Plymouth entries, entering them into the ledger, I made so many changes, inserting more and more facts as I remembered them, that I spoiled the first ledger and began again with a new one.

I have continued this rewriting practice all through my grief over father's death, and it does seem to be helping somewhat.

To avoid brooding about father's death and what's to become of us, I spend a lot of time working on the journal.

January 4, at about noon, my darling Chase returned— and he was limping. Mr. Carey was safe and sound, but they both had quite a story to relate. On their way down to the Cherokee Nation Mr. Carey's pack mule drowned trying to cross the Arkansas River. Chase had been kicked by one of the horses just yesterday.

Chase and Mr. Carey, who were escorted by Mr. Freshean and his cousin, stopped to rest up at Mr. Bell's place at Requah on Grand River. We learned before he left that Mr. Carey is an acquaintance. During the night, while Chase and Mr. Carey were sleeping, they were robbed of part of their money. The next morning Mr. Riley, Mr. Freshean's cousin, was gone. They searched for him, but could find no trace of him. Chase, Mr. Carey and Mr. Freshean rode on over to the Lynch claim. But their troubles didn't stop. Chase said that they were treated with suspicion by the ranch hands.

Chase expressed the opinion that, perhaps unbeknownst to Judge Lynch, some of the ranch hands might be thieves, who were dealing in stolen horses and perhaps both Worldy and Hildebrand knew that; after all why did Worldy go south to that particular place. He could have gone in any direction. Yet, if they were horse thieves, why did they allow Mr. Freshean to ride Tom Cordis' black horse up here?

Chase explained that one of the ranch hands claimed that Billy Palmer's horse had been killed in a farming accident, struck down when a hayrack fell on top of it. "The story sounded fishy," Mr. Carey said. "Our little wagon, which Chase had taken, broke down about eighty miles south of here, halfway to the Lynch ranch, so they were forced to abandon it and one of the Cherokees had to take turns walking.

"What about Puss?" I asked Chase.

"Well, Puss was still alive but she was so poor with distemper we thought it best to leave her." Chase added that the horse seemed to have been "tampered with" or abused in some way. Chase said that the two saddles had just disappeared, and so had Father's gun belt and his new Colt revolver. So, they've come back more or less empty-handed.

I asked Chase if he reported the missing saddles to Judge Lynch or Mr. Harrison? He said, "No."

Chase replied that both of them were cordial but businesslike and as a northerner, he felt that he should not press his inquiries too far.

Chase speculated that Worldy, on the way to the court at Van Buren, might have been allowed to escape, since he was a Southerner and was being escorted by Southerners. Chase's story has credibility.

Augusta notes in her journal that some months later she and Adda received "out of the blue" a condolence note and an offer of help, carried to Eldorado by a Doctor Crabtree who said he was a business partner of Captain John Wesley Stewart, who lived in Texas and had heard a Mr. Worldy, who was boasting that he had killed in self-defense in a dispute over in the Cherokee Nation Sam Stewart, a Territorial politician. Captain Stewart's offer is enlarged in Chapter 38.

At supper, I asked Chase "When you visited with Mr. Bell, did he give you any more information about Father's death than what he mentioned in his letter?"

"No."

January 5,   Now that Chase has returned, safely thank God, I thought to myself, "Well, he hasn't brought back any news about father, that differs from Mr. Bell's letter or what the two Cherokees told us, so I'll just have to face up to writing the obituary. How I dread that task.

Following mother's death Aunt Bertha sent me a book from a church in Boston, with a note that said the book was about death. I read it cover to cover but it was not about death.

Death, I knew, was a peculiar brand of sorrow that could reduce me to long fits of sobbing—that and a pervasive, limitless, agony. Aunt Bertha's book was about life hereafter. That's not death, nor does the promise of life hereafter mean anything to a ten-year-old girl who's lost her mother. I have no quarrel with these ideas, but to be told that my mother was alive with Jesus, gave me very little comfort. Jesus has plenty of company. I only had one mother. After Mother died, whenever I had to sing the hymn "Jesus Loves Me, This I Know" in Sunday school, I'd just hum along. I couldn't bring myself to sing the words. If Jesus loves me so much, why did he take my mother?

I can recall when door-to-door salesmen would come by our house and inquire, "Is the lady of the house in?" I'd say, "Well, yes, but she's uptown shopping, you shouldn't wait. Come back another time." I didn't intend it as a lie. I just wanted to believe that my mother was alive. Pretending to strangers helped. I continued to do things like this for several years after she died. I simply didn't discuss it with anybody.

30.

A Conspiracy to Murder Sam Stewart?
January 6 and 7, 1859

This afternoon Jerry Jordan came by. Jerry usually exudes a "happy-go-lucky" aura. Today he was unusually serious. I've been careful about my relationship with Jerry. He is a valued friend and was one of father's closest friends, with their friendship dating back to their confinement at Lecompton. They were brothers-in-arms and each in his own way held similar beliefs about the righteousness of the abolitionist movement.

There is a delicate matter between Jerry and me. He had proposed sweetly and with such good timing (after I felt so ignored by Chase last March, prior to our engagement), and I had declined politely, quickly and as gently as I knew how. In saying no, I knew I had to find a graceful way to do it, that wouldn't abrade our friendship or the friendship between Jerry and father. Grace is a virtue I'm trying to learn. I think, in this sensitive matter with Jerry, I've been successful, if for no other reason than Jerry is still here. And that's something to "crow" about what with all the gold seekers coming through here who are trying to persuade the men in our community to go with them.

During our visit Jerry quickly got to the point. Mr. Hildebrand is back. That news is very disconcerting. Chase saw him down on the Verdigris * and he has been seen over around

*The Verdigris River, which runs south of Eldorado

281

Conner's store, which is near his claim.

When Jerry mentioned this, Adda interrupted him. "He was ordered in writing to get out and stay out of this town. He must be touched in the head to come back."

Jerry said he had been doing some serious thinking about Billy Palmer's death. Jerry knows full well that under normal circumstances he would have been Father's traveling companion, not Billy, who, after all, was a stranger here. It would have been natural for Jerry to have gone with Father to recover his own horse. He has already implied, in some other conversations we have had recently, that had he gone, things might have turned out differently, for, after all, he's had some military experience and is twenty-eight, more than a decade older than Billy. But he didn't go. In the haste of that morning Billy did and Billy's dead.

Jerry seemed to need to discuss this situation with someone he could trust and I'm flattered that he felt he could talk about it with me.

Jerry said that he thought Hildebrand might pose a threat to us. "If Chase has to go away, to do a carpentry job out of town, I could pop in for supper and spend the night up in the loft." Jerry thinks there ought to be a man around. Well, that's fine with me.

The following morning Jerry returned and sat down at the table, didn't say anything, just sat down. Since he had just been here yesterday to tell us that Hildebrand had been seen in the vicinity, I wondered what it could be that would bring him back to our place so soon. His stopping by was not unusual, since he is our main sawmill operator, and sometimes he drops in if he has some business relating to the mill, or to take a meal with us. I could tell something more important than a question about the mill was bothering him, but I didn't have time just then for a heart-to-heart talk.

I had a rather large roast in the oven and to take advantage of the extra oven space and heat I was putting in a pan of new sweet potatoes to roast.

Jerry confided that he is now keeping a side arm nearby.

"Hildebrand probably has the same grudge against me, like he did towards your father."

Adda was sitting at the table, working on her journal, developing another article she intends submit for publication. I was "smarting" in a sisterly way from her recent success. Our relatives in Michigan had encouraged her to try getting an article published in some newspapers there. When she had her first article accepted, I was surprised. Adda had based it on her journal entries but it was pretty old news: it was about our coming out to Eldorado, life on the prairie, the episode with Paul, the Osage, etc. During her first attempts to get published all of her articles were rejected. One of them carried a note from an editor who wrote that half the U. S. population thinks they are pioneers— those not on the frontier have an uncle or a brother in western Missouri, western Iowa, Minnesota, etc.—so, he said, an article needed to be unique and contain human interest. The letter was addressed to Mr. A. Stewart. Adda said this gave her an idea: Any article she wrote must appear to have been written by a man to be treated seriously. She signed her name as Mr. Adamont Stewart to one of the previously rejected articles—and mailed it to a different newspaper…which immediately published it.

Nothing I've written has pleased me enough to risk sending it to an editor, so I guess I shouldn't be envious. But if I do send out an article someday, I will sign the article as Mr. Augustus Stewart.

Jerry had remained silent for several minutes, but finally, and with some hesitation and long pauses, he began to speak. "Do you mind if I talk about an idea, that I've been mulling over about your father's death? I have been reluctant to bring it up since you two might find it offensive."

Looking at me, but addressing his comment more to Adda, he said, "Have you two ever given any thought to the notion that Worldly or Worldy—whatever his name—might actually have been paid or somehow encouraged by Eastern proslavers to dispose of your father?" A long pause followed.

I could hear Adda put her pen down. I wiped my hands

on my apron and leaned against a wall log for support. I had been so preoccupied with the realities imposed on us by father's death, like what's to become of Adda and me, what we should do about our property claims, whether we should continue to improve the sawmill, should we use the saw's idle time to build up an inventory of timbers, etc., that I hadn't given any thought at all about the root causes of father's death, other than pondering the facts recited in Mr. Bell's letter.

Jerry continued to expand on the suspicions he had about father's death. "Where did Hildebrand get all the money he was spending right after your father left? He went around pricing claims. He wouldn't have done that without some means that he didn't have before. Worldy and Hildebrand could have had a plan to lure your father out of the Territory and kill him, but do it so it wouldn't look like it had anything to do with proslavery or Worldy, was instructed and paid by proslavers back east to contact Hildebrand in Eldorado. We know now that a stranger was at his claim for a few days before the theft. Hildebrand is a known proslaver and could have had contacts at Lecompton who had a score to settle with your father. How much time did Hildebrand and Worldy spend together? You know, stealing our horses might simply have been a ruse to get your father into the Cherokee Nation, which doesn't have U. S. territorial protection. Selling the horses could have provided Mr. Worldy with a little extra revenue…"

Adda interrupted him, "Wait a minute. We don't know that either horse was sold. Chase said Puss was at the Lynch ranch. He could have brought her back but didn't. And Mr. Freshean rode old Bill back up here and Tom Cordis has him now. So, yes our horses were stolen, but I don't see that they were stolen to be sold, and if those people at the Lynch ranch were really horse thieves, why hadn't they sold Puss, and why did they bother getting a lawyer to write that long letter disclosing the details of father's death, and going to the trouble of getting two men to come all this distance with the letter, then inviting us to send someone to bring back their belongings?"

"Well, you helped to make my point. If the stolen horses weren't sold by Worldy, we've removed a financial motive for the theft. That leaves another party providing those two the money to kill your father," Jerry said. He continued, "As the Free State legislator for this area, your father could easily have had proslavery enemies in high places up at Lecompton. For them to cook up a scheme to do him in is not all that far-fetched. Your father was working on our Free State Constitution and attended all the Constitutional conventions. You know he never missed a single meeting. Do you have any idea of the bitterness they hold for those who wrote it deleting slavery? Well, the proslavers hate us and they hate our political leaders even more, because now we have more people in the Territory than they do and we've been able to vote down their Constitution. We've now got the vote. Their constitution has been voted down. Our Constitution is finished and has now been delivered to Congress, so we've beaten them at their own. game. They invented popular sovereignty. We didn't.

"When we were in prison, we experienced first hand with Sheriff Jones and his deputies just how much they hated us. That sheriff wanted to shackle your father and several of the leaders with iron balls, six inches in diameter. To even come up with an idea like that takes diabolical hatred, to his credit Governor Geary wouldn't authorize it. And do you know, Sheriff Jones is still alive? In Lecompton, they wouldn't even feed us. After a time your father was allowed to go up to Lawrence and beg for food, blankets, extra clothing. In hindsight I'm surprised they allowed him out to do that, though in spite of it we still had deaths among the prisoners from excessively harsh conditions, no medicine, no doctors; I can tell you from being there, that was one cold winter.

Jerry said that the resentment they feel towards us is different from the rancor we feel towards them. "We have both been aggressive in fighting for our cause. But they take our presence here as a personal affront, and think we are denying them a God-given right. Slavery to them is both a cultural and an economic necessity. They see us as intending not only to prevent slavery in Kansas, but to destroy the institution altogether. So their response is to retaliate and put a stop to abolition.

"What really has aggravated their animosity is we have not only beaten them militarily but also politically The tide changed in October of last year, when we got more than half the seats in the Territorial Legislature and elected Andy Reeder for Congress. That's when the proslavers lost their hold on the Territory."

Jerry said that although the North is fighting for the abolition of slavery, seeing it like a religious cause, at the personal level, we are just as bigoted as the Southerners. "They tell Nigger jokes, we tell Nigger jokes. Even if there is a free Nigger roaming around over here we don't get social with him. We just want to help him get to Nebraska or points north. We may be fighting for a lofty idea, but some of our willingness to oppose slavery really contains more than just a few grains of revenge."

Adda asked, "What do you mean by that?"

"I mean we do these things more to aggravate the proslavers than to assist the slave. But by taking the slave we are imposing a form of eminent domain over their property; For example, there are 100,000 slaves in Missouri. If each of those slaves is worth at least $1,000, by freeing them all, we are taking away a hundred million of dollars of property from those slaveholders. If slavery becomes illegal in Missouri and the rest of the States, we will be obliterating the Southerners' plantation system and their economy.

"The Missouri slave owner who has lost his slave to an Underground Railroad conductor wants to get his slave back and punish the thief—pretty much what I expect your father felt when he went after the thief who stole Puss. But the difference between us abolitionists and the Southerners when it comes down to the slave is that they have the federal government on their side. They have been able to get the Supreme Court to put the death penalty on anyone who abets the freeing of a slave.

"The proslavers will never forgive our presence here, or the wrong they think we're doing them."

"The government and the army," he said, had sided with them until just recently. "Out here, none of us had a chance, because both Judge Lecompte and Judge Cato were dyed-in-the-wool proslavers.

"When your father and I were in Lecompton together, did you know that we were the only two men, out of the eighty-eight abolitionists tried for murder, who said we'd mount *no* defense and wouldn't accept the court-appointed lawyer? He was appointed by Judge Cato. What kind of defense could we expect from a proslaver lawyer? What I'm telling you is a matter of court record. And the trial wasn't for something minor—we were all being tried for murder!

"So when the news came from Washington that we would all be pardoned and released, well, you should have heard the profanity from the guards who had to carry out the order. Judge Cato resigned in protest against the order, though I think he resigned because Governor Geary demanded it of him. He quit, but old Judge Lecompte, he's still there, and is absolutely convinced that somehow slavery will survive and prevail. But now our Constitution is ready and Congress will have to use the principle of popular sovereignty to make the Territory a free state because we have the vote."

"The army didn't think about stopping all the fighting in the Territory until a year ago last fall, that's when their officers began to realize that we could beat the Southerners in the field. So the Army finally stepped in. But it wasn't just to stop the fighting. It was to protect their fellow Southerner's you know what."

Our "Likenesses" taken in Lawrence in November 1859 in Dagarian's studio, owned by Mr. John Bowles. John and his brother, William, fought with Sam's company, both captured and put in a POW camp. William died in the winter of 1857.

I was twenty years of age. Add, on the left, was eighteen.

31.

ADDA PLANS REVENGE
January 8, 1859

After Adda and I had fed our breakfast boarders and cleaned up, we decided to sit down and discuss Jerry Jordan's concern that Hildebrand might be a danger to us. Since her response to Father's death is so different from mine, it is important that I record our conversation as faithfully as memory allows.

Ever since we became aware that Hildebrand had been seen in the vicinity, I've been worrying and wondering what he was up to. Adda's response, on the other hand, has been to get ready, both physically and mentally, for a confrontation with the old rascal.

As we talked about Hildebrand, Adda became more and more animated; agitated might be a better description. In midsentence, she popped up from the kitchen table, walked over to the oak chest of drawers that we had brought out with us from Michigan (the piece of furniture that, in happier days, father used to refer to as "Sir Chester Drawers") pulled open a drawer and retrieved a small chamois leather bag from under some clothing. Standing next to me, she slid the contents of the bag onto her hand: It was a short ivory-handled revolver, so little it fit right in the palm of her hand. Adda held the gun up, bringing it unnecessarily close to my face, as if she wanted to provoke me. "You see what that trademark says?" she asked. Since it was overcast that morning, I had lit two candles on the little wall-mounted reflecting pan. The light allowed me to read the fine print beneath the cylinder. It was a Colt Repeater, the same kind of gun that Worldy had used to kill Billy Palmer, made somewhere in Connecticut.

"Adda, where did you get this thing? Is it loaded here in the house?"

"Of course it's loaded! You can't kill rats or snakes or skunks with an empty gun, stupid."

"Don't call me stupid. I'm your big sister and I'll thank you to remember that." I paused, thinking there was no need for a row even if Adda's attitude seemed a little rash to me. She hadn't told me about this gun before. All of this was sudden, disturbing, and unladylike and I was already upset because of Jerry Jordan's speculation that there might have been a conspiracy to kill father.

My silence quieted her down. In a calmer vein she told me how she had gotten the gun. "Several days ago I was over at Conner's store and he asked me if we had a gun for protection, now that father's gone. I told him about the Sharps carbine we have hanging on the lintel over the door. He said that by the time we took it down, someone could shoot us, so he suggested we buy a gun that's small and handy. It turns out Mr. Conner does a fairly brisk business in side arms. He showed me a couple of revolvers and explained how they worked. He seems very knowledgeable about these things. It was midafternoon and he had no customers, so he closed his shop, and grabbed two guns, some ammunition and said, 'Come on, Adda, let's go get some target practice,' just like that. We walked out over to that stand of timber where you and I waited for father to return from the Leavenworth Convention last April.

"He tacked four or five little white inventory tags on one of those trees. He stepped back ten or so paces, then swiftly lifted up his arm and fired six shots in such rapid succession the noise startled me. Without bothering to examine the tags, he turned to me and calmly said, 'Your turn, Miss Boone.' He said it with a contrived southern accent, which was really quite funny since he already has a rather thick Irish brogue. I held my gun more or less in front of me, aimed at the tree and pulled the trigger. Well, that gun almost jumped up out of my hand. After I recovered my senses, I realized the 'kick of the gun' had caused my hand to point in the air! I was so ashamed, I was about to give up, but he convinced me to try again. He said he had heard I was a good shot with the Sharps rifle, but a handgun wasn't like a rifle and eventually I'd get used to it. He told me I'd made two mistakes. I hadn't gripped the gun handle tightly enough and I'd bent my elbow. So I decided to see if I could hit the tags with the remaining bullets. Mr. Conner waited for me to 'get off' the five remaining shots and he was right—I did get better with each shot. We stayed out there for several more rounds and I guess I owe him for a whole box of bullets. I saved the brass shells.

"The gun I was using was bigger than this one," she said, pointing to the gun in her hand. "On the way back to the store, I made a remark that I couldn't go around town with a pistol that big strapped to my waist. As usual he had a solution, and as soon as we got back to his store, he pulled out this little gem. Augusta, do you know what we did then? He closed up his store, went back over to the timber and I shot this little beauty about fifty times, and after a while I got pretty good."

All this time I was amazed by what she was saying and trying to sort out why she had bought this gun. Was it for protection? Or was it more complicated than that? I knew she was angry and bitter about father's death. Could she be planning, in her action-oriented fashion, to concoct a confrontation with Hildebrand and exact some sort of revenge?

Adda quickly cleared up this mystery. "You seem afraid and Jerry seems worried about Hildebrand. Well, let me tell you, I'm not afraid and I'm not worried. I've converted my fear into anger. In fact, I'm looking forward to seeing him. I've asked around town, 'You seen old Hildebrand?' I've planned a dozen ways to shoot that murdering bastard. I confess, Augusta, when I can't sleep, I lie awake plotting revenge. Seeing him dead on the ground bleeding, like father must have bled, with his life, pumping out in little spurts on that Cherokee earth, that's what I want from Hildebrand. And by God, I'll get it! Sister dear, you have no idea what a smidgen of provocation it will take for me to cleanse this county of that corpulent bag of cow shit."

I was just aghast at this foul language. Adda has always been competitive with boys and young men and quick to pick up their slang. Now she seems to think she must talk like a mule driver and I said so.

She ignored my admonishment and went right on talking, "Sometimes I'll walk down to the stand of cottonwoods by the creek and pretend that one of those trees is Hildebrand. I imagine that we are coming face-to-face. Inconspicuously, I'd put my hand in my pocket and wrap my fingers around this little four-shot friend of mine, and then I'd watch for the slightest movement that I could take to be a provocation—if he raises an eyebrow or lifts his hand to adjust his hat or swat a fly or pick his runny nose, I don't care what he does. Anything that strikes me as provocative and Hildebrand is dead. Augusta, I can put four bullets into him as fast as you can say 'Hill-de-brand, sir.' I'd say, 'Are you dead yet, you bag of buffalo shit?' I'd examine where the bullets hit him, and if he wasn't bleeding enough to satisfy me, I'd calmly load and shoot that fat filthy stinking son-of-a bitch four more times."

"Adda, stop! Where did you learn such gutter language? It's disgusting."

"Who cares? Do you want to talk about proper language— or do you want to talk about Hildebrand and how he has just about devastated this family? I can conjure up as much decorum as you can, but Hildebrand is no respecter of social graces. Only someone touched in the head would come back here after the whipping our men gave him, followed by firm orders agreed upon by the whole town to get out and stay out of this county. You think you can treat a lunatic with decorum? Mr. Conner thinks he's crazy, and so do the Cordises."

"You've spoken to all of them about this?"

"You betcha. And by thunder, they not only agree with me, they are also of the opinion that Hildebrand plans to come after all of us, one-by-one, scaring us so we will clear out of Eldorado. He went after father because father founded this town, and he did it so cleverly that he can claim innocence. He also has it in for Jerry, because Jerry helped father recover our oxen. And he's angry with Chase interceding when Hildy had that fight with Mr. Carey. And of course Hildy also hates Doctor Weibley because of that argument they had last September just outside our door. And it seems you and I aren't safe from Hildy either. Well, by God, he won't intimidate me."

Adda said that he had already taunted her in the past. "Once last spring he was standing by his little wagon outside Howland's and he said to me, 'Well, lookey heah, it's the jail bird's daughtah.' Let me tell you, I look forward to his repeating those words. By the time he gets just two or three of them out of his filthy mouth, those words will be his last. I'll have shot him an' it won't bother me a smidgen to claim self-defense."

"Adda, father's dead, and his killing was a terrible wrong,

but two wrongs don't make a right! Worldy killed father! I'm sure Hildebrand was involved but he wasn't the murderer."

Adda was pacing back and forth by the kitchen table. Reciting her plans to kill Hildebrand had gotten her quite animated and she's never been at a loss for words—whether she's excited or not. "Two wrongs don't make a right." She kicked one of the table's chairs for emphasis. "Hah, that's just algebra. People who talk like that do so from the comfort of not having suffered a serious wrong, but if you want to talk about punishment and justice, I like the algebra of the Old Testament. It didn't take those old Jews long to figure out how to keep peace in the Promised Land. They figured out that justice was achieved through punishment; 'An eye for an eye, a tooth for a tooth.'—that's my kind of algebra. I'd even make that stronger and say, 'An eye for an eye, a life for a life.' Even old Hammurabi, who wrote his laws long before Moses, taught those same precepts, which father used to call 'symmetry in the law.' And anyway, shooting Hildebrand isn't a 'wrong'; it's just evening up the score. Out here we don't have a sheriff or a courthouse. Someone has to carryout this punishment. Who better than the next of kin? I've volunteered!"

She whirled around, pointed her little revolver at the candle reflector and shouted, "Blam, blam, blam, blam!"

For a few seconds I was afraid she was going to shoot that thing off in the house. "Adda, one of the reasons our family came out here was because we believe slavery is wrong and uncivilized, too, and taking the law into your own hands is uncivilized."

Adda cut me off in midsentence. "Civilized... civilized! Your thinking has become so addled that you think this place is civilized. That's your problem. For heaven's sake we don't have a school or a church or a preacher. We didn't even get a floor in this cabin until three months ago! Just talking about civilizing Eldorado doesn't make us civilized, Augusta. Why, if we were civilized, father wouldn't have chased the horse thieves. We would have had a sheriff and a deputy to take care of it, and if we were civilized, our settlement would have access to a federal marshal, and the aid of the U. S. Army. If the Indians around here ever get hostile, do you think we will settle *that* dispute in a civilized fashion? The nearest troops are at Fort Riley, and that's a hard day's ride away. And those soldiers are all proslavery anyway, so they might not even come. But even if they do, by the time they got here, we'll all be dead, or scalped—or for the women, worse.

"Augusta, neither Eldorado nor any other of the frontier towns out here will begin to take on the mantle of civilization until we have statehood, railroads, schools and thousands more people, and that may take fifty years or more. Until this place is as orderly as it was back home in Detroit, I'm advising you to know your adversary and be prepared to deal with him, expecting no protection from anyone in the army or the government. This little piece of well-crafted New England steel is *my* protection!" She turned and began pretending she was shooting at the candleholder again. "Blam!"

"If I can't cry, if I can't mourn for Father the way you can," she replied, "then, by God, I need to do something for this anguish I feel. An' I need to do something to square-up the situation that the old bastard has put us in. Augusta, we are orphans, you don't seem to recognize that. Hildebrand should pay for what he's done. And I think you'd better be a little less sanctimonious. You don't need to roll your eyes heavenward and tsk tsk your tongue about a little salty language when father's murderer is walking around the neighborhood free as a bird. You ain't mad enough to suit me. Oh, you're indignant all right and you are suitably offended, but I'd feel better if you were indignant enough to shoot him yourself. Frank once said you are a professional indignant."

"What did he mean?"

"That you can always find something to be indignant about."

I let this comment pass.

"Augusta, how far does your indignation go? Are you willing to avenge father? Would you shoot Hildy yourself?"

"No. Well not without serious provocation."

"Well, would you shoot him in self-defense? Better think about that, big sister, 'cause you might just have to face that situation," she added, "I want to deal out some punishment to him. In hindsight, I wish they'd assigned me to lay on ten lashes. You and I counted those lashes. Would you have laid on the whip if the jury had asked you—since you were a daughter?"

"NO!"

"Why not? For heaven's sakes, how much punishment must you take before you dish out a little yourself? We've lost our father an' his death is going to change everything. Wait an' see. I know as well as you that shooting Hildebrand won't bring father back but my, what glorious satisfaction we'd have, knowing Hildy was dead. I've given a little thought to what I'd like to see on his tombstone. Using her finger to punctuate the lines, she recited:
Eldorado, Kansas Territory

February 1859

Here Lies William Hildebrand,

Conspirator in the Death of Eldorado's President,

Samuel Stewart,

November 1858

Killed by Adelaide Henrietta Stewart,

as she bravely defended herself in a dispute "You want to know what I'd chisel on the back of his tombstone? 'Vengeance is mine'—and I don't know yet whether I'll finish it the usual way or like this: 'Sayeth Adelaide Henrietta Stewart.'"

I guess I thought I could change the subject. This whole

discussion was so offensive.

"Adda, you are quoting Paul out of context. In his letter to the Christians in Rome he didn't instruct them to seek revenge. Here's what Paul really says, 'Dearly beloved, avenge not yourselves.' When he goes on to say, 'Vengeance is mine, I will repay,' Paul's saying only God can mete out justice; not you."

Adda paused, but not for long. She shot back, "Well, I never thought I'd concede a point to you in a debate. I guess I'll have to read that passage in Paul more carefully. But anyway, I'm beginning to think that the teachings of the New Testament stopped at the Missouri River. All this 'Love thy neighbor, turn the other cheek, forgive transgressions, all that New Testament-Sunday school stuff is for minor offenses, and it works I guess when you've got an orderly society. The Old Testament better serves us settlers to a new land.

"It's all right for us to argue—we're flesh and blood—but we have a real enemy and we better have a real plan to deal with him. You don't have a plan, an' I'll tell you this, I don't think the elders in this town have a plan either."

Adda said that she wished she could cry a little more about father's death, but that it didn't seem to be in her nature. "On the other hand," she added, "it's my opinion that you cry too much. Too much crying isn't healthy either. It's not good for you to indulge yourself in misery. Well, thank God we've got plenty to keep us busy. We've got all that syrup to sell, and we have to keep that sawmill going, and in a couple of months we'll have to start the spring planting. And I suppose we now have some new problems caused by father's death."

"Like what?" I asked.

"We'll need to establish that you and I now own everything that belonged to father; his claim, the syrup mill and the sawmill. Maybe Judge Wakefield can handle that for us. Augusta, that's something you should take care of. Maybe that will take your mind off father."

Having gotten all this off her chest, my sister suggested we have some tea. She picked up our old speckled gray enamel teapot, which had been heating on the stove, and made us both a cup of what in our family we call "tea kettle tea" (hot water, a little sugar, a little milk) and brought the two warm cups over to the table. After she set the cups down, she gave me a little hug and a kiss on the back of my neck. "I'm sorry if my new language offended you. I must have picked it up from Davenport and the freighters when they were here."

"I was over there so often that when they stopped noticing my presence, they didn't hold back in cussing and some of their words were really more funny than filthy. After seeing what the skinners went through trying to get some of the mules shoed, I'm convinced the only way to get mules to do what you want is to cuss 'em and pop 'em on the butt."

Adda said that there were three Quakers in their outfit and even they had their own brand of salty language. "They never take the Lord's name in vain or use Jesus or Jesus Christ when they swear, but they cuss all right and it's really funny because whenever they do, they use the words 'thee' and 'thou' dozens of ways.

"Luella was Davenport's lead mule. He called her his belle mare, which he said a French-Canadian mule driver had told him meant mother-in-law. Every good skinner gets himself a belle mare if he knows what he's doing. Davenport said he once worked with a Mexican mule driver who had been hired by the U.S. Army during the Mexican War. After the war, he had come up North and had worked for Russell and Majors. He called his belle mare 'Madrina.' It was Davenport's opinion that nobody can work mules like an experienced Mexican. They cuss their mules too, but in Spanish.

"Davenport could always spot Luella, even when she was standing in a group with all of the others. How he could tell them apart beats me, but he could. They all looked the same to me. He had a name for each of the six mules in his mule team and he said he could identify them by their ears and eyes."

"The day they left I watched him round up all of his mules and let me tell you, that was quite a sight. First he had to harness Luella because she was his lead mule. He walked up to her and when he got to within ten to twelve feet of her, he said, 'Lu, you get your big Missouri ass over here.' Well, Luella didn't move a muscle. She just looked at him, and flicked one of her ears. By then Davenport had worked his way in among the mules and was standing alongside her. Using the butt end of his bullwhip as a small club, he popped old Luella on the behind, hard! I told him he was being mean. But he said, he wasn't mean; he had to do it to get her attention. Luella and he were old friends but mules stick together and he had to get her away from her buddies. When he smacked her with the whip, Luella did a little crow-hop. Davenport said that was Luella's way of saying in mule language, 'I'm ready, boss.' Then he slipped a halter over her head and led her to his wagon. He repeated the same procedure, more or less, with his five other mules, except he had to cuss them more."

Later in the morning when Adda was down by the saw, Doctor Weibley and Mrs. Weibley came by. Despite the pleasantries, I sensed this was more than a social call.

Doctor Weibley had, as usual, been drinking. Drinking before ten in the morning. But he was sober enough to convey that he was worried about Adda. He said she had dropped in recently to ask if she could browse through his library. "At first," he told me, "I assumed she wanted to look for a book on poetry or literature and she did pretend some interest, but it quickly became apparent to me that what she was really interested in was seeing a book on anatomy and soon she got to the point. She started firing off questions, asking me about the jugular vein. Where was it? How big was it? What does it do? She was as detailed in questioning me as my old medical professors back in Philadelphia. So I showed her in one of my anatomy books and then showed her on my head and neck where it was.

"I explained to her that there is both a jugular artery and a jugular vein though professionally we refer to it as the carotid artery. But my explanations annoyed her and made her impatient. She seemed angry and said she wanted to know exactly how the bullet that killed your father went through his neck and severed his jugular vein. I told her he probably bled to death. She had heard through Chase that one of the bullets severed his spinal chord.

"Augusta, we'll all need to be a little patient with your sister. You can expect some strange behavior for a while. It's a normal reaction to a death in the family. Has she cried a great deal?"

"No, but she cried some, though certainly not as much as I have. But she does seem unusually angry and has concocted a bizarre scheme to shoot Hildebrand. Did you know he's back?"

"Yes dear," Mrs. Weibley said, "we've heard. You girls must be very careful."

I told them how much Adda wanted to punish Hildebrand. "Adda is in such a vengeful frame of mind that I think she will actually go out hunting for him, like he was a skunk or a coyote."

"Yes, dear, we know about the gun."

A little surprised and perturbed I asked her, "How do you know about it?"

"Adda took me into her into her confidence and told me

about it after she bought it."

I asked Doctor Weibley what other types of behavior I could expect from Adda (and from myself,) for that matter. He began a long, rambling speech about grief. Doctor Weibley went on with his impromptu lecture; I thought to myself, "Why you presumptuous old sot, for you to tell me that grieving is natural and that we all get over it—what do you know?"

Humph! I was eight years old when my mother died and, yes, I cry less, but that has more to do with growing up than it does with grieving. A week ago a sparrow fluttering in our window reminded me of a song my mother used to sing. The song was so sad it brought tears to my eyes. It was about a bird fluttering at a windowpane. Mother said that the bird was a messenger angel, sent to tell a mother that the Angel of Death was about to take her child to heaven. I am always being reminded of Mother.

Last spring, when I visited with Mrs. Dempsey, the graceful turn of her neck, the whiff of her talcum powder, revived in an instant the image of my mother on a summer Sunday morning, as we dressed up for church. A few weeks ago, as Adda and I were making biscuits, Adda got a little baking soda on her forearm, and the graceful way she wiped her arm and wrist with her apron, for an instant made me think I was seeing my mother's arm, rather than Adda's. Maybe that's not grieving, maybe that is just memory. But when it's a memory of someone you loved, someone who died before her time, what's the difference?

For him to stand there and tell me that we'll get over it tells me he doesn't know what he's talking about. I suppose in his profession he must keep the patient at a distance, so that if death does come, the doctor's judgment isn't personally affected. I understand that.

It has been a busy day. Chase stopped by this morning, then the Weibleys, and now Mr. Conner has come around for a visit. Since father's death he's been very solicitous about our well being. As it is late afternoon, Adda and I invited him to join us for tea—our "tea kettle tea"—and we made a little small talk as we drank it, then he left.

After he left, Adda and I started to talk about some of our feelings about father's death, and I told her that in the last few days I'd seen him in my dreams. "When we first heard about his death, I would wake up in the middle of the night, wide awake and have some rational reason for why Father couldn't be dead, reasoning that Mr. Bell's affidavit described the wrong men as being killed. I was sure father was all right and he'd come riding up the valley one of these days. But now that Chase has seen the grave and spoken with the people down there, I guess I've gotten it pretty well into my head that father's dead and isn't coming back. Lately, when I wake up in the middle of the night, even though I'm half asleep, I carry on some comforting conversations with father."

"Like what?"

"Oh, we talk about all kinds of things."

"Well, give me an example."

"Well, I've asked him what he thinks we should do about the syrup mill. Should we keep it or should we sell? And I've asked him who owes us money for his surveying, and if he thinks I should I marry Chase, and whether we should pack up and go back to Michigan and live with the Stewarts."

"Does he answer you?"

"Well, yes, and very satisfactorily, but in the morning, when I'm fully awake and try to recall our conversation, some important parts of it are either missing or I can't recall them, so it doesn't make total sense, certainly not the way it did when I was dreaming."

I told Adda that I thought having these kinds of

conversations might run in the family. Father's mother used to talk directly to God. "Grandma Hannah, didn't just talk to God while praying, she'd carry on long rambling conversations. She did it so often nobody in the family ever gave it a second thought. It was one of her gifts. Father said that grandma sometimes came away from those conversations with some pretty good advice for grandpa, like when they had that big long dispute over who owned the rights to the water that powered one of their mills in Onondaga County. She said that God had told her to stop all that fighting and move to Michigan to join a new community founded by religious visionaries from New York State. 'Like-minded brethren,' grandma called them. Even though they were one of the wealthiest families in the county where they owned a sawmill and a gristmill, grandma convinced him to leave. So they just up and moved.

"That wasn't the first time Grandma Hannah had persuaded grandpa to do something because of one of her conversations with God. Father had told me years ago about an incident that happened when they were still living near Truxton, in New York, and I related this story to Adda. Their community didn't have a cemetery and as the town grew, this became a problem, so grandma spoke to God about it, and God told her to donate some of their land and she got grandpa to do it."

I told Adda that, according to Doctor Weibley, some of these strange things we were experiencing, like the dream I had that father wasn't really dead and her feelings of revenge, were the natural results of Father's death. They really aren't strange. Doctor Weibley says that what we are going through is normal and we'll get over it.

"Well, I agree with Doctor Weibley," Adda said. "Revenge, Augusta, is not strange. It's normal, as normal as—apple pie, in spite of what old Paul says."

Earlier that week, I noticed Adda had started to "sport" the wide-brimmed hat she had gotten from the skinners, and on nice days she had begun to wear that red-and-white heavy cotton plaid shirt, with the big cuffs that she had gotten by trading the chocolate milk. She was also wearing Davenport's bright yellow bandanna, and she had added a new element to her getup. Last summer we had both ordered a pair of grayish tan corduroy trousers from a catalog. She's now wearing the corduroys with high-topped boots, again like the mule drivers.

A few weeks ago she did some sewing on her left-front trouser pocket, and I know now it was to accommodate her little four-shot revolver. When she goes out, she carries that little Colt Repeater. I know because after she leaves, I check in the chest of drawers and it's always gone. Adda is very serious about her plan to get Hildy. And I know my sister well enough to know that if I try to talk her out of her plan, all I'll do is strengthen her resolve.

32.

WE'VE SET THE DATE
January 9, 1859

Mr. Carey and Chase were here for the noon meal yesterday. After the meal, using a rather formal tone of voice, Chase asked how Adda and I were getting along. I suppose this inquiry stemmed from his concern about father's death and how we were reacting to it. Adda and I have certainly discussed some alternative plans. We've considered going back to Lawrence or to Michigan for that matter, or we could stick it out here with our friends in Eldorado. It's my opinion that's what father would have preferred. I think Chase misses father, too. They were becoming good friends. I know Chase relied on father's judgment on certain construction aspects of his jobs.

It commenced snowing last evening, snowed all night and was still snowing when I woke up this morning to a cold cabin. Though we "bank" the stove at night with chunks of hardwood and close off the flue damper to slow down the burning, the fire has usually consumed all the wood well before morning, leaving the cabin cold. This morning it was so cold the ink in my little ink well was frozen solid. That's the first time I recall that happening. I soon got the stove going again and warmed things up nicely. When I make ink next time, I'll try to use alcohol rather than water.

About half an hour after I got the cabin nicely warmed up, Chase came by. I asked him if he'd had breakfast. He said, "No." We are getting some nice eggs lately from a dozen white leghorns that I raised from chicks, so we had a couple soft-boiled eggs together with toasted corn meal muffins. It was quite a chummy breakfast. Chase was unusually congenial and I was in pretty fair spirits myself. During breakfast he said they'd seen Hildebrand again recently in the neighborhood. I suppose as a result of that sighting Chase has felt a need to come around on our behalf more often. It is rare that he's here so early. He seems to have discussed with Adda her intentions, that is, her welcoming plans for Hildebrand. I think he is impressed by and favors Adda's intentions, but doesn't want to engage me in a discussion of it.

He is concerned about our safety, our plans for both the sawmill and the Sorghum press.

He helped me clean up after breakfast and invited himself to supper, saying, as he made ready to leave, he thought it was time for a serious discussion.

Though I had plenty of chores after he left, I occasionally found myself idly staring into space, preoccupied with what it was that Chase wanted to talk about this evening and how seriously. I knew I mustn't overly exercise my optimism. I did that a year ago on our cold walk home from the Cordis place and got bitterly disappointed for it. Since it's hard for me to predict what Chase will do, I vacillate between rosy expectations and a dark, foreboding apprehension, which I don't think I care to tolerate much longer.

I planned what I would fix for supper and settled on chicken stew and dumplings: not all those Leghorn hens have been laying their fair share. Two of those hens think they run the place. One of them even bosses the rooster. I don't think either one of them have laid an egg since Thanksgiving. That sets a bad example for those that do lay. This is not an old peoples' home for chickens. But I just hate to pluck feathers outside when it's so cold and I don't like to do it inside either. It takes almost as long to clean-up as it does to pluck. It turned dark early this evening, though the snowing stopped. For my big supper with Chase I decided to wear the same dress without a collar I had worn last March on the night of our engagement, and that night I had fixed my hair the same way that Chase had found attractive. I borrowed a little of Adda's cologne, the bottle that Howland had given her after he discovered that Glennis Beamis had left for the goldfields. While I prepared the chicken stew, I wore a high-bibbed apron to protect my dress, but I took it off near sundown, since I knew Chase would soon be here.

A little after dusk Chase came in alone and heaven be blessed no one else came around.

The chicken stew couldn't have been better and the dumplings stayed plump and tender. I was relieved about that because usually when chickens get old enough to lay eggs, their meat gets tastier but tougher and stringier. The secret with dumplings is to use just a little cornmeal mixed with meal from unleavened bread and a spoonful of melted chicken fat, that gives them flavor. But here's the real secret. I cook the dumplings in a broth made from the chicken wings, back and neck all flavored with a chopped onion. Aggie Rourke, who taught me that, said it was an ancient Jewish recipe, but the Jews don't call them dumplings. Oh, yes, you need to beat a fresh egg into the dumpling mixture.

I explained to Chase just why it was we were having chicken stew. He looked up at me with a twinkle in his eye. "In Massachusetts, they got better eggs from Rhode Island Reds than from Leghorns," he said, "but Bufforfingtons are the best to fry."

He chuckled. "How do you know we aren't eating a couple of pullets?"

I thought he was teasing me but I wasn't sure. "Don't you think I know the difference between a pullet and a full-grown hen? For heaven's sakes, what kind of woman do you think you're marrying?" I hadn't planned on bringing up marriage. It just popped out. It sure put a stop to the chicken talk. In fact, for a few minutes it put a stop to all talk. But marriage must have been on Chase's mind as well, because after the pause in our conversation, during which we both felt shy and embarrassed, Chase simply said, "That's what I think we should talk about tonight."

I made us a pot of tea and hoped no one would drop in. (I had a fleeting thought that I should go out and hang a quarantine sign on the front door.) I had saved a few sweet barley cookies for a special occasion, so I arranged them on a fancy little fruit plate one of my aunts had given me before we left Detroit.

For our tea, I thought it would be cozier to have it sitting next to each other on the bench, instead of at the table. Both the settee and the kitchen table had belonged to Mr. and Mrs. Benton. They had given them to us last September, when they left for the goldfields. Their kitchen table was certainly an improvement over the one we'd had and their long hardwood bench had a tall slotted back, and it was also rather nice. Both pieces of furniture were very practical, but too cumbersome for them to carry west. I made a cushion for the bench of a patterned brown upholstery fabric and it stretches across the entire seat, so the bench is now quite comfortable to sit on. I store my books, correspondence and writing materials in a box on one end of it, the bench is so long.

I put a little utility table in front of the bench and sat down. Patting the cushion, I said to Chase, who was standing with his back to the stove, "Why not come over here, and sit down next to me." As he sat down, he put his arm very lightly around my shoulder and, with more charity than affection, rationed out a little hug.

Our after-supper tea seemed to put us both in a friendly and compatible mood. Rather offhandedly, Chase said he had been thinking a lot about our future lately and had made some New Year's resolutions. Speaking with tenderness, which he rarely does and almost never so openly, he said he thought we'd been engaged long enough. And he said it as if he were seeking my opinion on the subject; another rarity, usually he doesn't solicit my opinion.

"Yes, since last March," I said, reminding him of how long it had been.

"Then it's time for us to think about marriage," he said matter-of-factly.

"Let's pick a date for the wedding."

What he said didn't come as a surprise. I knew in advance every word he was going to say!   I'd had a premonition while making the tea of what he would tell me."

"Chase," I said, "I've also been thinking about our getting married. Perhaps now that we have an evening to ourselves, we should start doing some planning." Chase told me that he had enough jobs to provide us with a good nest egg. It seems his carpentry and wood-business has picked up nicely.

Of course, I knew about his work on the Cordises' house and on Mr. Conner's Store, but it appears he's also been working on two framed houses, and planning two or three more. "I don't think any more log cabins will be built in Eldorado," he said. "Now that the mill is producing such good lumber, and with so much wood hereabouts." Chase seems more pleased with his prospects here than at any time that I can remember.

"And with this new framing method, using sawed lumber, I can now build a house faster than before," he declared. "I can get windows and window frames and whole staircases, complete with treads, and risers shipped to me from a factory in Illinois and I can assemble them on the job." These products were saving me time and were reducing the amount of skilled handwork required for a job, good carpenters were scarce out here. He reported that he could now build chimneys faster, too, because someone had started a brick factory over in Leavenworth so he had a ready supply of bricks. "I've already used some of them to build a couple of chimneys. Even little things, like the bigger and better variety of nails being made, are helping my business—but I wish Frank were still here and could assist me. I definitely could use a helper." I kept quiet, but it's my opinion that Chase acts much more mature now that Frank Robinson is gone. I don't miss Frank at all.

I guided the conversation back to our wedding plans, reminding him that Eldorado has no church, so we'd have to make our house "do" for the wedding. Chase said he would ask around about the availability of a preacher.

"I've heard that there are two preachers in Chelsea," I said, "Reverend George Perkins and Reverend James Saxby. And I know that in Otoe County there's a farmer, Israel Scott, who occasionally preaches thereabouts. Father said Mr. Scott was also a self-appointed justice of the peace. If we need to go as far as Emporia to find someone, I hear there is a Freemason up there who is also a preacher. Father once told me that if a Mason who has attained the fourteenth degree, performs a marriage ceremony at the time of the full moon, that portends well for a marriage, which will be long and fruitful.

Considering Chase's past reluctance to discuss a wedding date, I didn't want to suggest a date that would seem too soon or appear so urgent that it would put pressure on him, nor did I want to suggest one that was so far away, like the fourth of July—

that I'd tire of waiting! "How about March 21st?" I asked him. That would be the anniversary of our engagement, the tenderness of which I have so often recalled, especially when things weren't going well between the two of us.

"No! I don't want to wait that long."

His response just delighted me and seemed to be a measure of his ardor, which so far has been so "irregular" during our courtship.

"Well, what's a good date for you?" I said.

He suggested we marry by the end of the month, and after a short discussion we both agreed to Saturday or Sunday, January 22nd or 23rd, depending on the preacher. I was too excited to remain sitting. I had so much trouble containing my elation, I jumped up to see if there were any more cookies, though I knew there weren't any and on the way back threw a couple of unnecessary sticks of wood in the stove, and busied myself with a few other unnecessary chores. January 22nd makes it just two weeks away! Well, hallelujah!

I told him that I could have my wedding dress ready by then. When business started picking up at the sawmill, I sent away for material and the pattern for a dress I had seen in a catalog. (When I sent my order, Adda also mailed one off at the same time. Now she doesn't need to make any new dresses. Thanks to Howland's generosity and his failed romance with Glennis Bemis, Adda has plenty of dresses. Lucky for her she is Glennis' size.

When the material and the pattern for the dress arrived, I showed it to Mrs. Rackliffe and Mrs. Weibley and they volunteered to help cut it out and to help with the fitting. When they learn that this dress will be my wedding dress, working on it should add to our mutual pleasure.

Chase and I decided that we would not keep our wedding date a secret. But I suspect he has already talked about it with the

Martins, because he mentioned that the Martins told the doctor's wife that they planned to have a supper party for us in advance of the "big day."

Chase started to leave about 11 P.M., but some affectionate lingering delayed his departure. He left about midnight. It was snowing and blowing so hard I hated to see him go out into such a disagreeable night. Before he left, I suggested he sell his claim and move in here after the wedding.

"Well, what about Adda?" he said. It had never occurred to me to think about what would happen to Adda if Chase and I ever really got married and set up housekeeping.

Marriage until now was just a dream, just an idea. I hadn't given any thought to specific household arrangements. My sister and I have always been together, so the notion of Adda not being here was something I had never contemplated, didn't even want to. On the other hand Adda is sensitive to the importance of privacy, so I suppose we'll find a solution that will work for all of us and there'll be no need for a big discussion. Adda will simply realize that 'Two's company, three's a crowd"—but it will be hard not to live with my sister anymore. Needless to say, I didn't drop off to sleep that night.

This evening with Chase has put me in such a fine elated mood. After all these months of uncertainty, now that we've settled our differences and have actually picked a wedding date, I can't believe it! It's such a shame that father won't be here as a witness and to give me away, and there is simply no one else qualified to do it. December was the darkest, bleakest month I've ever had, with such terrible news, and until tonight I didn't hold out any prospects that this month would be any better. Then I recalled from my Latin lessons that January was named after Janus, an old Roman god with two faces: one looking back to the past, one looking forward to the beginning. I like that idea. This month began so sadly but by the end of January, Chase and I can start to look forward toward to a new beginning, our future together.

I had just about resigned myself to a long, perhaps endless engagement, particularly so when Chase went off to the goldfields. Maybe that adventure got the Argonaugt vapors out of his system. I considered other "sisters" who had long engagements; like Rachel, who had to wait for Jacob to work seven years for her hand. Then Laban deceived them both and tricked him into marrying Leah because she was the older sister. But Jacob had always wanted Rachel so Laban demanded he work another seven years. I love that story, but what a long engagement! Mine's been about ten months. I could have tolerated the delay if we had set a date when we got engaged, but until tonight we hadn't even discussed it. It was the uncertainty that was so unsettling. I dropped off to sleep wondering what our preacher would look like.

The next day—late in the afternoon—I received a beautifully written invitation from Mr. and Mrs. Henry Martin for supper Wednesday, January 19th. My, my, word travels fast.

While I was still admiring the Martins' invitation, Chase brought in a stranger who asked about city lots. There was something about this individual that caused me to suspect that he was looking for something other than just city lots, but I couldn't put my finger on what it was. I was glad Adda was around because that meant her little pistol would be in the drawer if we needed it..

This fellow made himself right at home. He inquired about supper and a night's lodging. But something about his appearance and his behavior continued to cause me concern. I asked Chase if he would bring in a few sticks of wood and as he went out the door, I followed him outside.

I tried to explain to him what my intuition was telling me, and thankfully he understood. "Chase," I suggested, "take him up valley to look at some claims, but away from down here, maybe beyond the Cordises', even up towards the Martins'."

"All right," he said. When we went back inside, Chase carried an armful of wood, and as he set it down by the stove, he said to the stranger that he would be too busy to show him around tomorrow but was free now, and since it was still light out, they could look for claims this afternoon. After a "round of tea", they left. They went so far north the stranger tired out his horse and couldn't get back for supper; he must have stayed someplace quite north of here. Chase came part way back and spent the night with the Cordises.

My plan had worked. We were rid of this worrisome nuisance and haven't heard from him since.

John Brown, 1850s

John Brown
With Permission from the Kansas State Historical Society

Helped defend Plymouth from Missouri raiders shortly after Sam's party arrived in August, 1856. John Brown gave both girls a Bowie knife. He was a frequent patron of the Whitney House, a small inn in Lawrence, favoring abolitionists, where Adda worked in 1857 and 1858. In the summer of 1959 Brown laid his plans to commence a Southern slave uprising. To get the arms, he and his followers would raid a Government Armory at Harper's Ferry, Virginia.

INDEX